Houghton Mifflin

Spelling and Vocabulary

A moth on a
prayer plant,
Washington State

Senior Authors
Edmund H. Henderson
Shane Templeton

Consulting Authors
Barbara Coulter
Joyce A. M. Thomas

Consultants
Jane Adrian
Judith Pierce Jefferson
Catherine Leeker
Jane Ann Malakosky
Elisabeth L. Rowlands

Houghton Mifflin Company   **Boston**

Atlanta   Dallas   Geneva, Illinois   Palo Alto   Princeton   Toronto

Acknowledgments

Select definitions in the Spelling Dictionary are adapted and reprinted by permission from the following Houghton Mifflin Company publications. Copyright © 1986 *The Houghton Mifflin Intermediate Dictionary*. Copyright © 1986 *The Houghton Mifflin Student Dictionary*.

Literature excerpts:
from *Dragon Stew* by Tom McGowen. Copyright © 1969 by Tom McGowen. Adapted and reprinted by permission of Tom McGowen.

from *An Oak Tree Dies and a Journey Begins*. Copyright © 1979 by Louanne Norris and Howard E. Smith, Jr. Used by permission of Crown Publishers Inc.

from *Through Grandpa's Eyes* by Patricia MacLachlan, illustrations by Deborah Ray. Text copyright © 1979 by Patricia MacLachlan; illustrations copyright © 1980 by Deborah Ray. Reprinted by permission of Harper & Row, Publishers, Inc. and Curtis Brown Ltd.

from *When Winter Comes* by Russell Freedman. Text copyright © 1981 by Russell Freedman. Adapted and reprinted by permission of the publisher, E. P. Dutton, a division of Penguin Books USA Inc.

How to Study a Word

1   **LOOK at the word.**
- What letters are in the word?
- What does the word mean? Does it have more than one meaning?

2   **SAY the word.**
- What are the consonant sounds?
- What are the vowel sounds?

3   **THINK about the word.**
- How is each sound spelled?
- Did you see any familiar spelling patterns?
- What other words have the same spelling patterns?

4   **WRITE the word.**
- Think about the sounds and the letters.
- Form the letters correctly.

5   **CHECK the spelling.**
- Did you spell the word the same way it is spelled in your word list?
- Do you need to write the word again in your Notebook for Writing?

Your Notebook for Writing

A Notebook for Writing is a good way to build your own personal word list. What words should you write in your notebook?

- new words from your reading and your school subjects
- words from your writing that you have trouble spelling
- spelling words that you need to study

When should you use your Notebook for Writing?

- when you are looking for exact or interesting words to use in your writing
- when you are proofreading your writing for misspelled words
- to help you study spelling

1

First, fold eight pieces of paper lengthwise. Also fold a cover sheet.

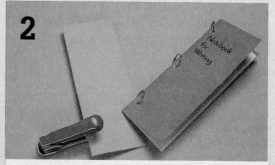

2

Staple the sheets, or punch holes and fasten with rings. Write **Notebook for Writing** and your name on the cover.

3

Beginning on the first page, write the numbers for the 36 units you will study. Write two numbers on each page.

    As you begin a unit, use this part of your notebook to write the spelling words that you especially need to study.

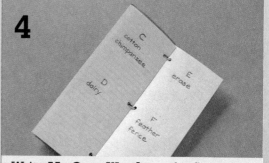

4

Write **My Own Words** on the first page of the second part. Write two alphabet letters on each page.

    In this part of your notebook, keep your own personal word list.

Contents

Cycle One

Cycle Two

Cycle Four

Cycle Six

Student's Handbook

1 Short Vowels

Theme: Baking

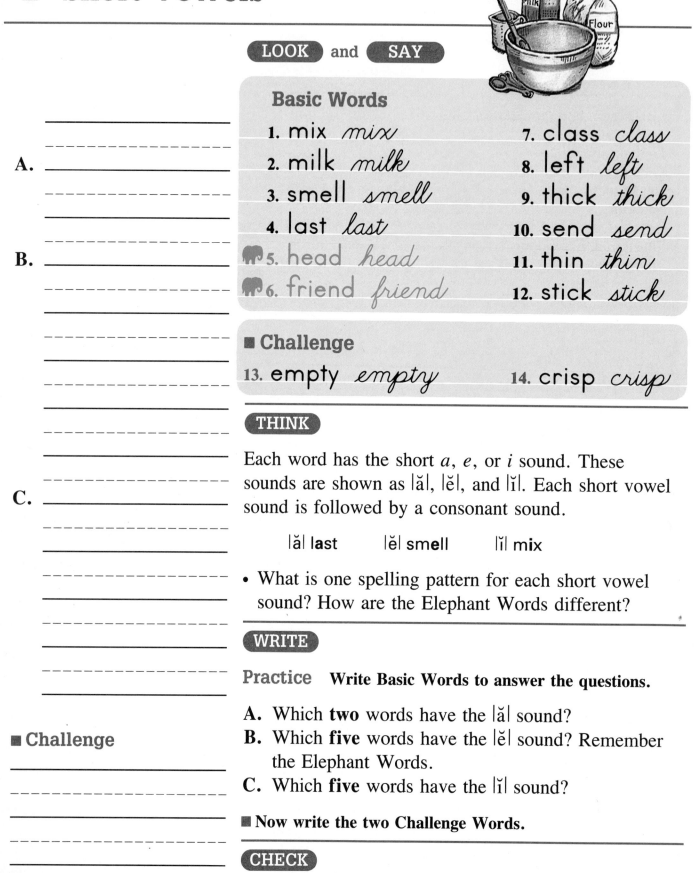

LOOK and **SAY**

Basic Words

A.

B.

1. mix *mix*
2. milk *milk*
3. smell *smell*
4. last *last*
🐘 5. head *head*
🐘 6. friend *friend*
7. class *class*
8. left *left*
9. thick *thick*
10. send *send*
11. thin *thin*
12. stick *stick*

■ Challenge

13. empty *empty*
14. crisp *crisp*

THINK

Each word has the short *a*, *e*, or *i* sound. These sounds are shown as |ă|, |ĕ|, and |ĭ|. Each short vowel sound is followed by a consonant sound.

C.

|ă| **last** |ĕ| **smell** |ĭ| **mix**

- What is one spelling pattern for each short vowel sound? How are the Elephant Words different?

WRITE

Practice   **Write Basic Words to answer the questions.**

A. Which **two** words have the |ă| sound?
B. Which **five** words have the |ĕ| sound? Remember the Elephant Words.
C. Which **five** words have the |ĭ| sound?

■ **Now write the two Challenge Words.**

CHECK

■ **Challenge**

Independent Practice

Word Attack   Use Basic Words in these exercises.

1-4. Write four words by adding the missing letters.
   1. _ _ in   **3.** _ end
   2. m _ _ _   **4.** _ ix

5-6. Write the two words that end with the same sounds as *pick* and *trick*.

Classifying   Both words in each group begin or end with the same two letters. Write the Basic Word that belongs in each group.
   7. best, fist, ___
   8. soft, lift, ___
   9. clap, club, ___
   10. tall, fill, ___

Elephant Words   Write the Elephant Word that completes each sentence.
   11. My best ___ Chris and I baked some muffins.
   12. Maria bumped her ___ when she fell.

Challenge Words   Write the Challenge Word that fits each meaning below. Use your Spelling Dictionary.
   13. firm but breaks easily
   14. having nothing in it

1.
2.
3.
4.
5.
6.
7.
8.
9.
10.
11.
12.
13.
14.

Summing Up

A short vowel sound is usually spelled with one vowel and is followed by a consonant sound.
- The |ă| sound is usually spelled *a*.
- The |ĕ| sound is usually spelled *e*.
- The |ĭ| sound is usually spelled *i*.

Basic

1. mix
2. milk
3. smell
4. last
5. head
6. friend
7. class
8. left
9. thick
10. send
11. thin
12. stick

■ Challenge

13. empty
14. crisp

Review

1. step
2. dish

Expanding Vocabulary

Rhyming Words **Rhyming words** end with the same sounds, such as *milk* and *silk*.

Practice   **Write a word for each clue.**

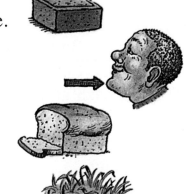

1. It rhymes with *smell*.
   It is found at the beach.

2. It rhymes with *thick*.
   It is used to build a house.

3. It rhymes with *thin*.
   It is part of your face.

4. It rhymes with *head*.
   You can eat it.

5. It rhymes with *class*.
   It is found outdoors.

1. _____

2. _____

3. _____

4. _____

5. _____

Dictionary

ABC Order   Put words in ABC order by looking at the first letter of each word. Decide which of those letters comes first in the alphabet. If the first letters are the same, go to the first pair of letters that are different.

head	**sa**nd	**mil**k
left	**se**nd	**mix**

Practice   **1–5. Write these words in ABC order.**

step   dish   stick   left   last

1. _____

2. _____

3. _____

4. _____

5. _____

Review: Spelling Spree

Letter Swap   Write a Basic or Review Word by changing the first letter of each word.

1. fish   **5.** silk
2. bend   **6.** fast
3. fix   **7.** glass
4. dead

Proofreading   8–14. Find and cross out seven misspelled Basic or Review Words. Then write each word correctly.

My frend and I made pizza. We rolled out the crust. It wanted to stik to everything. It was too thik in some spots and too thine in others. The next stap was to add the sauce and the cheese. At last we baked the pizza. A wonderful smel filled the air. Soon nothing was laft.

```
    c
f r i e n d
i       i
s       s
e m p t y  h
```

■ Challenge Words
Make a puzzle. Write the Challenge Words so that they cross. Add other spelling words.

Writing Application: A Description   Write a paragraph describing a tasty new food, such as Sun Soup. What does it look, taste, and smell like? Try to use three words from the list on page 14.

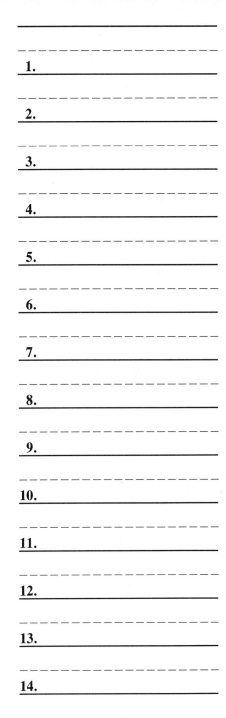

1. _____
2. _____
3. _____
4. _____
5. _____
6. _____
7. _____
8. _____
9. _____
10. _____
11. _____
12. _____
13. _____
14. _____

1   Spelling Across the Curriculum

Home Economics: *Baking*

Theme Vocabulary

flour
batter
oven
bread
stir

Using Vocabulary   Write the Vocabulary Words to complete the paragraph. Use your Spelling Dictionary.

Making a loaf of __(1)__ is fun. Mix salt, baking powder, sugar, __(2)__, and milk in a bowl. Then __(3)__ everything together, and pour the __(4)__ into a pan. Bake it in a hot __(5)__ for about an hour.

Understanding Vocabulary   Is the underlined word used correctly? Write *yes* or *no*.

6. An <u>oven</u> will bake food.
7. Use a <u>batter</u> to mix the milk and the eggs.
8. Look at the red <u>flour</u> in the garden!

1. _____

2. _____

3. _____

4. _____

5. _____

6. _____

7. _____

8. _____

FACT FILE

Salt and sugar look alike, but the taste buds on your tongue know the difference. Taste buds send flavor signals to your brain.

Enrichment

1

👥 *What's Baking?*

As a class, make a bakery of words with short vowel sounds. First, write |ă|, |ĕ|, or |ĭ| on three construction paper "cookie sheets." Next, tack them to a bulletin board. Then cut out round paper "cookies." On each cookie write a Basic or Review Word. Tack each word on the cookie sheet that has the same vowel sound. Add other words with the |ă|, the |ĕ|, and the |ĭ| sounds.

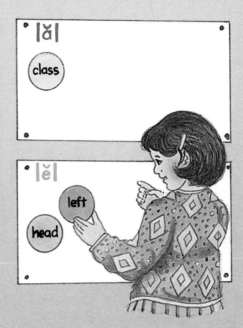

📖 *Writing*
Monster Meal

How would *you* make Monster Stew? Write a recipe that tells what you would use. Then explain each step for making the stew. Try to use words from the unit lists. Be sure to proofread your paper.

ALPHABET SOUP

Draw a large bowl of soup on colored paper. Then choose five words from the lists in this unit. Write the letters for these words as well as other letters in the soup. Then make words by connecting the letters!

Theme: Fishing

2 More Short Vowels

A. _____

B. _____

■ Challenge

_____

LOOK and SAY

Basic Words

1. pond *pond*
2. luck *luck*
3. drop *drop*
4. lot *lot*
5. rub *rub*
🐘6. does *does*
7. drum *drum*
8. sock *sock*
9. hunt *hunt*
10. crop *crop*
11. shut *shut*
🐘12. front *front*

■ **Challenge**

13. dodge *dodge*   14. crumb *crumb*

THINK

Each word has the short *o* sound or the short *u* sound. These sounds are shown as |ŏ| and |ŭ|. Each vowel sound is followed by a consonant sound.

|ŏ| **lot** |ŭ| **rub**

• What is one spelling for the |ŏ| sound? What is one spelling for the |ŭ| sound? How are the Elephant Words different?

WRITE

Practice   **Write Basic Words to answer the questions.**

A. Which **five** words have the |ŏ| sound?
B. Which **seven** words have the |ŭ| sound? Remember the Elephant Words.

■ **Now write the two Challenge Words.**

CHECK

Independent Practice

Word Attack   Use Basic Words in these exercises.

1-2. Write the words that start with the sounds you hear at the beginning of *shop* and *help*.

3-4. Write the two words that start with the sounds you hear at the beginning of *dress*.

5-7. Write the word that rhymes with each word.
    5. tub
    6. duck
    7. dot

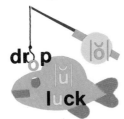

Classifying   Write the Basic Word that belongs in each group.
    8. hat, shirt, ____
    9. farm, seed, ____
    10. stream, lake, ____

Elephant Words   Write the Elephant Word that completes each sentence.
    11. Where ____ Elena usually go fishing?
    12. Mom is in ____ of the sporting goods store.

Challenge Words   Write the Challenge Word that completes each sentence. Use your Spelling Dictionary.
    13. Look at those fish ____ the rocks!
    14. The ducks ate every ____ of bread.

1. _____
2. _____
3. _____
4. _____
5. _____
6. _____
7. _____
8. _____
9. _____
10. _____
11. _____
12. _____
13. _____
14. _____

Summing Up

A short vowel sound is usually spelled with one vowel and is usually followed by a consonant sound.
• The |ŏ| sound is usually spelled *o*.
• The |ŭ| sound is usually spelled *u*.

Basic

1. pond
2. luck
3. drop
4. lot
5. rub
6. does
7. drum
8. sock
9. hunt
10. crop
11. shut
12. front

■ **Challenge**

13. dodge
14. crumb

Review

1. spot
2. much

Proofreading Marks

¶ Indent
∧ Add something
ℰ Take out something
≡ Capitalize
/ Make a small letter

Expanding Vocabulary

Word Clues   What does the word *scour* mean?

I will **scour** this burned pan to clean it.

The words *burned*, *pan*, and *clean* are clues that *scour* means "to clean something by rubbing."

Practice   **Write the word that means almost the same as the underlined word. Use word clues.**

1. A silver <u>trout</u> leaped into the air and dived back into the water. Then it swam away.
   a. butterfly   **b.** turtle   **c.** fish
2. The <u>fee</u> for renting a rowboat is $5.00.
   a. day   **b.** cost   **c.** time
3. Dad usually hums a <u>melody</u> as he fishes.
   a. whistle   **b.** word   **c.** tune

1. _____   3. _____

2. _____

Proofreading

End Marks   Use correct end marks.

STATEMENT: Lea went fishing.
QUESTION: Did she go to the lake?

Practice   **Proofread Will's story. Use proofreading marks to correct the three misspelled words. Add two missing end marks.**

Example: ~~Dose~~ Does Ray like to fish?

I fish at the pand I often hont for a new spot and just drap my line. How many fish do I catch I catch a lot!

Review: Spelling Spree

Hidden Words   Write the Basic or Review Word hidden in each group of letters. Do not let the other words fool you.

Example: e t i p o n d p e   *pond*

1. l o v d r u m k s
2. f o s h u s h u t
3. m u r m u c h o r
4. s p o f r o n t e

5. d o s s d r o p t
6. t r e n h u n t e
7. d e d o e s t o s
8. e b l b u r u b b

Code Breaker   Use the code to figure out each Basic or Review Word below. Then write the word.

● = c	□ = l	⊥ = p	↑ = t
▲ = d	∞ = n	↕ = r	☆ = u
⊖ = k	⊠ = o	> = s	

Example: ▲ ↕ ⊠ ⊥   *drop*

9. □ ⊠ ↑   11. □ ☆ ● ⊖   13. > ⊥ ⊠ ↑

10. ● ↕ ⊠ ⊥   12. ⊥ ⊠ ∞ ▲   14. > ⊠ ● ⊖

■ **Challenge Words**   Make up a code. Write each Challenge Word and five Basic Words in your code. Then write the words correctly on the back of your paper. Have a friend try to decode the words.

>  *Writing Application:* Creative Writing
> Pretend that you are a fish. Write a paragraph about people trying to catch you. What happened? How did you feel? Try to use three words from the list on page 20.

1. _____
2. _____
3. _____
4. _____
5. _____
6. _____
7. _____
8. _____
9. _____
10. _____
11. _____
12. _____
13. _____
14. _____

2   Spelling Across the Curriculum

Recreation: *Fishing*

Theme Vocabulary

fishing rod
hook
nibble
river
bait

Using Vocabulary   Write the Vocabulary Words to complete the paragraph. Use your Spelling Dictionary.

At last Kay found a fishing spot by the __(1)__. She threw the line of her __(2)__ into the air. The shiny __(3)__ at the end fell into the water. Then she waited eagerly for hungry fish to __(4)__ at the tasty __(5)__.

Understanding Vocabulary   Is the underlined word used correctly? Write *yes* or *no*.

6. Gulls <u>nibble</u> their fish in big gulps.
7. My dad uses <u>bait</u> to keep fish away.
8. My family goes rowing on the <u>river</u>.

1. _____
2. _____
3. _____
4. _____
5. _____
6. _____
7. _____
8. _____

FACT FILE

Every year salmon leave the ocean. They fight swift rivers and may jump over ten-foot-high waterfalls to return to their place of birth.

Enrichment

2

👪 *Go Fish!*

Players: 2-3 **You need:** 24 cards with each Basic Word written on two cards
How to play: Each player takes five cards. Player 1 spells a word on one of his or her cards and asks another player for the matching card. If a match is made, Player 1 lays down both cards. If not, Player 1 draws a card from the pile, and the next player takes a turn. The first player to "go out" wins.

📖 *Writing*
A Fishy Tale

People often tell fish stories in which the fish are much bigger than usual and do surprising things. Write this kind of fish story. How strong was the fish? What happened? Try to use words from the lists in this unit. Be sure to proofread your paper.

A-B-SEA FISH

Have your fish swim through the sea in ABC order. First, cut fourteen fish out of colored paper. Then write a Basic or Review Word on each. Next, draw a sea on a big sheet of paper. Last, put the fish in alphabetical order, and glue them on the sea.

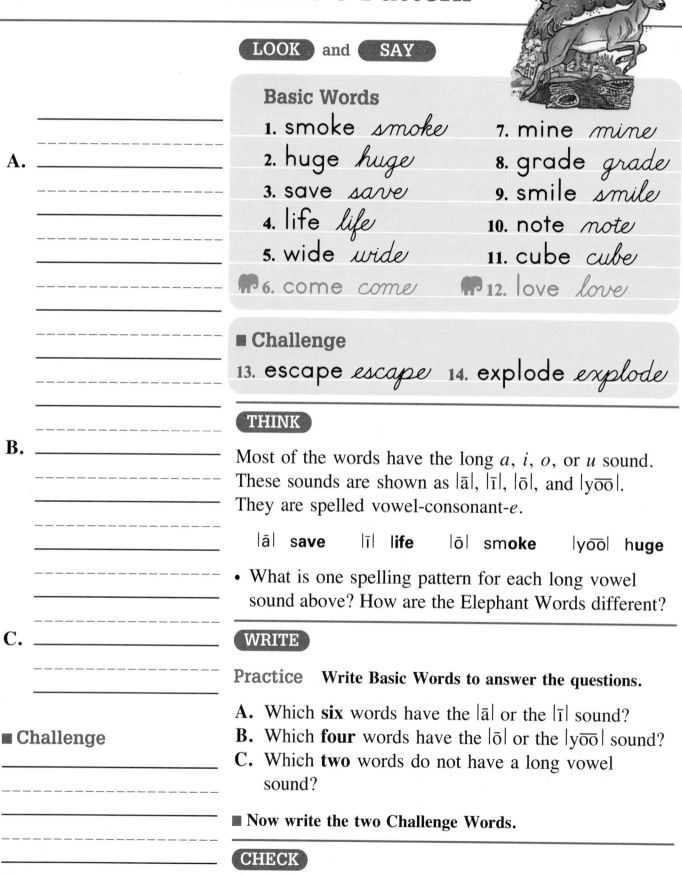

Theme: Forest Fires

3 Vowel-Consonant-e Pattern

LOOK and **SAY**

Basic Words

1. smoke *smoke*
2. huge *huge*
3. save *save*
4. life *life*
5. wide *wide*
🐘 6. come *come*
7. mine *mine*
8. grade *grade*
9. smile *smile*
10. note *note*
11. cube *cube*
🐘 12. love *love*

■ Challenge

13. escape *escape*   14. explode *explode*

THINK

Most of the words have the long *a, i, o,* or *u* sound. These sounds are shown as |ā|, |ī|, |ō|, and |yōō|. They are spelled vowel-consonant-*e*.

|ā| **save** |ī| **life** |ō| **smoke** |yōō| **huge**

• What is one spelling pattern for each long vowel sound above? How are the Elephant Words different?

WRITE

Practice   **Write Basic Words to answer the questions.**

A. Which **six** words have the |ā| or the |ī| sound?
B. Which **four** words have the |ō| or the |yōō| sound?
C. Which **two** words do not have a long vowel sound?

■ Now write the two Challenge Words.

CHECK

A. _____

B. _____

C. _____

■ Challenge

Independent Practice

Word Attack   Use Basic Words in these exercises.

1. Write the word that ends with the same sound that you hear at the end of *page*.

2-5. Write four words by adding one or two consonants to these vowel-consonant-*e* patterns.
   2. ＿ ide   **4.** ＿ ube
   3. ＿ ＿ ade   **5.** ＿ ＿ ile

Context Sentences   Write the Basic Word that completes each sentence.

6. We saw the gray ＿＿ from the fire.

7. The firefighters tried to ＿＿ the animals.

8. A deer saved its ＿＿ by standing in a lake.

9. Al wrote the firefighters a thank-you ＿＿.

10. This drawing of the fire is not hers but ＿＿.

ǀōǀ   **smoke**

o·consonant-e

🐘 **Elephant Words**   Write the Elephant Word that matches each meaning.

11. to move toward   12. to have warm feelings for

■ **Challenge Words**   Write the Challenge Word that fits each clue. Use your Spelling Dictionary.

13. Deer do this when they run from a fire.

14. People like to watch fireworks do this.

1.	
2.	
3.	
4.	
5.	
6.	
7.	
8.	
9.	
10.	
11.	
12.	
13.	
14.	

Summing Up

A long vowel sound is often spelled with the vowel-consonant-*e* pattern.

Basic

1. smoke
2. huge
3. save
4. life
5. wide
6. come
7. mine
8. grade
9. smile
10. note
11. cube
12. love

■ Challenge

13. escape
14. explode

Review

1. side
2. hope

_____
1. _____
2. _____
3. _____
4. _____
5. _____
6. _____

Expanding Vocabulary

Meanings for *save* When you save your money, do you rescue it from danger? *Save* has more than one meaning.

save   **a.** to rescue from danger
        b. to keep from wasting or spending

Practice **Which meaning of *save* is used in each sentence? Write the meaning.**

1. I <u>save</u> part of my allowance each week.
2. Police know how to <u>save</u> people in trouble.
3. I hope the firefighter can <u>save</u> my cat!
4. Dad will <u>save</u> that bone for the dog.

1. _____
2. _____
3. _____
4. _____

Dictionary

Parts of a Dictionary A dictionary lists words in ABC order. How could you find the word *cube* quickly? Turn to the beginning, where you will find the words starting with *c*.

BEGINNING	MIDDLE	END
abcdefg	hijklmnopq	rstuvwxyz

Practice **Write *beginning*, *middle*, or *end* to tell the part of the dictionary where you would find each word below.**

1. note   4. wide
2. save   5. mine
3. come   6. life

Review: Spelling Spree

Hink Pinks   Write the Basic Word that fits each clue and rhymes with the given word.

Example: a burning wheel   **tire** ___ *fire*

1. a message carrier   ___ **tote**
2. a changed test score   ___ **trade**
3. a place for happy faces   ___ **file**
4. a square straw   ___ **tube**
5. a fancy, deep hole in the ground   **fine** ___
6. a daring rescue   **brave** ___

Proofreading   7–14. Find and cross out eight misspelled Basic or Review Words. Then write each word correctly.

A hugh cloud of smok rose into the sky. Firefighters were able to save the homes, but they could not stop the fire from climbing up the sid of a wid hill. People luv this land. They hopp it will com to lif again soon.

■ **Challenge Words**   Make up two movie titles, using both Challenge Words. Begin the first, last, and each important word in each title with a capital letter. Underline your titles. Then write two sentences that tell what each movie is about.

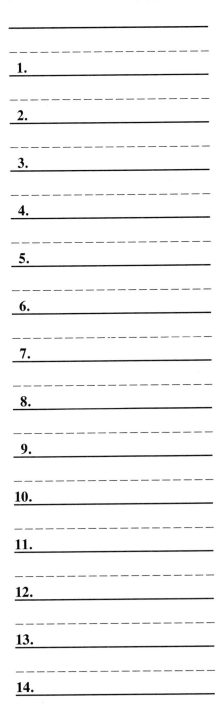

Writing Application: A Description   Write a description of a fire in the woods. Tell what you saw, heard, and felt. Try to use three words from the list on page 26.

1. ___
2. ___
3. ___
4. ___
5. ___
6. ___
7. ___
8. ___
9. ___
10. ___
11. ___
12. ___
13. ___
14. ___

3   Spelling Across the Curriculum

Science: *Forest Fires*

Theme Vocabulary

blaze
forest
animals
ranger
spark

Using Vocabulary   Write the Vocabulary Words to complete the paragraph. Use your Spelling Dictionary.

From her lookout tower, the park **(1)** could see miles of green **(2)**. No rain had fallen in weeks, and she was worried. Just one **(3)** from a match might start a **(4)**. This would harm the woodlands and the **(5)** that lived there.

Understanding Vocabulary   Write the Vocabulary Word that fits each clue.

6. You can hike or camp in this place.
7. This roars, crackles, and leaps.
8. This person watches over the woods.

1. _____
2. _____
3. _____
4. _____
5. _____
6. _____
7. _____
8. _____

FACT FILE

In 1950 a bear cub was saved from a forest fire. Now pictures of that bear, named Smokey, tell people to prevent forest fires.

Enrichment

👪 *Just What Do You Do?*

What is it like to be a forest ranger or a firefighter? Work with three or four of your classmates to find out about these jobs. Then write questions and answers for a TV interview. Role-play the interview by having one person play the firefighter or ranger and the other people play TV reporters.

POSTER POWER

Make a colorful poster to tell people how to prevent forest fires. Draw a forest scene. Write one or more sentences telling ways people can be careful. Try to use words from the lists in this unit.

📖 *Writing*
Wanted: Ranger

You work for a big park that needs to hire a forest ranger. Write a help wanted ad. Describe what a ranger does and what type of person should answer the ad. Try to use words from the lists in this unit. Be sure to proofread your ad.

Theme: Art Class

4 More Long Vowel Spellings

LOOK and **SAY**

A. _____

Basic Words

1. paint *paint*
2. clay *clay*
3. feel *feel*
4. leave *leave*
5. neighbor *neighbor*
6. eight *eight*
7. seem *seem*
8. speak *speak*
9. paid *paid*
10. lay *lay*
11. need *need*
12. weigh *weigh*

■ **Challenge**

13. easel *easel*   14. crayon *crayon*

THINK

Each word has the long *a* sound or the long *e* sound.

|ā| **paint, clay** |ē| **leave, feel**

B. _____

- What are two spelling patterns for the |ā| sound? Which pattern is used at the end of a word? How is the |ā| sound spelled in the Elephant Words? What are two spelling patterns for the |ē| sound?

WRITE

Practice   **Write Basic Words to answer the questions.**

■ **Challenge**

A. Which **seven** words have the |ā| sound? Remember the Elephant Words.
B. Which **five** words have the |ē| sound?

■ **Now write the two Challenge Words.**

CHECK

Independent Practice

Word Attack   Use Basic Words in these exercises.

1. Write the word that ends with two consonant sounds.

2-3. Write the two words that end with the |ā| sound spelled *ay*.

4-6. Write the three words that have the |ē| sound spelled *ee*.

Synonyms   A **synonym** is a word that means the same or almost the same as another word. Write a Basic Word that is a synonym for each word below.

7. talk
8. spent
9. go

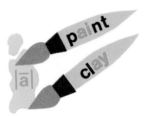

Elephant Words   Write the Elephant Word that completes each sentence.

10. Sid needs seven brushes, not ___.
11. This clay is heavy. It must ___ ten pounds.
12. My ___ Mrs. Ling is a famous painter.

■ **Challenge Words**   Write the Challenge Word that fits each meaning. Use your Spelling Dictionary.

13. a coloring stick
14. a stand for painting

1. _____
2. _____
3. _____
4. _____
5. _____
6. _____
7. _____
8. _____
9. _____
10. _____
11. _____
12. _____
13. _____
14. _____

Summing Up

The |ā| and the |ē| sounds can have these spelling patterns.
• The |ā| sound can be spelled *ai* or *ay*.
• The |ē| sound can be spelled *ea* or *ee*.

Basic

1. paint
2. clay
3. feel
4. leave
5. neighbor
6. eight
7. seem
8. speak
9. paid
10. lay
11. need
12. weigh

■ Challenge

13. easel
14. crayon

Review

1. green
2. play

Proofreading Marks

¶ Indent
∧ Add something
ℓ Take out something
≡ Capitalize
/ Make a small letter

Expanding Vocabulary

Thesaurus Look in a **thesaurus** for the best word to say what you mean. The entry for *put* shows that *lay* might be used instead of *put*.

main entry word   part of speech   definition

sample sentence
subentry

put *v.* to cause to be in a certain place.
Put the spoons in the drawer.
lay to put or set down.
He **lays** his coat on the bed.

Practice **Read pages 251–252. Then find each word below in your Thesaurus. Write the two subentries given for each word.**

1. new   **2.** hurry   **3.** walk

1. _____
2. _____
3. _____

Proofreading

End Marks End a sentence with the correct mark.

COMMAND: Please clean the paintbrush now.
EXCLAMATION: Sue's painting won first prize!

Practice **Proofread this ad. Use proofreading marks to correct three misspelled words. Add two missing end marks.**

Example: You can ~~leve~~ *leave* your troubles behind.

Do you paint or pla with clay?

Join the town art class You'll feal great

To sign up, spek to Mr. Hanks.

Review: Spelling Spree

Letter Math Write a Basic or Review Word by adding and taking away letters from the words below.

Example: gray − ay + een = *green*

1. clay − c =
2. see + m =
3. p + maid − m =
4. f + heel − h =
5. leaf − f + ve =
6. pl + spray − spr =
7. n + weigh − w + bor =
8. p + rain − r + t =
9. w + sleigh − sl =

Silly Rhymes Write a Basic or Review Word to complete each silly sentence. Each answer rhymes with the underlined word.

10. Did you ever ___ from a mountain <u>peak</u>?
11. Have you ever <u>seen</u> a sky that is ___?
12. A turtle has a ___ to <u>speed</u>.
13. That blue <u>jay</u> is made out of ___.
14. Does your <u>weight</u> include the number ___?

■ **Challenge Words** Look at the Letter Math activity. Then write three letter math problems for each Challenge Word. Put the answers on the back of your paper. Have a classmate figure out the problems.

Example: please − pl + l = *easel*

Writing Application: Instructions How do you clean paintbrushes or mix paint? Write step-by-step directions. Tell how to do something you learned in art class. Try to use three words from the list on page 32.

1. _____
2. _____
3. _____
4. _____
5. _____
6. _____
7. _____
8. _____
9. _____
10. _____
11. _____
12. _____
13. _____
14. _____

4   Spelling Across the Curriculum

Art: *Art Class*

Theme Vocabulary

picture
paste
poster
trace
marker

Using Vocabulary   Write the Vocabulary Words to complete the paragraph. Use your Spelling Dictionary.

Toby made a big __(1)__ to tell people about the art show. First, he cut out a __(2)__ of a famous painting from a magazine. Then he used glue to __(3)__ it onto heavy paper. Last, he used a blue __(4)__ to __(5)__ over words that he had written in large letters in pencil.

1. _____
2. _____
3. _____
4. _____
5. _____
6. _____
7. _____
8. _____

Understanding Vocabulary   Write a Vocabulary Word to answer each question.

6. What can you use to color?
7. What can make things stick together?
8. What can you make to announce a fair?

FACT FILE

The American painter Mary Cassatt studied in France. She often painted children and women taking part in everyday happenings.

FAMILY GROUP — READING (Detail), Mary Cassatt

Enrichment

👥 *Famous Painters*

With a small group, choose a painter. You might like Grandma Moses, Georges Seurat, Mary Cassatt, or Winslow Homer. Find out three facts about the artist. When and where did the artist live? What subjects did he or she usually paint? What are some of the artist's best-known paintings? Share your facts and pictures of the artist's paintings with your class.

📖 *Writing*
Art News

Which art project at school have you liked best? Write someone special a letter about it. Tell what you did, and explain why you liked it. Try to use words from the unit lists. Be sure to proofread your paper.

HIDDEN WORDS

Draw a picture of anything you want. As you draw, hide five or more spelling words in your art. For example, hide the word *play* in some grass. Can your classmates find the hidden words?

Theme: Swimming Race

5 Spelling the Long o Sound

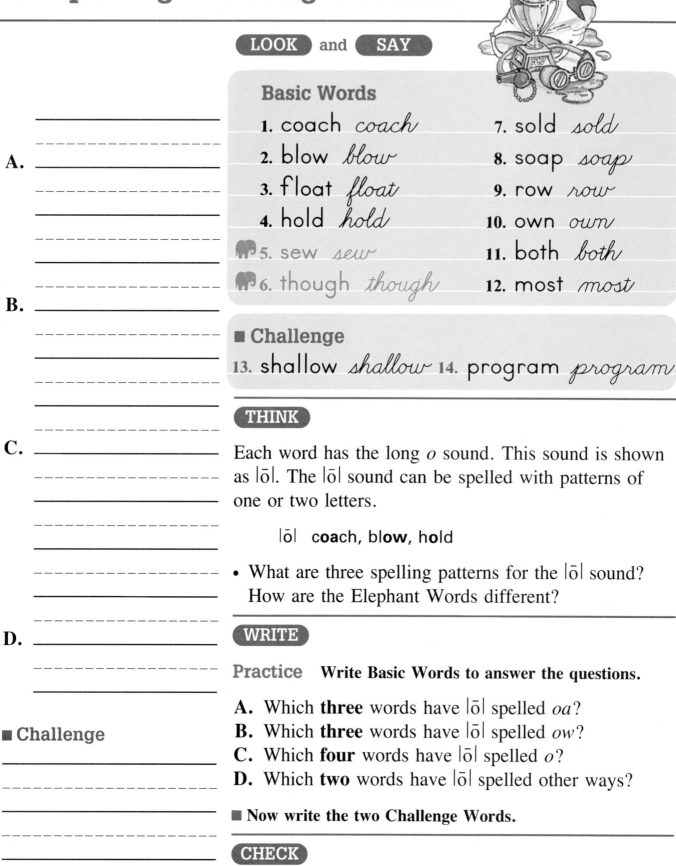

LOOK and **SAY**

Basic Words

1. coach *coach*
2. blow *blow*
3. float *float*
4. hold *hold*
5. sew *sew*
6. though *though*
7. sold *sold*
8. soap *soap*
9. row *row*
10. own *own*
11. both *both*
12. most *most*

■ Challenge

13. shallow *shallow* 14. program *program*

THINK

Each word has the long *o* sound. This sound is shown as |ō|. The |ō| sound can be spelled with patterns of one or two letters.

|ō| c**oa**ch, bl**ow**, h**o**ld

• What are three spelling patterns for the |ō| sound? How are the Elephant Words different?

WRITE

Practice   **Write Basic Words to answer the questions.**

A. Which **three** words have |ō| spelled *oa*?
B. Which **three** words have |ō| spelled *ow*?
C. Which **four** words have |ō| spelled *o*?
D. Which **two** words have |ō| spelled other ways?

■ Now write the two Challenge Words.

CHECK

A. _____
   _____
   _____
   _____

B. _____
   _____
   _____
   _____

C. _____
   _____
   _____
   _____
   _____

D. _____
   _____

■ Challenge
   _____
   _____
   _____
   _____

Independent Practice

Word Attack   Use Basic Words in these exercises.

1. Write the word that ends with the consonant sound you hear at the end of *each*.

2-3. Write the two words that rhyme with *cold*.

Context Sentences   Write the Basic Word that completes each sentence.

4. Do you sink in the water, or can you ___?

5. Jessie and Lianna are ___ good swimmers.

6. Carrie will ___ the boat beside the swimmer.

7. Can you ___ bubbles in the water?

8. Do you ___ this swimsuit, or is it Jason's?

9. Ms. Clark coaches ___ of these ten swimmers.

10. Please use ___ and warm water to wash your hands.

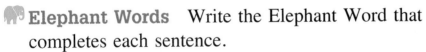

Elephant Words   Write the Elephant Word that completes each sentence.

11. Sam needs a needle and thread to ___ this rip.

12. Nan tried to smile even ___ she was sad.

Challenge Words   Write the Challenge Word that matches each meaning. Use your Spelling Dictionary.

13. not deep

14. a list of events and names

1.
2.
3.
4.
5.
6.
7.
8.
9.
10.
11.
12.
13.
14.

Summing Up

The lōl sound can be spelled with the pattern *oa, ow,* or *o.*

Basic

1. coach
2. blow
3. float
4. hold
5. sew
6. though
7. sold
8. soap
9. row
10. own
11. both
12. most

■ Challenge

13. shallow
14. program

Review

1. cold
2. slow

1. _____
2. _____
3. _____
4. _____

Expanding Vocabulary

Antonyms   *Sink* is the opposite of *float*.

Metal will **sink**, but wood will **float**.

Words with opposite meanings are **antonyms**.

Practice   Write the antonym for each underlined word. Use your Spelling Dictionary.

most	sold
hold	slow

1. Dena <u>bought</u> an old wagon at the yard sale.
2. Is Ed a <u>quick</u> swimmer?
3. Which movie is the <u>least</u> frightening?
4. Did Mr. Rice ask you to <u>drop</u> those books?

1. _____ 3. _____
2. _____ 4. _____

Dictionary

Guide Words   **Entry words** are the main words in a dictionary. They are in ABC order. Two **guide words** at the top of each page help you find words quickly. They tell the first and last entry words on the page.

---

lively | load

live·ly |līv′ lē| *adj.* **livelier, liveliest 1.** Full of life;

Practice   **1–4.** Write the four words that would be on the same page as the guide words *sky/sore*.

smell	sew	sold
spot	slow	soap

Review: Spelling Spree

Letter Swap   Change the underlined letter in each word to make a Basic Word. Write the Basic Words.

Example: l̲oad   *road*

1. ow̲e
2. p̲ost
3. sol̲o
4. bl̲ew
5. soa̲k
6. sa̲w
7. ba̲th
8. l̲ow

Proofreading   **9–14.** Find and cross out six misspelled Basic or Review Words. Then write each word correctly.

Last year Tanya could hardly flot, but she swam in a race today. She took holed of her cap and walked up to the dock. The koach yelled, "Go!" The girls dived into the cald water. Tanya was too slo today, thow. Both of her friends beat her.

■ **Challenge Words**   Make a pictionary. Write each Challenge Word and three other unit words on five half sheets of paper. Write one word on each sheet. Draw a picture that shows the meaning of each word.

Writing Application: An Opinion   Would you like to be in a swimming race? If not, what kind of race *would* you like to enter? Why? Write a paragraph that explains your choice. Try to use three words from the list on page 38.

1. _____
2. _____
3. _____
4. _____
5. _____
6. _____
7. _____
8. _____
9. _____
10. _____
11. _____
12. _____
13. _____
14. _____

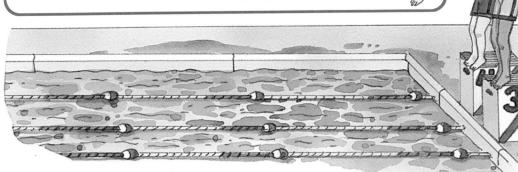

5 Spelling Across the Curriculum

Physical Education: *Swimming Race*

Theme Vocabulary

whistle
goggles
meet
lane
scoreboard

Using Vocabulary   Write the Vocabulary Words to complete the paragraph. Use your Spelling Dictionary.

The last race of the swim __(1)__ was about to begin. The racers pulled their __(2)__ over their eyes. The timer blew his __(3)__. Each racer dived into the pool and swam as quickly as possible down a __(4)__. The winning time was shown on the __(5)__.

Understanding Vocabulary   Is the underlined word used correctly? Write *yes* or *no*.

6. Do not eat <u>meet</u> before the race.
7. <u>Goggles</u> will keep your hair dry.
8. A red rope separated each <u>lane</u>.

1. _____
2. _____
3. _____
4. _____
5. _____
6. _____
7. _____
8. _____

FACT FILE

The butterfly stroke is often used in racing. As the swimmers move, they arch their arms forward like wings.

Enrichment

5

👥 *Ready, Set, Go!*

Players: 2 players and 1 reader **You need:** a drawing of a swimming pool with 2 racing lanes, each one divided into 8 spaces; game markers; a list of Basic and Review Words

How to play: Each player chooses a lane. The reader reads a spelling word to Player 1. If Player 1 spells the word correctly, he or she moves ahead one space. Players take turns until one player wins.

📖 *Writing*
Safety Rules

Should you dive into a crowded pool? How can you have fun in the water and stay safe too? Write a list of rules for safe swimming. Try to use words from the lists in this unit. Be sure to proofread your paper.

SWIMMER'S GUIDE

Make a swimmer's guide. Draw pictures that show what swimmers can do and what they wear. Do they float or blow bubbles? Do they wear caps or flippers? Label each picture. Try to use words from the lists in this unit.

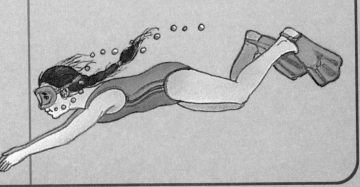

6 Review: Units 1–5

Unit 1 Short Vowels pp. 12–17

last	head	friend
thin	left	class

Remember: In most words, the |ă| sound is spelled **a**, the |ĕ| sound is spelled **e**, and the |ĭ| sound is spelled **i**.

smell mix

last

Write the word that is the opposite of each word below.

1. foot   3. first
2. right   4. fat

Write the word that completes each sentence.

5. Every Tuesday we have our music ___.
6. Uncle Mike, this is my best ___ Anna.

_____
1. _____

_____
2. _____

_____
3. _____

_____
4. _____

_____
5. _____

_____
6. _____

Unit 2 More Short Vowels pp. 18–23

luck	drop	does
sock	shut	front

Remember: In most words, the |ŏ| sound is spelled **o** and the |ŭ| sound is spelled **u**.

drop

luck

Write the word that rhymes with each word below.

7. but   8. knock

Write the word that completes each sentence.

9. Be careful you do not ___ those dishes.
10. What ___ Mr. Wood do for a living?
11. Someone is ringing the ___ doorbell.
12. It was just ___ that Andy found his glasses.

_____
7. _____

_____
8. _____

_____
9. _____

_____
10. _____

_____
11. _____

_____
12. _____

Half of the words from each unit are reviewed on these pages.
The rest are reviewed on pages 229–231.

Unit 3 Vowel-Consonant-e Pattern pp. 24–29

save	smoke	come
cube	smile	love

Remember: A long vowel sound is often spelled vowel-consonant-**e**.

Write the word that means the opposite of each word.

13. frown **14.** hate **15.** go

Write the word that completes each sentence.

16. Trisha needs another ice ___ for her juice.
17. Clouds of ___ came from the forest fire.
18. Chuck is trying to ___ money for a bike.

13. ___
14. ___
15. ___
16. ___
17. ___
18. ___

Unit 4 More Long Vowel Spellings pp. 30–35

leave	clay	eight
paid	seem	weigh

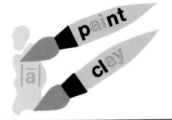

Remember: In many words, the |ā| sound is spelled **ai** or **ay**. The |ē| sound may be spelled **ea** or **ee**.

Write the word that completes each sentence.

19. Where is the ___ for art class?
20. Nina has ___ cousins, not seven.
21. How much does your new baby brother ___?
22. Uncle Bob has already ___ for the tickets.
23. Eva and Li ___ to have lost their money.
24. Did Adam ___ the party already?

19. ___
20. ___
21. ___
22. ___
23. ___
24. ___

6   Review

Unit 5   Spelling the Long *o* Sound   pp. 36–41

coach	sew	though
most	own	soap

Remember: The |ō| sound is often spelled **oa**, **ow**, or **o**.

Write the word that belongs in each group.
25. needle, cloth, ____   **26.** game, team, ____
Write the word that completes each sentence.
27. I hate ____ in my eyes when I wash my hair.
28. Who has the ____ baseball cards?
29. Teresa wants her ____ skateboard.
30. Lou likes to jog, ____ he is often too busy.

25. _____
26. _____
27. _____
28. _____
29. _____
30. _____

■ Challenge Words   Units 1–5   pp. 12–41

empty	crumb	escape
crayon	program	

Write the word that completes each sentence.
31. Dad, you have a ____ of toast on your tie.
32. Lee needs a purple ____ to color her picture.
33. Mary Ann's dog keeps trying to ____ from the yard.
34. Pam's piggy bank is ____ because she bought several gifts.
35. Look at the ____, and tell me which band will play next.

31. _____
32. _____
33. _____
34. _____
35. _____

44

Word Forms

Like people, words have families. The words in a family look alike in some ways. They also have a common "family" meaning. They are related to each other. Read this paragraph.

Lisa collects **stickers**. She **sticks** some on her backpack, but she keeps most of them in books. Her favorite ones show boats.

Think

- How are *stickers* and *sticks* alike in meaning?
- How are *stickers* and *sticks* alike in spelling?

Here are words in the *stick* family.

stick	stickier	stickers
sticky	stickiest	stickiness

Apply and Extend

Complete these activities on another piece of paper.

1. Look up the meaning of each word in the Word Box above in your Spelling Dictionary. Write six sentences, using one word in each sentence.

2. With a partner list words related to *thick*, *mix*, and *luck*. Then look in your Spelling-Meaning Index beginning on page 268. Add any other words in these families to your list.

A Story About Yourself

John is visiting his grandfather. How can you tell that his grandfather is blind?

The sun wakes Grandpa differently from the way it wakes me. He says it touches him, *warming* him awake. When I look in the room, Grandpa is already up and doing his morning exercises, bending and stretching by the bed. He stops and smiles because he hears me.

"Good morning, John."

I exercise with Grandpa. Up and down. Then I try to exercise with my eyes closed.

"One, two," says Grandpa, "three, four."

"Wait!" I cry. I am still on one, two when Grandpa is on three, four.

I fall sideways. Three times. Grandpa laughs as he hears me falling on the floor.

from Through Grandpa's Eyes
by Patricia MacLachlan

Think and Discuss

1. What **details** tell you that Grandpa has a special way of seeing?
2. Why does the **beginning** of the story make you want to learn more about Grandpa?
3. Who is the **I** in the story? How do you know?

The Writing Process

In the story on page 46, John shares an experience. You can too. Write a **beginning** that makes the reader want to know more. Use **details** that make the story seem real. Use *I* in the story.

Assignment: Write a Story About Yourself

Step One: Prewriting

1. List interesting things you have done, and discuss them with a partner. Choose a topic.
2. Write two beginnings. Choose your favorite.

Step Two: Write a First Draft

1. Think about your purpose and your audience.
2. Do not worry about mistakes—just write!

Step Three: Revise

1. Where could details make your story clearer?
2. Use your Thesaurus to find exact words.
3. Read your story to a friend. Make changes.

Step Four: Proofread

1. Did you begin and end each sentence correctly?
2. Did you correct any misspelled words? Add them to your Notebook for Writing.

Step Five: Publish

Copy your story. Add a title. Share your story.

Composition Words

friend
last
does
come
huge
neighbor
most
own

Proofreading Marks

¶ Indent
⋀ Add something
ℒ Take out something
≡ Capitalize
/ Make a small letter

Theme: Baseball

7 Three-Letter Clusters

LOOK and **SAY**

A. _____

Basic Words

1. spring *spring*
2. throw *throw*
3. strong *strong*
4. three *three*
5. straight *straight*
6. scream *scream*
7. stream *stream*
8. spray *spray*
9. screen *screen*
10. street *street*
11. spread *spread*
12. string *string*

B. _____

■ **Challenge**

13. strength *strength*   14. struggle *struggle*

C. _____

THINK

Each word begins with three consonants. You can hear their different sounds. When two or more consonants with different sounds are written together, they form a **consonant cluster**.

scream   **spr**ing   **str**ong   **thr**ow

• What consonant cluster begins each word above?

D. _____

WRITE

Practice   Write Basic Words to answer the questions.

A. Which **two** words begin with *scr*?
B. Which **three** words begin with *spr*?
C. Which **five** words begin with *str*?
D. Which **two** words begin with *thr*?

■ **Challenge**

■ **Now write the two Challenge Words.**

CHECK

Independent Practice

Word Attack   Use Basic Words in these exercises.

1. Write the word that ends with the |ō| sound.

2. Write the word that rhymes with *long*.

3. Write the word that rhymes with *bread*.

4-5. Write the two words that have the |ā| sound.

6-7. Write the two words that have the |ē| sound spelled *ea*.

Classifying   Write the Basic Word that belongs in each group.

8. path, road, ____
9. ribbon, thread, ____
10. winter, fall, ____
11. one, two, ____
12. movie, theater, ____

 **str**ing

■ **Challenge Words**   Write the Challenge Word that completes each sentence. Use your Spelling Dictionary.

13. Two teams, the Screaming Eagles and the Fighting Tigers, are in a ____ for first place.

14. Does Tommy Joe have the ____ to pitch all nine innings?

1. _____
2. _____
3. _____
4. _____
5. _____
6. _____
7. _____
8. _____
9. _____
10. _____
11. _____
12. _____
13. _____
14. _____

Summing Up

When you hear the different sounds of two or more consonants written together, the consonants form a **consonant cluster**. Some words begin with the consonant clusters *scr*, *spr*, *str*, and *thr*.

Basic

1. spring
2. throw
3. strong
4. three
5. straight
6. scream
7. stream
8. spray
9. screen
10. street
11. spread
12. string

■ **Challenge**

13. strength
14. struggle

Review

1. glad
2. start

Expanding Vocabulary

Rhyming Words You can have fun with rhyming words, such as *stream*, *cream*, and *team*.

Practice **Write a rhyming word for each clue.**

1. It rhymes with *scream*. It happens during sleep.

2. It rhymes with *street*. It is a red vegetable.

3. It rhymes with *spray*. It is used in art class.

4. It rhymes with *spread*. It is used for sewing.

1. _____

2. _____

3. _____

4. _____

Dictionary

Definitions A dictionary entry has one or more **definitions**, or meanings, for the entry word. A **sample sentence** helps to make a meaning clear.

definition

street |strēt| *n. pl.* **streets** A road in a city or town: *I live on this street.*

sample sentence

Practice **Use your Spelling Dictionary to complete the exercises.**

1. Look up *strong*. Write the definition.
2. Look up *spread*. Write the sample sentence.

1. _____

2. _____

Review: Spelling Spree

Letter Math   Write Basic or Review Words by
solving the problems below.
Example: thr + bee − b = *three*
1. gl + had − h =   5. spr + play − pl =
2. str + dream − dr =   6. scr + green − gr =
3. spr + head − h =   7. str + cling − cl =
4. st + dart − d =   8. spr + thing − th =

Proofreading   9–14. Find and cross out six
misspelled Basic Words in Leroy's letter. Then write
each word correctly.

Dear Grandpa and Grandma,

   The Smalltown baseball team is strog
this spring. Our players thro hard! Bigtown
hit first today. The team made thee strait
outs. Then Smalltown scored a string of
runs. Our fans really did screem! Mom
heard them all the way up the streat!

■ **Challenge Words**   Write two sayings for T-shirts.
Use each Challenge Word in one of the sayings.
Example: Red Sox, struggle on and win!

📖 *Writing Application:* Creative Writing
Write a short story about the picture on this page.
Who is in it? What is happening? Try to use three
words from the list on page 50.

1.
2.
3.
4.
5.
6.
7.
8.
9.
10.
11.
12.
13.
14.

7 Spelling Across the Curriculum

Physical Education: *Baseball*

Theme Vocabulary

home run
base
mitt
pitch
bleachers

Using Vocabulary Write the Vocabulary Words to complete this paragraph. Use your Spelling Dictionary.

Jill is a great baseball player. Today she hit Jim's first __(1)__ beyond third __(2)__ . The fans in the __(3)__ cheered. It was the first __(4)__ this year! Later, Jill caught a fly ball in her __(5)__ .

Understanding Vocabulary Is the underlined word used correctly? Write *yes* or *no*.

6. Meg has a sore arm and cannot <u>pitch</u>.
7. Fred's <u>home run</u> tied the score.
8. The team used <u>bleachers</u> to clean their uniforms.

1. _____

2. _____

3. _____

4. _____

5. _____

6. _____

7. _____

8. _____

FACT FILE

Babe Ruth was a great baseball hero. He hit 714 home runs in 22 seasons. He broke or tied 76 batting and pitching records. Ruth was called the Sultan of Swat.

Enrichment

👨‍👩‍👧‍👦 *Home Run*

Players: two teams of 4 or more, a "pitcher" **You need:** a list of Basic and Review Words

How to play: The "pitcher" reads words to "batters" on one team. Each batter must correctly spell his or her word to score a home run, or one point. If the word is not spelled correctly, the batter is out. After three outs, the other team is up to bat.

📖 *Writing*
Start Playing!

What is your favorite sport or game? Think about why you enjoy playing it. Write a paragraph, giving reasons why someone should play your game or sport. Try to use unit list words. Be sure to proofread your paper.

AUTOGRAPH MITT

Draw a big mitt on heavy paper, and cut it out. Then choose nine words from the unit lists, and make up funny names for a baseball team. Write the team names on your mitt.

Example: Zing the Spring

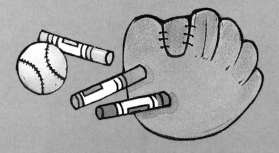

(Theme: Flowers)

8 Spelling the Long i Sound

LOOK and SAY

A. _____

B. _____

C. _____

■ Challenge

_____

Basic Words

1. wild *wild*
2. bright *bright*
3. die *die*
4. sight *sight*
5. child *child*
6. pie *pie*
7. fight *fight*
8. lie *lie*
9. tight *tight*
10. tie *tie*
11. might *might*
12. mind *mind*

■ Challenge

13. lilac *lilac*   14. delight *delight*

THINK

Each word has the long *i* sound. This sound is shown as |ī|. The |ī| sound can be spelled with patterns of one, two, or three letters.

|ī| br**igh**t, w**i**ld, d**ie**

• What are three spelling patterns for the |ī| sound?

WRITE

Practice **Write Basic Words to answer the questions.**

A. Which **five** words have |ī| spelled *igh*?
B. Which **three** words have |ī| spelled *i*?
C. Which **four** words have |ī| spelled *ie*?

■ Now write the two Challenge Words.

CHECK

Independent Practice

Word Attack   Use Basic Words in these exercises.

1. Write the word that begins with the sound you hear at the beginning of *wide*.

2. Write the word that rhymes with *kind*.

3-4. Write the two words that begin with the sounds you hear at the beginning of *brave* and *chop*.

Context Sentences   Write the Basic Word that completes each sentence.

5. Use string to ___ the sunflowers to a stick.

6. Those fresh flowers are a beautiful ___.

7. I often ___ in the garden and look at the sky.

8. Plants ___ if they do not get enough water.

9. Those flowers look too ___ in that small vase.

10. If Jamie smells those flowers on your desk, he ___ sneeze.

11. Do not have a ___ over who will do the dishes.

12. These cherries will taste good in a ___.

■ **Challenge Words**   Write the Challenge Word that completes each sentence. Use your Spelling Dictionary.

13. A ___ may be pink, purple, or white.

14. What a ___ to see such colorful flowers!

1. _____
2. _____
3. _____
4. _____
5. _____
6. _____
7. _____
8. _____
9. _____
10. _____
11. _____
12. _____
13. _____
14. _____

Summing Up

The |ī| sound can be spelled with the pattern *igh*, *i*, or *ie*.

Basic

1. wild
2. bright
3. die
4. sight
5. child
6. pie
7. fight
8. lie
9. tight
10. tie
11. might
12. mind

■ Challenge

13. lilac
14. delight

Review

1. find
2. night

Expanding Vocabulary

Antonyms Which word is an antonym for *bright*: *dull* or *shining*? *Dull* is the antonym because it means the opposite of *bright*.

Practice Write the word below that is an antonym for each numbered word.

| night | tight | wild | lie | die | child |

1. adult
2. loose
3. tame
4. truth
5. live
6. day

1. _____
2. _____
3. _____
4. _____
5. _____
6. _____

Dictionary

Pronunciation Key A dictionary entry has a **pronunciation** that helps you say the entry word.

tie |tī| ←—pronunciation

The **pronunciation key** tells you what sounds the symbols in the pronunciation stand for. It gives a sample word for each sound. For example, *ice* has the vowel sound shown by ī.

ī ice

Practice Write the word in the key below that helps you say the vowel sound in each pronunciation.

Example: |rŭb| *cut*

| ā pay | ē be | ō go | ŭ cut |

1. |lŭv| 2. |nēd| 3. |grād| 4. |sōk|

1. _____
2. _____
3. _____
4. _____

Review: Spelling Spree

Hink Pinks   Write the Basic or Review Word that fits the clue and rhymes with the given word.

Example: you and two friends   **we** ____ *three*

1. a quiet little boy or girl   **mild** ____
2. a shining fighter for a king   ____ **knight**
3. a bedtime lamp   ____-**light**
4. a gentle brain   **kind** ____
5. a crowded plane   ____ **flight**
6. a correct argument   **right** ____

Proofreading   7–14. Find and cross out eight misspelled Basic or Review Words. Then write each word correctly.

   I will fin some flowers for my mom's birthday. I can ti them with bright ribbon and put them in water so they won't diy. Then I mite pick wil berries to make piy. That will be a pretty site! When it's ready, I'll ly down and rest.

■ **Challenge Words**   Pretend that you have a garden shop. Write an ad to sell flower bushes. Use both Challenge Words in your ad.

📖 *Writing Application:* A Poem   Write a short poem about flowers, using pairs of rhyming words. Try to use three words from the list on page 56.

1.
2.
3.
4.
5.
6.
7.
8.
9.
10.
11.
12.
13.
14.

8   Spelling Across the Curriculum

Science: *Flowers*

Theme Vocabulary

April
May
daisy
tulip
violet

Using Vocabulary   Write the Vocabulary Words to complete the paragraph. Use your Spelling Dictionary.

Where I live, spring flowers bloom in **(1)** , the fourth month of the year. The tiny **(2)** is first, followed by the bright red **(3)** . Next we see the white or yellow **(4)** . Then it is the month of **(5)** !

1. _____
2. _____
3. _____
4. _____
5. _____
6. _____
7. _____
8. _____

Understanding Vocabulary   Write *yes* or *no* to answer each question.

6. Does a violet grow tall?
7. Does April come before May?
8. Is May the sixth month of the year?

FACT FILE

A sunflower looks like a giant daisy. It may grow to be ten feet tall, with a blossom one foot wide. Its seeds are used as food.

Enrichment

Flower Facts

Make a class flower display. With a partner, find out facts about a flower shown on this page or another flower that interests you. What colors can it be? Where does it grow? When does it bloom? Draw a picture of your flower. Label it, and list facts about it. Pin it on the bulletin board.

WORD DAISY

Make a big paper daisy with twelve petals. Write |ī| in the center. On each petal write a spelling word that has the |ī| sound. Can you think of even more |ī| words? Write them on bumblebees flying around your daisy.

child
sight
|ī|

Writing
Flower Tale

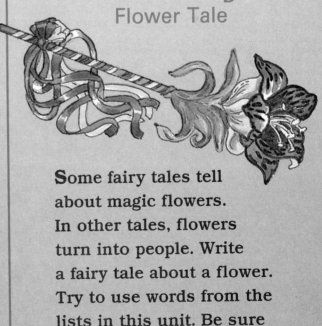

Some fairy tales tell about magic flowers. In other tales, flowers turn into people. Write a fairy tale about a flower. Try to use words from the lists in this unit. Be sure to proofread your story.

9 The Vowel Sound in clown

A. _____

B. _____

C. _____

■ Challenge

LOOK and SAY

Basic Words

1. clown *clown*
2. crowd *crowd*
3. round *round*
4. sound *sound*
5. bow *bow*
🐘 6. would *would*
7. loud *loud*
8. ground *ground*
9. crown *crown*
10. count *count*
11. cloud *cloud*
12. mouth *mouth*

■ Challenge

13. bounce *bounce*   14. sprout *sprout*

THINK

Most of the words have the vowel sound you hear in *clown*. This sound is shown as |ou|.

> |ou| cl**ow**n, r**ou**nd

• What are two spelling patterns for the |ou| sound? How is the Elephant Word different?

WRITE

Practice   Write Basic Words to answer the questions.

A. Which **four** words have |ou| spelled *ow*?
B. Which **seven** words have |ou| spelled *ou*?
C. Which **one** word has the *ou* pattern but does not have the |ou| sound?

■ Now write the two Challenge Words.

CHECK

Independent Practice

Word Attack   Use Basic Words in these exercises.

1-2. Write the two words that begin with the same consonant cluster as *creek*.

3-5. Write the three words that rhyme with *found*.

Making Inferences   Write the Basic Word that matches each clue.

6. Sometimes the moon hides behind this.
7. You do this when you say 1–2–3–4.
8. This part of the face smiles or frowns.
9. You might do this if you met a king or a queen.
10. This is the funny person in the circus.
11. This is how a plane sounds when it takes off.

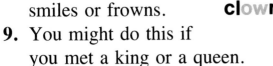

round
clown
|ou|

Elephant Word   Write the Elephant Word that completes the sentence.
12. Charleen ___ like to be a clown in a circus or a play.

■**Challenge Words**   Write the Challenge Word that completes each sentence. Use your Spelling Dictionary.
13. Look at that little seal ___ a ball on its nose.
14. Flowers are starting to ___ in my grandfather's garden.

1. _____
2. _____
3. _____
4. _____
5. _____
6. _____
7. _____
8. _____
9. _____
10. _____
11. _____
12. _____
13. _____
14. _____

Summing Up

The |ou| sound, as in *clown* and *round*, is often spelled with the pattern *ow* or *ou*.

Basic
1. clown
2. crowd
3. round
4. sound
5. bow
6. would
7. loud
8. ground
9. crown
10. count
11. cloud
12. mouth

■ Challenge
13. bounce
14. sprout

Review
1. town
2. out

Proofreading Marks
¶ Indent
∧ Add something
ℓ Take out something
≡ Capitalize
/ Make a small letter

Expanding Vocabulary

The Word bow *Bow* has different pronunciations and meanings. What are two meanings of |bou|? What is one meaning of |bō|?

a. bow |bou| to bend the body, head, or knee
b. bow |bou| the front part of a ship or a boat
c. bow |bō| a weapon for shooting arrows

Practice   Which meaning of bow is used in each sentence? Write the letter of the meaning.
1. Waves crashed over the <u>bow</u> of the rowboat.
2. Actors <u>bow</u> at the end of a play.
3. Native Americans used the <u>bow</u> for hunting.

1. _____   2. _____   3. _____

Proofreading

Proper Nouns   A proper noun names a special person, place, or thing. Capitalize proper nouns.

Pablo Gomez   Maine   Big Top Circus

Practice   Proofread part of Ed's post card to Stacy. Use proofreading marks to correct three misspelled words and two missing capital letters.

Example: I saw old ~~cloun~~ clown costumes in florida.

Dear stacy,

There was a croud at the Ringling Circus Galleries in the toun of sarasota.

You wood like the huge clown shoes.

Review: Spelling Spree

Finding Words   Write the Basic or Review Word in each of these words.

1. clowning
2. outside
3. crowded
4. loudest
5. underground
6. counting

Silly Rhymes   Write the Basic or Review Word that best completes each silly sentence. Each answer rhymes with the underlined word.

7. A circus <u>clown</u> is king of our ____.
8. If the pig <u>could</u> dance, it ____.
9. The bear looked <u>south</u> and opened its ____.
10. I clapped for the <u>cow</u> that was taking a ____.
11. The king has a <u>brown</u> hat on top of his ____.
12. Would you be <u>proud</u> to sit on a soft white ____?
13. Listen to the happy <u>hound</u> make a sad ____.
14. The lucky horse <u>found</u> a merry-go-____.

```
Brown bears
One pony
U
N
C
E
```

■ **Challenge Words**   Write the Challenge Words down a piece of paper. For each letter, write a word or group of words about the circus. Two examples are shown.

📖 *Writing Application:* A Description
Describe the circus act you like best. Who is in it? How do they look? What do they do? Use details in your "picture." Try to use three words from the list on page 62.

1. _____
2. _____
3. _____
4. _____
5. _____
6. _____
7. _____
8. _____
9. _____
10. _____
11. _____
12. _____
13. _____
14. _____

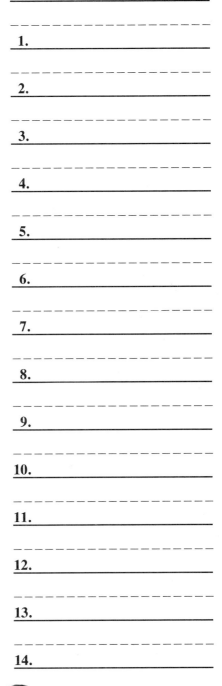

9 Spelling Across the Curriculum

Recreation: *The Circus*

Theme Vocabulary

elephant
trainer
roar
acrobat
juggler

Using Vocabulary Write the Vocabulary Words to complete the paragraph. Use your Spelling Dictionary.

The circus parade was led by an __(1)__ walking on his hands. Next, Tommy heard a loud, angry __(2)__ and saw a lion with its __(3)__. Then a huge gray __(4)__ marched by, swinging its trunk. Last, Tommy saw a __(5)__ throwing seven oranges into the air and catching them.

Understanding Vocabulary Write a Vocabulary Word to answer each riddle.

6. What kind of bat does flips?
7. What animal carries a big trunk?
8. What can be heard but not seen?

1. _____

2. _____

3. _____

4. _____

5. _____

6. _____

7. _____

8. _____

FACT FILE

P.T. Barnum began the most famous circus in the world. One star was an elephant named Jumbo. *Jumbo* came to mean "very big."

Enrichment

TALKING CLOWNS

Make a talking clown! Draw a large clown face on heavy paper. Draw an open mouth, and make a cut at each end. Then cut out long strips of cardboard. Write a sentence, using a unit word, on each strip. Have the clown "talk" to a classmate by sliding the strips through its mouth as you read the sentences.

The crowd elled.

📖 *Writing*
The Greatest Act

Write a tale about an animal that becomes a circus star. What is its greatest act? How does the star get the circus owner to let it perform? What happens when the star performs for a crowd? Try to use words from the unit lists. Be sure to proofread your story.

👥 *Circus Train*

With a group of classmates, make an |ou| circus train. First, draw and cut out cars for the train. Next, write |ou| on the engine. Then write a Basic or Review Word on each car. Last, tape the cars together to form a train.

loud |ou|

Theme: A Cookout

10 The Vowel Sound in lawn

LOOK and SAY

A. _____

B. _____

C. _____

■ Challenge
_____

Basic Words

1. lawn *lawn*
2. raw *raw*
3. cloth *cloth*
4. talk *talk*
5. straw *straw*
6. almost *almost*
7. soft *soft*
8. also *also*
9. wall *wall*
10. law *law*
11. walk *walk*
12. cost *cost*

■ Challenge

13. scald *scald*
14. flaw *flaw*

THINK

Each word has the vowel sound you hear in *lawn*.
This sound is shown as |ô|. The |ô| sound can be
spelled with patterns of one or two letters.

|ô| **la**wn, c**lo**th, **al**most

- What are three spelling patterns for the |ô| sound?
  What consonant follows |ô| when it is spelled *a*?

WRITE

Practice **Write Basic Words to answer the questions.**

A. Which **four** words have |ô| spelled *aw*?
B. Which **three** words have |ô| spelled *o*?
C. Which **five** words have |ô| spelled *a* before *l*?

■ **Now write the two Challenge Words.**

CHECK

Independent Practice

Word Attack Use Basic Words in these exercises.

1. Write the word that begins with a three-letter consonant cluster.

2. Write the word that ends with a double consonant.

3-4. Write the two words that have the |ō| sound.

Context Sentences Write the Basic Word that completes each sentence.
5. I will ___ to Frank about the cookout plans.
6. The cookout will be held on the back ___.
7. The potato salad will ___ less than one dollar.
8. Chen likes his steak well done, not ___.
9. Clean the picnic basket with a wet ___.
10. Carmen and Ellen are taking a ___ by the pond.
11. Is there a ___ against burning leaves in town?
12. This thick grass feels very ___.

lawn | talk | cost
|ô|

■ **Challenge Words** Write the Challenge Word that completes each sentence. Use your Spelling Dictionary.
13. I knitted a perfect sweater. There was not one ___ in it.
14. If I spill that hot soup, I might ___ myself.

1. _____
2. _____
3. _____
4. _____
5. _____
6. _____
7. _____
8. _____
9. _____
10. _____
11. _____
12. _____
13. _____
14. _____

Summing Up

The |ô| sound can be spelled with these patterns:
- *aw*, as in *lawn*
- *a* before *l*, as in *almost*
- *o*, as in *cloth*

Basic

1. lawn
2. raw
3. cloth
4. talk
5. straw
6. almost
7. soft
8. also
9. wall
10. law
11. walk
12. cost

■ Challenge

13. scald
14. flaw

Review

1. saw
2. small

Proofreading Marks

¶ Indent
∧ Add something
℮ Take out something
≡ Capitalize
/ Make a small letter

Expanding Vocabulary

Exact Words for *talk* Which word more clearly tells that Tim and Sandy do not agree?

Tim and Sandy **talk.**   Tim and Sandy **argue.**

Argue means "to disagree." It is more exact than *talk*. Always try to use exact words.

Practice **Write the exact word for** *talk* **below that best fits each sentence. Use your Thesaurus.**

gossip   answer   scold

1. I ___ my puppy when it chews the rug.
2. It is unkind to ___ about your neighbors.
3. Did you ___ that question correctly?

1. _____   3. _____

2. _____

Proofreading

Singular Possessive Nouns A **possessive noun** shows ownership. Add an **apostrophe** (') and an *s* to a singular noun to make it possessive.

boy + 's = boy's bike   Eli + 's = Eli's cat

Practice **Proofread this paragraph from a story. Use proofreading marks to correct three misspelled words. Add two missing apostrophes.**

Example: I ~~sow~~ saw Lee's friend Tom.

When I went to Toms cookout, I also

took my smal dog. It ate a mans strow hat

that cost allmost six dollars.

Review: Spelling Spree

Classifying   Write the Basic or Review Word that belongs with each group of pictures.

1.

2.

3.

4.

Questions   Write a Basic or Review Word to answer each question.

5. What has doors or windows in it?
6. How does a rabbit like its carrot?
7. How does a pillow feel?
8. What is it rude to do if your mouth is full?
9. What word means ''nearly''?
10. What size shirt does a baby wear?
11. What is written on a price tag?
12. What word means ''too''?
13. What is a rule everyone must obey?
14. What can you do if you are too tired to run?

■ **Challenge Words**   Write two questions that can be answered by one Challenge Word and two that can be answered by the other Challenge Word. Trade papers with a partner, and answer each other's questions.

📖 *Writing Application:* A Bulletin Board Note
Write a note about a school cookout. Include when the cookout will be and what people should bring. Write complete sentences. Try to use three words from the list on page 68.

1. _____
2. _____
3. _____
4. _____
5. _____
6. _____
7. _____
8. _____
9. _____
10. _____
11. _____
12. _____
13. _____
14. _____

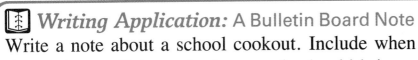

10   Spelling Across the Curriculum

Recreation: *A Cookout*

Theme Vocabulary

grill
hamburger
charcoal
apron
table

Using Vocabulary Write the Vocabulary Words to complete the paragraph. Use your Spelling Dictionary.

   Uncle Ted is starting a fire in the __(1)__ for our cookout. He is using a big bag of black __(2)__. Now he has tied on his cook's __(3)__. Please put the cups and plates on the __(4)__. The first juicy __(5)__ will soon be ready!

Understanding Vocabulary Write a Vocabulary Word to match each clue.

6. It protects your clothes when you cook.
7. It is often eaten with ketchup or pickles.
8. You use it for outdoor cooking.

1. _____
2. _____
3. _____
4. _____
5. _____
6. _____
7. _____
8. _____

FACT FILE

One kind of cookout is a clambake. Rocks are heated in a pit and covered with seaweed. Then lobsters, clams, and corn are baked on the hot rocks.

Enrichment

📖 *Writing*
Menu Magic

Plan a cookout menu. List four or five things to eat and drink. Write a sentence that describes each one. Would you like to have chicken, hamburgers, and salad? Or do you like to make up silly foods, such as peanut butter burgers and potato-raisin juice? Try to use words from the lists in this unit. Be sure to proofread your menu.

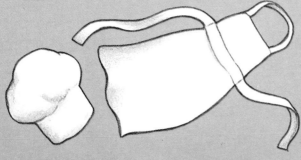

A COOK'S CLOTHES

Design a cook's hat and apron. First, draw pictures of them. Then add some funny sayings that use spelling words, such as "I can cook *almost* anything." How many words can you use?

👥 *Burger Mix-Up*

Write steps for making your favorite hamburger. Try to use words from the unit lists. Begin a new line for each step. Then cut apart the steps. Trade your steps with a partner. Try to put each other's steps in order.

11 Unexpected Consonant Patterns

LOOK and **SAY**

A. _____

B. _____

C. _____

Basic Words

1. knee *knee*
2. scratch *scratch*
3. patch *patch*
4. wrap *wrap*
5. knot *knot*
6. wrong *wrong*
7. watch *watch*
8. knife *knife*
9. write *write*
10. knock *knock*
11. match *match*
12. know *know*

■ Challenge

13. stretcher *stretcher*   14. knuckle *knuckle*

THINK

Each word has an unexpected spelling for a consonant sound. One letter is ''silent,'' or not pronounced.

|n| **kn**ee |r| **wr**ap |ch| scra**tch**

• What are unexpected spelling patterns for the |n|, the |r|, and the |ch| sounds? Which letter in each pattern is silent?

WRITE

Practice   **Write Basic Words to answer the questions.**

A. Which **five** words begin with the |n| sound?
B. Which **three** words begin with the |r| sound?
C. Which **four** words end with the |ch| sound?

■ **Now write the two Challenge Words.**

■ Challenge

_____

CHECK

Independent Practice

Word Attack   Use Basic Words in these exercises.

1. Write the word that ends with |ē| spelled *ee*.

2. Write the word that ends with |ō| spelled *ow*.

3-4. Write the two words with |ī| spelled
   i-consonant-*e*.

Context Sentences   Write the Basic Word that
completes each sentence.

5. With a broken hand,
   Dad cannot tie the ___.

6. The nurse checked the
   time on his ___.

7. Did you ___ the sick
   cat in a warm blanket?

8. The cat made a long
   red ___ on my hand.

9. Just walk in after you ___ on the nurse's door.

10. The burn from a ___ can be very painful.

11. It is ___ to put anything greasy on a burn.

12. After Dina walked through a ___ of poison oak,
    her legs itched.

■ Challenge Words   Write the Challenge Word that
completes each sentence. Use your Spelling Dictionary.

13. The two men carried the hurt girl on a ___.

14. Alice scraped the ___ of her thumb.

1. _____
2. _____
3. _____
4. _____
5. _____
6. _____
7. _____
8. _____
9. _____
10. _____
11. _____
12. _____
13. _____
14. _____

Summing Up

Some words have unexpected consonant patterns.
- A beginning |n| sound may be spelled *kn*.
- A beginning |r| sound may be spelled *wr*.
- A final |ch| sound may be spelled *tch*.

Basic

1. knee
2. scratch
3. patch
4. wrap
5. knot
6. wrong
7. watch
8. knife
9. write
10. knock
11. match
12. know

■ **Challenge**

13. stretcher
14. knuckle

Review

1. catch
2. two

Expanding Vocabulary

Words That Begin with *wr* Long ago the *w* in *wrap* was pronounced. Now it is silent. Here are other words with the |r| sound spelled *wr*.

wrench   wren   wreath   wring

Practice **Write the word above that fits each meaning. Use your Spelling Dictionary.**

1. a circle of flowers
2. to twist or squeeze
3. a small brown bird
4. a tool for turning

1. _____

2. _____

3. _____

4. _____

Dictionary

Choosing the Correct Meaning When an entry word has more than one meaning, the meanings are numbered. A sample sentence may be given to make a meaning clear.

wrong |rông| *adj.* **1.** Not correct. **2.** Bad: *It is wrong to lie.* **3.** Not working correctly.

Practice **Write the meaning of *wrong* that is used in each sentence.**

1. It is <u>wrong</u> to steal.
2. Two names on the map were <u>wrong</u>.
3. Is something <u>wrong</u> with Billy Joe's radio?

1. _____

2. _____

3. _____

Review: Spelling Spree

Word Web   1–8. Find eight Basic or Review Words by matching the letters. One word has been shown. Write the eight words.

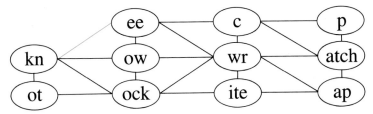

Proofreading   9–14. Find and cross out six misspelled Basic or Review Words. Then write each word correctly.

Everything went rong today. First, I broke too shoelaces. I had to use ones that were too long and did not mach.Then I did not wach where I was going. I tripped and knocked a nife off the table. I was lucky that I got only a scrach on my knee.

■ **Challenge Words**   Make a pictionary. Write each Challenge Word at the top of a separate sheet of paper. Then write the meaning of each word. Last, draw a picture that shows the meaning of each word.

Writing Application: A List of Rules   It is no fun to hurt yourself and need help. Think of ways people get hurt at home or in school. Then list at least five safety rules. Try to use three words from the list on page 74.

1. _____
2. _____
3. _____
4. _____
5. _____
6. _____
7. _____
8. _____
9. _____
10. _____
11. _____
12. _____
13. _____
14. _____

FIRST AID

11   Spelling Across the Curriculum

Health: *First Aid*

Theme Vocabulary
bandage
sling
splint
blood
breathe

Using Vocabulary   Write the Vocabulary Words to complete the paragraph. Use your Spelling Dictionary.

Last week Tim got hurt skiing. He had a broken arm and __(1)__ on his face from a cut. The ski patrol put a __(2)__ on his cut and a __(3)__ on his arm to keep it straight. They told Tim to __(4)__ slowly. When I saw Tim again, his arm was in a __(5)__ tied around his neck.

Understanding Vocabulary   Is each underlined word used correctly? Write *yes* or *no*.

6. Can you <u>splint</u> the cloth into two pieces?
7. Cover a cut with a clean <u>bandage</u>.
8. I have a cold, so it is hard to <u>breathe</u>.

1. _____

2. _____

3. _____

4. _____

5. _____

6. _____

7. _____

8. _____

FACT FILE

There are four blood types—A, B, AB, and O. If someone needs blood, it must come from a person with the correct blood type.

Enrichment

👪 *Know Your Knots*

Players: 2 teams **You need:** pencils and paper

How to play: Each team writes ten sentences. The **Know** team uses *know* or *no* in each sentence. The **Knot** team uses *knot* or *not*. Then each team reads one of their sentences aloud. The other team decides if *know* or *no* or if *knot* or *not* is used. Each correct answer gets one point.

📖 *Writing*
Emergency!

Find out the emergency telephone number or the telephone numbers of the closest hospital, the fire department, and the police. Then write a story in which this information is used to get help for a hurt person. Try to use words from the unit lists. Be sure to proofread your paper.

FIRST AID WONDER

Think of something new that would make first aid less painful, such as a machine that can heal cuts instantly. Draw a picture of it. Label the parts, and give directions for using it. Try to use words from the unit lists.

12 Review: Units 7–11

Unit 7 Three-Letter Clusters   pp. 48–53

throw	spring	straight
screen	street	spread

Remember: Some words begin with the consonant clusters **scr**, **spr**, **str**, and **thr**.

st**ring**

Write the word that means the opposite of each word.

1. crooked   **2.** catch   **3.** autumn

Write the word that completes each sentence.

4. Mrs. Brink put a new ___ in this window.

5. We brought a blanket to ___ out on the sand.

6. Take a right turn at the next ___.

___

1. _____
2. _____
3. _____
4. _____
5. _____
6. _____

Unit 8 Spelling the Long *i* Sound   pp. 54–59

die	wild	bright
fight	lie	mind

Remember: The /ī/ sound can be spelled with the pattern **igh**, **i**, or **ie**.

w**i**ld s**igh**t t**ie** /ī/

Write the word that matches each clue.

7. A full moon may look this way on a dark night.

8. Crops do this if they do not get enough rain.

9. A person may tell this instead of the truth.

10. This is what jungle animals are.

11. You use this when you think.

12. Cats and dogs may do this.

___

7. _____
8. _____
9. _____
10. _____
11. _____
12. _____

Half of the words from each unit are reviewed on these pages.
The rest are reviewed on pages 232–234.

Review **12**

Unit 9 The Vowel Sound in *clown* pp. 60–65

crowd	sound	would
count	crown	ground

Remember: The |ou| sound, as in *clown* and *round*, is often spelled with the pattern **ow** or **ou**.

Write the word that completes each sentence.

A huge **(13)** of people had come to see Queen Ann. There were too many people to **(14)**. Many of them were sitting on the **(15)**. One person said that the queen **(16)** come in a horse-drawn coach. Then people heard the **(17)** of a cannon. Queen Ann arrived, wearing a long dress and a **(18)**.

13. _____

14. _____

15. _____

16. _____

17. _____

18. _____

Unit 10 The Vowel Sound in *lawn* pp. 66–71

almost	straw	cloth
walk	soft	law

Remember: These patterns can spell the |ô| sound:
- **aw**, as in *lawn*
- **o**, as in *cloth*
- **a** before **l**, as in *almost*

Write the word that completes each sentence.
19. Mom made me a skirt out of some red ____.
20. This soup is so hot I ____ burned my mouth.

Write the word that belongs in each group.
21. grass, hay, ____
22. crawl, run, ____
23. judge, court, ____
24. fluffy, fuzzy, ____

19. _____

20. _____

21. _____

22. _____

23. _____

24. _____

Unit 11 Unexpected Patterns pp. 72–77

| knot | scratch | wrong |
| write | knife | watch |

Remember: $|n| \rightarrow$ **kn**ee

$|r| \rightarrow$ **wr**ap

$|ch| \rightarrow$ scra**tch**

|ch|

Write the word that belongs in each group.

25. fork, spoon, ___   **26.** cut, burn, ___

Write the word that completes each sentence.

27. Read the question, and then ___ your answer.

28. Please tell me the time if you have a ___.

29. Is this answer right or ___?

30. Janice cannot get the ___ out of her ribbon.

25. _____

26. _____

27. _____

28. _____

29. _____

30. _____

■ **Challenge Words Units 7–11** pp. 48–77

| strength | delight | scald |
| bounce | stretcher | |

Write the word that means the opposite of each word.

31. freeze   **32.** weakness

Write the word that completes each sentence.

33. No one was badly hurt in the accident, so a ___ is not needed.

34. Going for a swim is a ___ on a hot day.

35. That window may break if you ___ a ball against it.

31. _____

32. _____

33. _____

34. _____

35. _____

Spelling-Meaning Strategy

Word Forms

You have learned that words belong to families. The words in a family are spelled alike in some ways. They are also related in meaning. Read this paragraph.

> One of my favorite sights is a **bright** full moon in a coal black sky. Its **brightness** lights my way in the dark.

Think
- How are *bright* and *brightness* alike in meaning?
- How are *bright* and *brightness* alike in spelling?

Here are words in the *bright* family.

bright	brighten	brighter
brightness	brightly	brightest

Apply and Extend

Complete these activities on another piece of paper.

1. Look up the meaning of each word in the Word Box above in your Spelling Dictionary. Write six sentences, using one word in each sentence.

2. With a partner list words related to *child*, *mind*, and *count*. Then look in your Spelling-Meaning Index beginning on page 268. Add any other words in these families to your list.

Instructions

Lisa wants to use puppets to act out the play Finn McCool *by May Lynch. She has decided to make a puppet, using the instructions below. What are the steps for making a puppet?*

Making a puppet from a cardboard tube can be easy and fun! First, find a cardboard tube from a roll of paper towels or toilet tissue. Cut the tube to the size you want. Next, use crayons or markers to draw your puppet's clothes, eyes, and mouth. Then make paper ears, nose, hair, and arms. Finally, glue them to the tube.

Now bring your puppet to life. Just put your middle fingers inside the tube. Then wiggle your fingers, and your puppet will move.

Think and Discuss

1. What **steps** for making a puppet are given in the first paragraph?
2. Which sentence in the first paragraph tells the **main idea** of the paragraph?
3. What **order words,** such as *first* and *next,* are used?

The Writing Process

You can write instructions like the ones on page 82. Begin with a **topic sentence** that tells the **main idea**. List the **steps** in order. Use **order words**, such as *next* and *then*.

Assignment: Write Instructions

Step One: Prewriting

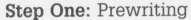

1. List things you do well, and discuss them with a partner. Choose a topic.
2. List the steps in correct order.

Step Two: Write a First Draft

1. Think about your purpose and your audience.
2. Do not worry about mistakes—just write.

Step Three: Revise

1. Are the steps in order? Did you forget any?
2. Did you use order words?
3. Use your Thesaurus to find exact words.
4. Read your instructions to a partner. Make more changes.

Step Four: Proofread

1. Does each sentence begin and end correctly?
2. Did you correct any misspelled words? Add them to your Notebook for Writing.

Step Five: Publish

Copy your paper. Act out your instructions.

Composition Words

three
straight
tight
round
soft
walk
wrap
knot

Proofreading Marks

¶ Indent
∧ Add something
℔ Take out something
≡ Capitalize
/ Make a small letter

Theme: Weather

13 Vowel + |r| Sounds

LOOK and SAY

Basic Words

1. storm *storm*
2. clear *clear*
3. dark *dark*
4. star *star*
5. fourth *fourth*
6. door *door*
7. smart *smart*
8. art *art*
9. near *near*
10. north *north*
11. ear *ear*
12. March *March*

■ Challenge

13. tornado *tornado*   14. argue *argue*

THINK

Each word has a vowel sound + *r*. These sounds are shown as |är|, |îr|, and |ôr|.

|är| **dark** |îr| **clear** |ôr| **storm**

- What are spelling patterns for the |är|, the |îr|, and the |ôr| sounds? How are the |ôr| sounds spelled in the Elephant Words?

WRITE

Practice   **Write Basic Words to answer the questions.**

A. Which **five** words have the |är| sounds?
B. Which **three** words have the |îr| sounds?
C. Which **four** words have the |ôr| sounds? Remember the Elephant Words.

■ **Now write the two Challenge Words.**

CHECK

A.

B.

C.

■ Challenge

Independent Practice

Word Attack   Use Basic Words in these exercises.

1. Write the word with the |ch| sound.

2-3. Write the two words that begin with *st*.

4-5. Write the two words that rhyme with *part*.

Context Sentences   Write the Basic Word that completes each sentence.
6. The wind is blowing from the ___.
7. Today will be cool, sunny, and ___.
8. Look at those huge, ___ rain clouds!
9. The cold air made Jason's ___ hurt.
10. I hear thunder, so a storm must be ___.

|är| d a r k

|ôr| st o r m

|îr| n ear

Elephant Words   Write the Elephant Word that completes each sentence.
11. This rainstorm is the ___ one in two weeks.
12. The strong wind blew open the ___.

Challenge Words   Write the Challenge Word that fits each meaning. Use your Spelling Dictionary.
13. disagree   14. a twisting, dangerous storm

_____
1. _____

_____
2. _____

_____
3. _____

_____
4. _____

_____
5. _____

_____
6. _____

_____
7. _____

_____
8. _____

_____
9. _____

_____
10. _____

_____
11. _____

_____
12. _____

_____
13. _____

_____
14. _____

Summing Up

These vowel + |r| sounds can be spelled with these patterns:
- |är| → *ar*, as in *dark*   • |ôr| → *or*, as in *storm*
- |îr| → *ear*, as in *clear*

Basic

1. storm
2. clear
3. dark
4. star
5. fourth
6. door
7. smart
8. art
9. near
10. north
11. ear
12. March

■ Challenge

13. tornado
14. argue

Review

1. hard
2. short

1. _____
2. _____
3. _____
4. _____
5. _____
6. _____

Expanding Vocabulary

Synonyms and Antonyms   Some words, such as *near*, have both synonyms and antonyms.

	SYNONYM	ANTONYM
near	close	far

Practice   Write a synonym for each numbered word below. Use words from the box below.

1. quick   **2.** hard   **3.** strong

powerful	easy	weak
difficult	slow	speedy

Now write an antonym of each word below. Use words from the box above.

4. quick   **5.** hard   **6.** strong

1. _____   4. _____
2. _____   5. _____
3. _____   6. _____

Dictionary

Guide Words   Use guide words to help you find an entry word in a dictionary more quickly. Remember that entry words are in ABC order.

Practice   Write the word that would be found on the same page as each pair of guide words.

star   storm   short   smart   screen   spray

1. stir | stun   **3. shirt | shy**   **5. spike | spy**
2. scarf | scuba   **4. sly | smell**   **6. squash | step**

Review: Spelling Spree

Letter Change   Change the order of the letters in each word. Write a Basic Word that begins with the underlined letter.

Example: rea<u>d</u>   *dear*

1. ear<u>n</u>   **3.** o<u>d</u>or   **5.** <u>t</u>ar
2. rat<u>s</u>   **4.** ar<u>e</u>   **6.** thor<u>n</u>

Proofreading   7–14. Find and cross out eight misspelled Basic or Review Words in this weather report. Then write the words correctly.

> The sky is cleer now, but expect a strom after darck. It will rain for a shot time, and a hrd wind will blow from the north. This will be the forth day of rain this Mach. Be smat, and carry an umbrella!

■ **Challenge Words**   Write two tongue twisters. Use a Challenge Word in each one. Use other words that begin with the same letters as the Challenge Words. Use your Spelling Dictionary to help you find words.

Example: Al and Andy always argue with acrobats.

📖 *Writing Application:* A Weather Report
What do you think the weather will be like tomorrow? Will it be rainy, cloudy, or sunny? Will it be warm or cool? Write a weather report. Try to use three words from the list on page 86.

1. _____
2. _____
3. _____
4. _____
5. _____
6. _____
7. _____
8. _____
9. _____
10. _____
11. _____
12. _____
13. _____
14. _____

13   Spelling Across the Curriculum

Science: *Weather*

Theme Vocabulary

fog
sleet
heat
cool
damp

Using Vocabulary   Write the Vocabulary Words to complete the paragraph. Use your Spelling Dictionary.

Forget the snow and icy __(1)__ of winter. Say good-by to chilly spring days with __(2)__ winds. No more __(3)__ raincoats and clouds of __(4)__ ! Come to Florida, where you can lie on the beach and feel the __(5)__ from the sun.

Understanding Vocabulary   Write a Vocabulary Word to match each clue.

6. This describes a rainy day.
7. This rain has ice in it.
8. This floats near the ground.

1. _____
2. _____
3. _____
4. _____
5. _____
6. _____
7. _____
8. _____

FACT FILE

Weather satellites fly over the clouds with cameras that take pictures of the earth. The pictures are used to predict the weather.

Enrichment

👨‍👩‍👧 *Rainbow Race*

Players: 2–6, one reader **You need:** a drawing of a rainbow with six colors, each color divided into eight spaces; game markers; a list of Basic and Review Words

How to play: Each player chooses a color. The reader reads a word to Player 1. If Player 1 spells the word correctly, he or she moves ahead one space. Players take turns until one player crosses the rainbow.

RAIN OR SHINE?

Make a weather pictionary. Fold a piece of paper in half. On each half write a word that describes or names a kind of weather, such as *windy*, *rainy*, *thunderstorm*, or *blizzard*. Draw a picture that shows the meaning of the word.

📖 *Writing*
Weather Control

You have just made a machine to control the weather. Write an ad for your machine. How does it work? How will it help people? Try to use words from the unit lists. Be sure to proofread your paper.

Theme: Dance Class

14 The Vowel + |r| Sounds in first

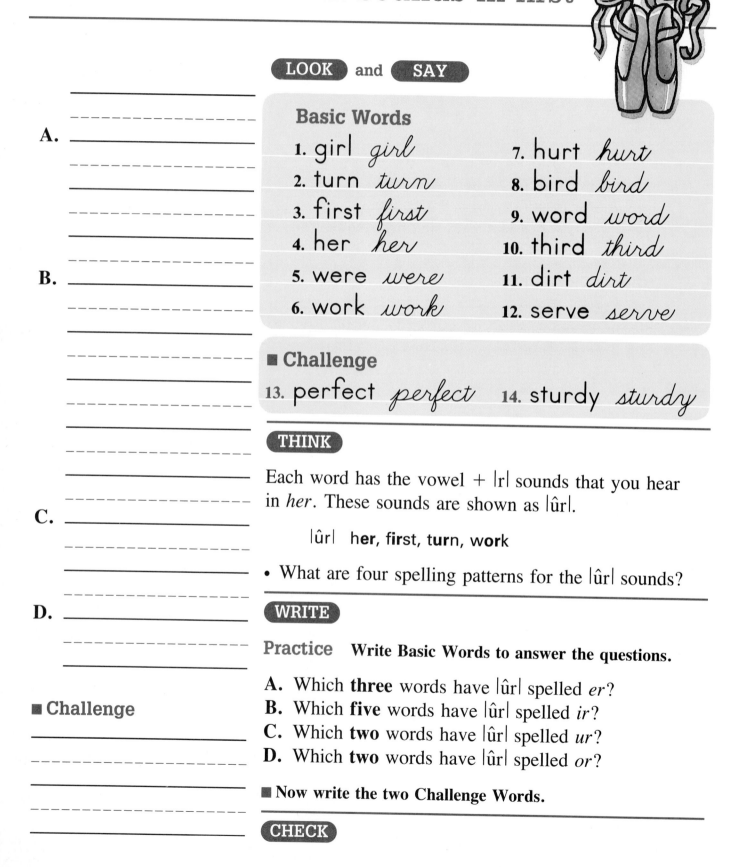

LOOK and SAY

Basic Words

1. girl *girl*
2. turn *turn*
3. first *first*
4. her *her*
5. were *were*
6. work *work*
7. hurt *hurt*
8. bird *bird*
9. word *word*
10. third *third*
11. dirt *dirt*
12. serve *serve*

■ **Challenge**

13. perfect *perfect*   14. sturdy *sturdy*

THINK

Each word has the vowel + |r| sounds that you hear in *her*. These sounds are shown as |ûr|.

|ûr| **her, first, turn, work**

• What are four spelling patterns for the |ûr| sounds?

WRITE

Practice   **Write Basic Words to answer the questions.**

A. Which **three** words have |ûr| spelled *er*?
B. Which **five** words have |ûr| spelled *ir*?
C. Which **two** words have |ûr| spelled *ur*?
D. Which **two** words have |ûr| spelled *or*?

■ Now write the two Challenge Words.

CHECK

A. _____

B. _____

C. _____

D. _____

■ Challenge

Independent Practice

Word Attack   Use Basic Words in these exercises.

1. Write the word that begins with *th*.

2-4. Write *work*. Then write two other words that begin with the same sound.

5-8. Write four words by adding a vowel and *r* to the letters below.

   5. s __ __ ve
   6. g __ __ l
   7. h __ __
   8. h __ __ t

Word Pairs   Write the Basic Word that completes each pair of sentences.

  9. A snake crawls on the ground.
    A ____ flies in the air.
10. You push a button.
    You ____ a steering wheel.
11. You rake leaves on a lawn.
    You shovel ____ into a hole.
12. The caboose is the last train car.
    The engine is the ____ train car.

■ **Challenge Words**   Write the Challenge Word that fits each meaning. Use your Spelling Dictionary.
13. strong
14. without any mistakes

1. _____
2. _____
3. _____
4. _____
5. _____
6. _____
7. _____
8. _____
9. _____
10. _____
11. _____
12. _____
13. _____
14. _____

Summing Up

The |ûr| sounds can be spelled with these patterns:
- *er*, as in *her*
- *ur*, as in *turn*
- *ir*, as in *first*
- *or*, as in *work*

Basic

1. girl
2. turn
3. first
4. her
5. were
6. work
7. hurt
8. bird
9. word
10. third
11. dirt
12. serve

■ **Challenge**

13. perfect
14. sturdy

Review

1. any
2. been

Proofreading Marks

¶ Indent
∧ Add something
ℒ Take out something
≡ Capitalize
/ Make a small letter

Expanding Vocabulary

Exact Words Which sentence is more exact?

The **bird** flew at night.   The **owl** flew at night.

The second sentence is more exact because *owl* tells what kind of bird flew at night.

Practice Write one of the names below in place of *bird* in each sentence. Use your Thesaurus.

sea gull   crow   robin   canary

1. That <u>bird</u> has such a pretty red breast.
2. Look at that <u>bird</u> dive into the ocean!
3. I love to hear my yellow <u>bird</u> sing.
4. That black <u>bird</u> makes such a loud noise.

1. _____   3. _____

2. _____   4. _____

Proofreading

Good and *bad*   Use *good* and *bad* correctly.

	good	bad
COMPARING TWO:	better	worse
COMPARING MORE THAN TWO:	best	worst

Practice Proofread this paragraph. Use proofreading marks to correct three misspelled words and two wrong forms of *good* or *bad*.

Example: That ~~brid~~ ^{bird} costume is the ~~goodest~~ ^{best}.

Have you ben to the talent show? I did my worse turn of all in the frist dance. I hit the gril beside me. I got gooder at the end.

Review: Spelling Spree

Word Maze   1–8. Begin at the arrow and follow the Word Maze to find eight Basic or Review Words. Write the words in order.

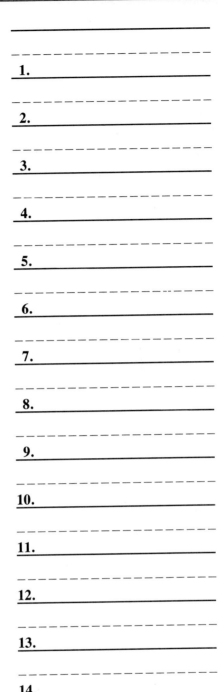

1.
2.
3.
4.
5.
6.
7.
8.
9.
10.
11.
12.
13.
14.

Letter Math   Write a Basic Word by solving each problem below.

Example: worry − ry + d = *word*

9. worst − st + k =   **12.** g + twirl − tw =
10. d + shirt − sh =   **13.** hurry − ry + t =
11. t + burn − b =   **14.** thirst − st + d =

```
      s e r v e
      t
      u
      p e r f e c t
      d
      y
```

■ **Challenge Words**
Make a puzzle. Write the Challenge Words so that they cross. Then add other spelling words. Part of a puzzle is shown.

Writing Application: An Invitation   Write a paragraph inviting someone to a show performed by your dance class. Tell when and where the show will be held. Try to use three words from the list on page 92.

14   Spelling Across the Curriculum

Performing Arts: *Dance Class*

Theme Vocabulary

music
partner
movement
sway
skip

Using Vocabulary   Write the Vocabulary Words to complete the paragraph. Use your Spelling Dictionary.

A dancer and his or her __(1)__ should move together easily. They must be able to __(2)__ across the stage or __(3)__ from side to side in time to the __(4)__. Each hand or body __(5)__ should be beautiful to watch.

Understanding Vocabulary   Is the underlined word used correctly? Write *yes* or *no*.

6. Trees often <u>sway</u> in the wind.
7. I watched the dancer's every <u>movement</u>.
8. Did he <u>skip</u> up the tree to get the cat?

1. _____
2. _____
3. _____
4. _____
5. _____
6. _____
7. _____
8. _____

FACT FILE

Edgar Degas was a great French painter. Some of his works show dancers practicing or relaxing after a class.

THE REHEARSAL ON THE STAGE (Detail), Edgar Degas

Enrichment

👥 *Square Dance*

Players: 4 or 6, one caller **You need:** a square with three boxes drawn on each side, game markers, a list of Basic and Review Words

How to play: Players form pairs of "square dance" partners. The caller reads a Basic or Review Word to the first pair. They must spell the word correctly to move ahead one space. The first pair to travel around the square wins.

📖 *Writing*
Stop the Show!

Write a funny story about a dance program that went wrong. What happened? Did the scenery fall down? Did a dancer do the wrong steps? How did the show end? Try to use words from the unit lists. Be sure to proofread your paper.

IT'S SHOE TIME!

Draw a funny scene in which the characters are dancing shoes. Make the shoes talk with cartoon balloons that use spelling words. For example, you might draw a sneaker asking a tap shoe, "Will you be my partner?"

15 The Vowel Sound in coin

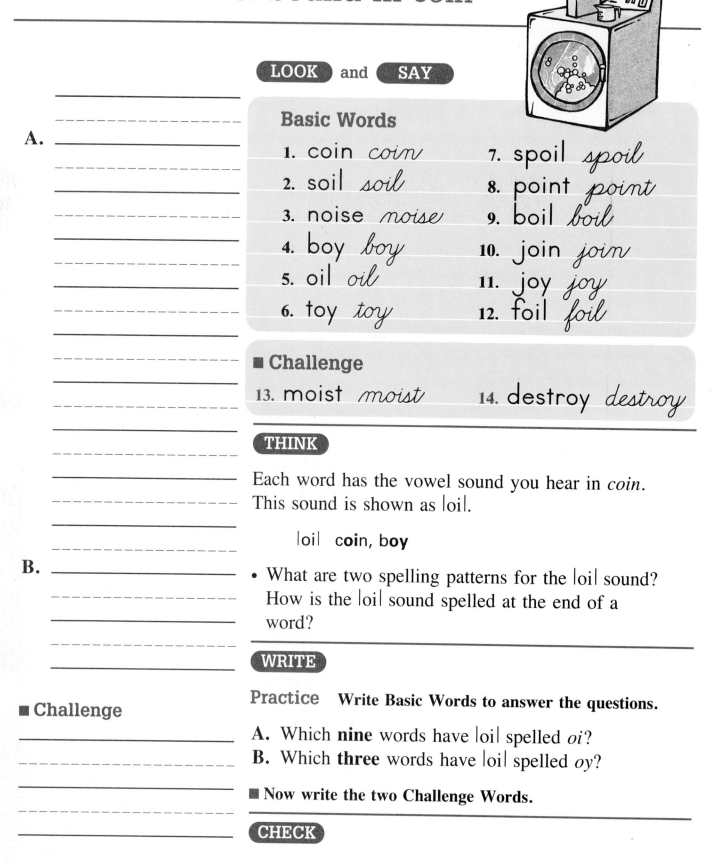

A.

LOOK and SAY

Basic Words

1. coin *coin*
2. soil *soil*
3. noise *noise*
4. boy *boy*
5. oil *oil*
6. toy *toy*
7. spoil *spoil*
8. point *point*
9. boil *boil*
10. join *join*
11. joy *joy*
12. foil *foil*

■ Challenge

13. moist *moist*   14. destroy *destroy*

THINK

Each word has the vowel sound you hear in *coin*.
This sound is shown as |oil.

    |oil **coin, boy**

B.

• What are two spelling patterns for the |oil sound?
How is the |oil sound spelled at the end of a
word?

WRITE

Practice   **Write Basic Words to answer the questions.**

A. Which **nine** words have |oil spelled *oi*?
B. Which **three** words have |oil spelled *oy*?

■ **Now write the two Challenge Words.**

CHECK

■ Challenge

Independent Practice

Word Attack   Use Basic Words in these exercises.

1. Write the word that begins with a consonant cluster.

2-3. Write *coin*. Then change the first letter to write another spelling word.

4-6. Write *boy*. Then write two other words that rhyme with *boy*.

Making Inferences   Write the Basic Word that matches each clue.

7. This part of a pin is sharp.
8. This is a way to cook eggs.
9. This is what you hear in an airport.
10. You can wrap food in this to keep it fresh.
11. A car needs this.
12. Seeds are planted in this.

■ **Challenge Words**   Write the Challenge Word that completes each sentence. Use your Spelling Dictionary.

13. Remove the stain with a ___ cloth and some soap.
14. This hot weather will ___ the crops if it does not rain soon.

1. _____

2. _____

3. _____

4. _____

5. _____

6. _____

7. _____

8. _____

9. _____

10. _____

11. _____

12. _____

13. _____

14. _____

Summing Up

The |oi| sound, as in *coin* and *boy*, is spelled with the pattern *oi* or *oy*.

15 Part C Spelling and Language Study

Basic
1. coin
2. soil
3. noise
4. boy
5. oil
6. toy
7. spoil
8. point
9. boil
10. join
11. joy
12. foil

■ Challenge
13. moist
14. destroy

Review
1. are
2. give

Expanding Vocabulary

Meanings of *spoil* *Spoil* has several meanings.

spoil   **a.** to make less perfect or useful
       b. to become unfit for use
       c. to give someone too much

Practice   **Which meaning of *spoil* is used in each sentence? Write the letter of the meaning.**
1. Meat will spoil if you leave it in the sun.
2. Does Grandpa spoil you with lots of toys?
3. A fence would spoil our view of the lake.

1. _____ 2. _____ 3. _____

Dictionary

Words That Look the Same   Some words are spelled the same but have different meanings. The words are numbered and listed separately in a dictionary. What are two meanings of *foil*?

> **foil¹** |foil| *v.* **foiled, foiling** To keep from success: *The alarm foiled the thief.*
> **foil²** |foil| *n., pl.* **foils** A thin sheet of metal: *Wrap the meat in foil.*

Practice   **Which meaning of *foil* is used in each sentence? Write *foil¹* or *foil².***
1. The rain will foil our wish to go camping.
2. Please cover the leftovers with foil.
3. Wrap the corn in foil, and then roast it.
4. How did Meg foil your plan to win the game?

1. _____ 3. _____

2. _____ 4. _____

Review: Spelling Spree

Missing Letters   Each missing letter fits in ABC order between the other letters. Write the missing letters to spell a Basic or Review Word.

Example: r _ t   n _ p   h _ j   k _ m   *soil*

1. s _ u   n _ p   x _ z
2. a _ c   n _ p   h _ j   k _ m
3. r _ t   o _ q   n _ p   h _ j   k _ m
4. f _ h   h _ j   u _ w   d _ f
5. o _ q   n _ p   h _ j   m _ o   s _ u
6. i _ k   n _ p   x _ z
7. e _ g   n _ p   h _ j   k _ m

Proofreading   8–14.   Find and cross out seven misspelled Basic or Review Words. Then write each word correctly.

Laundromats ar busy places with a lot of noize. Humming machines wash out sol. A coyn or a toy rattles in a dryer. Squeaky cart wheels need oll. A little boi yells to his mother. Come joyn the group!

■ **Challenge Words**   Make a Missing Letters game for each Challenge Word. Write the answers on the back of your paper. Have a partner play your game.

📖 *Writing Application:* Instructions   Write directions that tell how to wash clothes. What do you do first? When is the soap added? Try to use three words from the list on page 98.

1. _____
2. _____
3. _____
4. _____
5. _____
6. _____
7. _____
8. _____
9. _____
10. _____
11. _____
12. _____
13. _____
14. _____

15 Spelling Across the Curriculum

Life Skills: *The Laundromat*

Theme Vocabulary

laundry
washer
soak
load
fold

Using Vocabulary Write the Vocabulary Words to complete this note. Use your Spelling Dictionary.

Theresa, please wash and dry a __(1)__ of dark-colored clothes. Remember to __(2)__ the stains in your jeans. Pour only a cup of soap into the __(3)__ before you put in the clothes. Please __(4)__ the clean __(5)__, and put it away.

Understanding Vocabulary Is the underlined word used correctly? Write *yes* or *no*.

6. <u>Soak</u> the socks to dry them.
7. A <u>washer</u> dries clothes.
8. There is another <u>load</u> of light-colored shirts to wash.

1. _____
2. _____
3. _____
4. _____
5. _____
6. _____
7. _____
8. _____

FACT FILE

Wool and cotton cloth are made from animal and plant products. Some kinds of cloth, such as nylon, were created by scientists.

Enrichment

Laundry Adventure

With a partner write a short skit about a real or an imaginary trip to a laundromat. What adventures do you have? Do you use too much soap? Do you drop someone's wet clothes on the floor? Does something happen to one of the machines? What do you say and do? Try to use words from the unit lists. Act out your skit for your classmates.

FUTURE-MAT

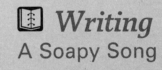

Draw a picture of a laundromat of the future. What machines would people use? How would the machines work? Add labels that explain the things in your picture. Try to use words from the unit lists.

Writing
A Soapy Song

Write a song to sing as you do your laundry. You may want to use a well-known tune and add new words. Try to use unit list words. Be sure to proofread your song.

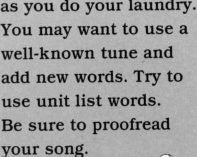

16 Spelling the |j| Sound

Theme: Field Day

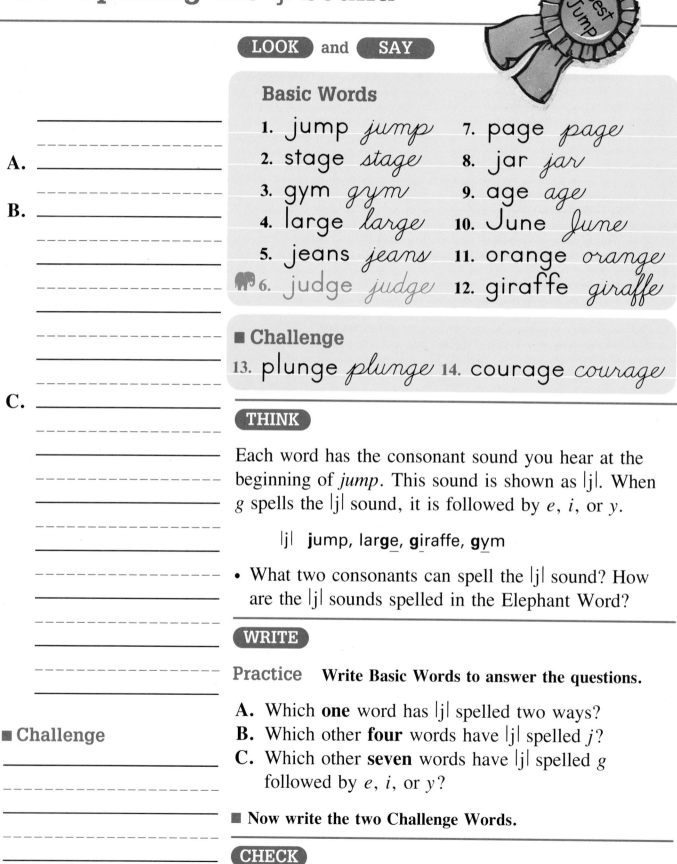

LOOK and **SAY**

Basic Words

1. jump *jump*
2. stage *stage*
3. gym *gym*
4. large *large*
5. jeans *jeans*
6. judge *judge*
7. page *page*
8. jar *jar*
9. age *age*
10. June *June*
11. orange *orange*
12. giraffe *giraffe*

■ Challenge

13. plunge *plunge*
14. courage *courage*

THINK

Each word has the consonant sound you hear at the beginning of *jump*. This sound is shown as |j|. When *g* spells the |j| sound, it is followed by *e*, *i*, or *y*.

|j| **j**ump, lar**ge**, **gi**raffe, **gy**m

- What two consonants can spell the |j| sound? How are the |j| sounds spelled in the Elephant Word?

WRITE

Practice   **Write Basic Words to answer the questions.**

A. Which **one** word has |j| spelled two ways?
B. Which other **four** words have |j| spelled *j*?
C. Which other **seven** words have |j| spelled *g* followed by *e*, *i*, or *y*?

■ **Now write the two Challenge Words.**

CHECK

A. _____

B. _____

C. _____

■ **Challenge**

102

Independent Practice

Word Attack   Use Basic Words in these exercises.

1. Write the word that has the |ĭ| sound spelled *y*.

2-3. Write a word that rhymes with each word below.
   2. charge
   3. car

4-6. Write the three words with the |ā| sound spelled *a*-consonant-*e*.

Classifying   Write the Basic Word that belongs in each group.
   7. red, blue, ____
   8. hop, skip, ____
   9. April, May, ____
   10. shoes, coat, ____
   11. elephant, hippo, ____

Elephant Word   Write the Elephant Word to complete the sentence.
   12. Who will ____ the three o'clock race in the gym?

Challenge Words   Write the Challenge Word that completes each sentence. Use your Spelling Dictionary.
   13. Jason likes to watch divers who can ____ into a pool from a high board.
   14. Who has the ____ to run against Speedy Sue in the next race?

_____
1. _____
2. _____
3. _____
4. _____
5. _____
6. _____
7. _____
8. _____
9. _____
10. _____
11. _____
12. _____
13. _____
14. _____

Summing Up

The |j| sound can be spelled with the consonant *j* or with the consonant *g* followed by *e*, *i*, or *y*.

Basic

1. jump
2. stage
3. gym
4. large
5. jeans
6. judge
7. page
8. jar
9. age
10. June
11. orange
12. giraffe

■ **Challenge**

13. plunge
14. courage

Review

1. job
2. brother

Proofreading Marks

¶ Indent
∧ Add something
℘ Take out something
≡ Capitalize
/ Make a small letter

Expanding Vocabulary

Words from Other Languages   Did you know that *giraffe* comes from the Italian word *giraffa*? Many English words come from other languages.

Practice   **Write the word that fits each clue. Use your Spelling Dictionary.**

mosquito   octopus   walrus   skunk

1. a Greek word for an animal with eight arms
2. a Native American word for a small animal with a bad smell
3. a Spanish word for a biting bug
4. a Dutch word for a sea animal

1. _____   3. _____

2. _____   4. _____

Proofreading

Introductory Words   Use a comma after words such as *first* or *next* when they begin a sentence.

First, step up to the starting line.

Practice   **Proofread this paragraph. Use proofreading marks to correct three misspelled words. Add two missing commas.**

Example: Next, put the ~~pag~~ page of names over there.

Pablo's brouther went to the jym for Sports Day. First he gave a juge his name and age. Next he showed how far he could jump. He won a toy giraffe!

Review: Spelling Spree

Hink Pinks Write the Basic or Review Word that fits the description and rhymes with the given word.

Example: what a washer does **cleans** ___ *jeans*

1. a song for the month after May ___ **tune**
2. a list of birth dates ___ **page**
3. a tearful task **sob** ___
4. a kangaroo's bruise ___ **bump**
5. a big cost ___ **charge**
6. a glass container for an auto **car** ___
7. a home for a bird in a play ___ **cage**

Comparisons Write the Basic or Review Word that completes each comparison.

8. This hose is longer than the neck of a ___.
9. This robe is as comfortable as a pair of ___.
10. Mrs. Lyon is as wise as a ___ in a court.
11. This desk is as shiny as a waxed ___ floor.
12. This drink is as tasty as fresh ___ juice.
13. Stan is as helpful as an older ___.
14. Jan's face is as readable as a ___ in a book.

(deep)
(water)
(plunge)

■ **Challenge Words** Make a cluster for each Challenge Word. Then write at least four sentences, using the Challenge Words and other words in the clusters. A cluster is shown.

Writing Application: A Story Write a story about being in a race. What happened? Try to use three words from the list on page 104.

1. _____
2. _____
3. _____
4. _____
5. _____
6. _____
7. _____
8. _____
9. _____
10. _____
11. _____
12. _____
13. _____
14. _____

16 Spelling Across the Curriculum

Physical Education: *Field Day*

Theme Vocabulary

field
track
medal
prize
contest

Using Vocabulary Write the Vocabulary Words to complete the paragraph. Use your Spelling Dictionary.

Everything is ready for tomorrow. Ropes mark the dirt __(1)__ circling the baseball __(2)__. Once again a crowd will watch Ted and Al race for the title of fastest runner. They each have two wins in this __(3)__. Who will finally win first __(4)__ and receive the gold __(5)__?

Understanding Vocabulary Write the Vocabulary Word that belongs in each group.

6. game, race, ____
7. path, course, ____
8. meadow, lawn, ____

1. _____

2. _____

3. _____

4. _____

5. _____

6. _____

7. _____

8. _____

FACT FILE

Wilma Rudolph could not walk until she was eight, but she was the first American female runner to win three Olympic gold medals.

106

Enrichment

👥 *Relay That Word*

Players: 2 relay teams, judge **You need:** a list of Basic and Review Words

How to play: The judge reads a word to Team 1. The first player says the first letter of the word, the next player says the second letter, and so on until the word is spelled. The team gets a point if the word is spelled correctly. Teams take turns spelling words. The team with the most points wins.

📖 *Writing*
A Ball of Fun

What kind of field day would you like? Would you have races? Would there be an unusual contest? Write a paragraph that describes the day. Try to use words from the unit lists. Be sure to proofread your paper.

SPORTS AFIELD

Make a poster to tell about a school field day. Make colorful drawings, and name the events. Tell when and where the field day will take place. Try to use words from the unit lists.

17 Spelling the |k| and |kw| Sounds

(Theme: Bees)

A. _____

B. _____

C. _____

LOOK and **SAY**

Basic Words

1. park *park*
2. queen *queen*
3. skin *skin*
4. picnic *picnic*
5. quick *quick*
6. school *school*
7. quart *quart*
8. week *week*
9. quit *quit*
10. squeeze *squeeze*
11. second *second*
12. crack *crack*

■ Challenge

13. insect *insect*   14. freckles *freckles*

THINK

Each word has the |k| sound, as in *park*, or the |kw| sounds, as in *queen*.

|k| park, qui**ck**, pi**c**nic |kw| **qu**een

- What are three spelling patterns for the |k| sound? How is the |k| sound spelled in the Elephant Word? What is a spelling pattern for the |kw| sounds?

WRITE

Practice   **Write Basic Words to answer the questions.**

A. Which **one** word has the |kw| and the |k| sounds?
B. Which other **four** words have the |kw| sounds?
C. Which other **seven** words have the |k| sound? Remember the Elephant Word.

■ **Now write the two Challenge Words.**

CHECK

■ Challenge

_____

_____

Independent Practice

Word Attack   Use Basic Words in these exercises.

1. Write the word that has the |k| sound spelled both *c* and *ck*.

2-5. Write the four words with the |ĭ| sound.

Context Sentences   Write the Basic Word that completes each sentence.

6. Ty and I visited Mr. Day, a beekeeper, last ___.
7. We saw some bees ___ through a tiny hole.
8. One bee landed on a flower. Then a ___ bee landed beside it.
9. "The most important bee is the ___ bee," I said.
10. Tim asked, "Do bees live in trees in the ___?"
11. At lunch Mr. Day shared a ___ of milk with us.

Elephant Word   Write the Elephant Word to complete the sentence.

12. Ellen and I are learning about bees in ___.

Challenge Words   Write the Challenge Word that completes each sentence. Use your Spelling Dictionary.

13. The bee is an ___ that is related to the ant.
14. You cannot see where a bee stung Jack because he has so many ___ on his arm.

1. _____
2. _____
3. _____
4. _____
5. _____
6. _____
7. _____
8. _____
9. _____
10. _____
11. _____
12. _____
13. _____
14. _____

Summing Up

The |k| sound may be spelled with the pattern *k*, *ck*, or *c*. The |kw| sounds may be spelled with the *qu* pattern.

Basic

1. park
2. queen
3. skin
4. picnic
5. quick
6. school
7. quart
8. week
9. quit
10. squeeze
11. second
12. crack

■ **Challenge**

13. insect
14. freckles

Review

1. black
2. coat

Expanding Vocabulary

Measurements   Do you usually buy a quart or a gallon of milk? *Quart* and *gallon* are measurements, or amounts.

Practice   Write the word that fits each meaning. Use your Spelling Dictionary.

cup   pint   quart   gallon

1. a measurement equal to two cups
2. a measurement equal to four quarts
3. a measurement equal to sixteen tablespoons
4. a measurement equal to two pints

1. _____   3. _____

2. _____   4. _____

Dictionary

Part of Speech   A dictionary entry shows if a word is used as a noun, a verb, or another **part of speech**. Abbreviations are used.

n. = noun   *v.* = verb

park |pärk| *n.*, *pl.* **parks** An area of land used for recreation: *We play in the park.* *v.* **parked**, **parking** To stop and leave a car for a time: *Where did you park the car?*

1. _____

2. _____

3. _____

Practice   Write *noun* or *verb* to tell how *park* is used in each sentence.

1. Many children play in the park on Saturday.
2. Teachers park their cars behind the school.
3. Jim's baseball team practices in the park.

Review: Spelling Spree

Classifying   Write the Basic or Review Word that belongs in each group.

1. mittens, hat, ___
2. month, day, ___
3. hair, fingernails, ___
4. snap, break, ___
5. pint, gallon, ___
6. king, princess, ___
7. library, bank, ___
8. stop, finish, ___

Proofreading   **9–14.** Find and cross out six misspelled Basic or Review Words. Then write each word correctly.

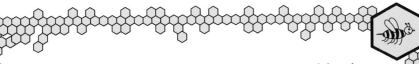

   Have you ever been in a parck and had a tiny blak and yellow bee visit your picknick? Don't squeez it if it crawls on your skin or coat. Don't be quik to scare it away. It is a tiny wonder! Watch its wings. They beat about 250 times a sekund.

■ **Challenge Words**   Make a pictionary. Write each Challenge Word at the top of a half sheet of paper. Then write the meaning of each word. Last, draw a picture that shows the meaning of each word.

Writing Application: Creative Writing
Pretend that you are a bee. How do you spend your days? How do you have fun? When are you in danger? Write a description of your life. Try to use three words from the list on page 110.

1. ___
2. ___
3. ___
4. ___
5. ___
6. ___
7. ___
8. ___
9. ___
10. ___
11. ___
12. ___
13. ___
14. ___

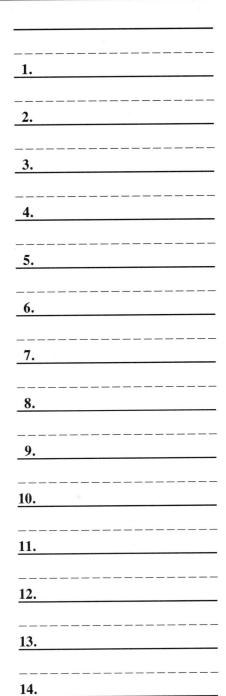

17 Spelling Across the Curriculum

Science: *Bees*

Theme Vocabulary

bumblebee
buzz
honey
hive
sting

Using Vocabulary Write the Vocabulary Words to complete the paragraph. Use your Spelling Dictionary.

The black and yellow __(1)__ makes its home in thick grass or in the ground, not in a __(2)__. This bee will __(3)__ loudly as it gathers food from flowers to make golden __(4)__. Be careful if a bee is near you! It can __(5)__ many times if you scare it.

Understanding Vocabulary Write the Vocabulary Word that answers each question.

6. Which can you eat: a hive or some honey?
7. Which can you hear: a buzz or a sting?
8. Which can you feel: a buzz or a sting?

1. _____
2. _____
3. _____
4. _____
5. _____
6. _____
7. _____
8. _____

FACT FILE

Bees gather pollen for food. As bees go from plant to plant, some pollen drops into each flower, and new flower seeds begin to grow.

Enrichment

📖 *Writing*
Where's the Food?

When a bee returns home, it does a dance to tell where pollen can be found. Pretend that you are a bee. Write directions telling other bees how to find some pollen. Should they fly straight or make some turns? How far should they fly? Try to use words from the unit lists. Be sure to proofread your paper.

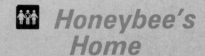

👫 *Honeybee's Home*

With a partner read about the inside of a beehive. Then make a shoe box model of it. Label the different parts. Try to use unit words. Share your model with the class.

SPELLING BEES

Draw a hive on construction paper. Write |kw| on the hive. Next, draw five bees flying to the hive. Write a unit list word with the |kw| sounds on each bee. You may want to add a |k| hive and bees labeled with unit list words that have the |k| sound.

18 Review: Units 13–17

Unit 13   Vowel + |r| Sounds   pp. 84–89

clear	fourth	door
north	near	March

Remember: |är| → d**ar**k
|îr| → cl**ear**
|ôr| → st**or**m

Write the word that fits each group.
1. east, south, ___
2. second, third, ___
3. January, February, ___

Write the word that completes each sentence.
4. I see the lake bottom when the water is ___.
5. Remember not to slam the ___ when you leave.
6. Patsy's house is ___ the old shoe factory.

1. _____
2. _____
3. _____
4. _____
5. _____
6. _____

Unit 14   Vowel + |r| Sounds in *first*   pp. 90–95

turn	first	were
word	third	serve

Remember: The |ûr| sounds can be spelled with the patterns **er, ir, ur,** and **or.**

Write the words to complete the paragraph.
   Today we had a surprise party for my brother Ben. The lights __(7)__ out when he came in. Dad jumped up to __(8)__ them on, and we all yelled the __(9)__ *surprise*! The __(10)__ thing we did after that was __(11)__ the cake. Then we gave Ben presents. He opened mine __(12)__, after Mom's and Dad's.

7. _____
8. _____
9. _____
10. _____
11. _____
12. _____

114

Half of the words from each unit are reviewed on these pages.
The rest are reviewed on pages 235–237.

Review **18**

Unit 15 The Vowel Sound in *coin* pp. 96–101

toy	soil	noise
joy	point	spoil

Remember: The |oil| sound, as in *coin* and *boy,* is spelled with the pattern **oi** or **oy**.

Write a word that means the same as each word.
13. dirt   **14.** ruin
Write the word that completes each sentence.
15. Will you ___ out the park as we drive by it?
16. Grandma says it is a ___ to watch the baby.
17. Sam gave Tony a ___ truck for his birthday.
18. You will wake Dad if you make too much ___.

13. _____
14. _____
15. _____
16. _____
17. _____
18. _____

Unit 16 Spelling the |j| Sound pp. 102–107

large	jeans	judge
giraffe	June	orange

Remember: The |j| sound can be spelled with **j** or with **g** followed by **e, i**, or **y**.

Write the word that matches each clue.
19. These pants are usually blue.
20. The first day of summer is in this month.
21. An elephant is this size.
22. This person is in charge of a courtroom.
23. This animal can eat leaves from tall trees.
24. You make this color by mixing red and yellow.

19. _____
20. _____
21. _____
22. _____
23. _____
24. _____

18 Review

Unit 17   The |k| and |kw| Sounds   pp. 108–113

picnic	quick	school
week	second	squeeze

Remember: The |k| sound may be spelled **k, ck,** or **c.** The |kw| sounds may be spelled with the **qu** pattern.

Write the word that completes each sentence.

25. There is only one ____ left until vacation!
26. I will miss all my ____ friends this summer.
27. Maybe we should all go on a ____ together.
28. I should make some ____ plans before vacation.
29. Dad says we can all ____ into his car.
30. Maybe we can even get together a ____ time.

■ Challenge Words   Units 13–17   pp. 84–113

insect	perfect	moist
plunge	tornado	

Write the word that belongs in each group.

31. fish, bird, ____
32. wet, damp, ____

Write the word that completes each sentence.

33. I only had one wrong answer on the test, but Ann got a ____ score.
34. Shelley likes to ____ into the cool lake on a hot day.
35. Dad says we should stay in the basement until the ____ has passed.

25. _____
26. _____
27. _____
28. _____
29. _____
30. _____

31. _____
32. _____
33. _____
34. _____
35. _____

Spelling-Meaning Strategy

Word Forms

Words belong to families, just as people do. The words in a family are spelled alike in some ways. They are also related in meaning. Read this paragraph.

I heard shouts of **joy** and ran downstairs. Our favorite uncle had arrived. Uncle Bob is very funny, and we always **enjoy** his stories.

Think

- How are *joy* and *enjoy* alike in meaning?
- How are *joy* and *enjoy* alike in spelling?

Here are words in the *joy* family.

joy	joyous	joyful
enjoy	enjoyable	enjoyment

Apply and Extend

Complete these activities on another piece of paper.

1. Look up the meaning of each word in the Word Box above in your Spelling Dictionary. Write six sentences, using one word in each sentence.

2. With a partner list words related to *serve*, *large*, and *quart*. Then look in your Spelling-Meaning Index beginning on page 268. Add any other words in these families to your list.

Story

A young man wants to make his fortune. What does this story beginning tell about him?

A shabby young man came trudging up the road toward the castle. He had patched knees and elbows, and the feather in his worn hat was bedraggled. But he had a merry grin, and he was whistling a cheerful tune. When he saw the long line of people, he asked a soldier standing nearby, "What's going on? Why are all these people lined up around the castle?"

"The king's looking for a new royal cook!" the soldier replied. "The cook with the most unusual recipe will get the job and will live in the palace off the best of the land!"

"I'm just the sort of cook the king wants," the young man answered, "and I have the most unusual recipe he's ever heard of!"

from Dragon Stew *by Tom McGowen*

Think and Discuss

1. How does the young man look and act? What do you learn about this **character**?
2. This story **beginning** makes you want to read more. Why?
3. Where and when do you think the story takes place?

The Writing Process

The **beginning** of a story introduces the main **character,** such as the young man in *Dragon Stew*. It tells where and when the story takes place. The **middle** tells what happens. The **ending** finishes the story in a way that makes sense.

Assignment: Write a Story

Step One: Prewriting
1. List three story ideas, and discuss them with a partner. Choose one idea to write about.
2. List the events in your story in order.

Step Two: Write a First Draft
1. Think about your purpose and your audience.
2. Do not worry about mistakes—just write.

Step Three: Revise
1. Does your story have a beginning, a middle, and an end? Did you describe your characters?
2. Use your Thesaurus to find exact words.
3. Read your story to a partner. Make changes.

Step Four: Proofread
1. Did you capitalize all proper nouns?
2. Did you correct any misspelled words? Add them to your Notebook for Writing.

Step Five: Publish
Copy your story. Add a title. Share your story.

Composition Words
dark
storm
girl
noise
boy
large
crack
squeeze

Proofreading Marks
¶ Indent
∧ Add something
℮ Take out something
≡ Capitalize
/ Make a small letter

19 The Vowel + |r| Sounds in hair

Theme: Hairdresser

A. _____

B. _____

C. _____

D. _____

■ Challenge

_____

LOOK and **SAY**

Basic Words

1. hair
2. care
3. chair
4. pair
5. bear
6. where
7. scare
8. air
9. pear
10. bare
11. fair
12. share

■ **Challenge**

13. flair   14. compare

THINK

Each word has the vowel + |r| sounds that you hear in *hair*.

|âr| **care, hair, bear**

• What are three spelling patterns for the |âr| sounds?

WRITE

Practice   **Write Basic Words to answer the questions.**

A. Which **four** words have |âr| spelled *are*?
B. Which **five** words have |âr| spelled *air*?
C. Which **two** words have |âr| spelled *ear*?
D. Which **one** word has |âr| spelled another way?

■ Now write the two Challenge Words.

CHECK

Independent Practice

Word Attack Use Basic Words in these exercises.

1. Write the word that begins with the |sh| sound.

2-3. Write *care*. Then add a letter to *care* to write another word.

4-6. Write the word that sounds like each word below but is spelled differently.

4. bear
5. pear
6. fare

Classifying Write the Basic Word that belongs in each group.

7. table, stool, ___
8. orange, apple, ___
9. land, sea, ___
10. deer, fox, ___
11. fur, feathers, ___

Elephant Word Write the Elephant Word to complete the sentence.

12. Melissa, ___ do you get your hair cut?

■ **Challenge Words** Write the Challenge Word that completes each sentence. Use your Spelling Dictionary.

13. Vic goes to different shops to ___ haircut prices.
14. Diane's haircuts always have ___ to them.

Summing Up

The |âr| sounds can be spelled with these patterns:

- *are,* as in *care*
- *ear,* as in *bear*
- *air,* as in *hair*

1. ___
2. ___
3. ___
4. ___
5. ___
6. ___
7. ___
8. ___
9. ___
10. ___
11. ___
12. ___
13. ___
14. ___

Basic

1. hair
2. care
3. chair
4. pair
5. bear
6. where
7. scare
8. air
9. pear
10. bare
11. fair
12. share

■ Challenge

13. flair
14. compare

Review

1. buy
2. could

Proofreading Marks

¶ Indent
∧ Add something
ℓ Take out something
≡ Capitalize
/ Make a small letter

Expanding Vocabulary

Rhyming Words *Hair*, *pear*, and *care* rhyme even though the final sounds are spelled differently. Here are more rhyming words.

| fare | repair | rare | beware | wear |

Practice **Write the word above that completes each sentence. Use your Spelling Dictionary.**

1. These coins are very old and ___.
2. I want to ___ my new hat to school.
3. Dad will ___ my broken bike.
4. Tim told me to ___ of the dog next door.
5. Nancy saves all her change for bus ___.

1. _____
2. _____
3. _____
4. _____
5. _____

Proofreading

Commas in a Series Use commas to separate a series of three or more words in a sentence.

Billy, Joe, and Kate had their hair cut.

Practice **Proofread this ad. Use proofreading marks to correct three misspelled words. Add two missing commas.**

Example: We need a comb, scissors, and a ~~char~~ *chair*.

Good Care for Your Hair

Get your hair washed cut and dried

for a fare price! Come to Sylvia's Shop,

were you always get a great by.

Sylvia's Shop

Review: Spelling Spree

Letter Math   Add and subtract letters from the words below to make Basic or Review Words. Write the new words.

Example: ch + fair − f = *chair*

1. c + would − w =
2. sh + fare − f =
3. p + chair − ch =
4. b + scare − sc =
5. c + stare − st =
6. sc + stare − st =
7. wh + there − th =
8. f + hair − h =
9. p + wear − w =

Silly Sentences   Write a Basic or Review Word to complete each silly sentence.

Example: Apples and a ___ grew on a tree. *pear*

10. I had a friendly talk with a big brown ___.
11. I saw a puppy comb its long ___.
12. Alexander saw a book rising into the ___.
13. An elephant likes to sit in a ___.
14. The dog has money to ___ a snack.

■ **Challenge Words**   Look at the Silly Sentences activity. Then write your own Silly Sentences. Use each Challenge Word in two sentences. You may want to draw cartoons to go with your sentences.

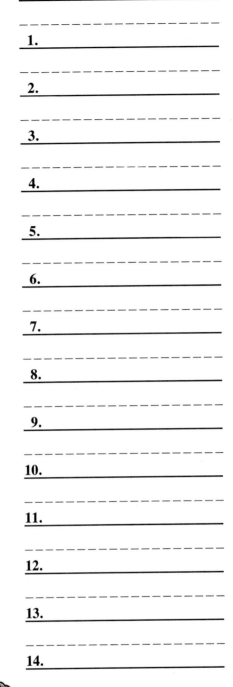

> *Writing Application:* A Description   Write a paragraph that describes what it is like to get your hair cut. What do you see, smell, hear, and feel? Does it tickle? Do you sneeze? Try to use three words from the list on page 122.

1. _____
2. _____
3. _____
4. _____
5. _____
6. _____
7. _____
8. _____
9. _____
10. _____
11. _____
12. _____
13. _____
14. _____

19 Spelling Across the Curriculum

Careers: *Hairdresser*

Theme Vocabulary

shampoo
trim
style
brush
dryer

Using Vocabulary   Write the Vocabulary Words to complete the paragraph. Use your Spelling Dictionary.

I use a good __(1)__ to wash my hair. It dries so fast that I do not need a __(2)__. Every month I have Todd, a hairdresser, __(3)__ my hair because it grows fast. He uses a comb and a soft __(4)__ to fix it in a new __(5)__.

Understanding Vocabulary   Is the underlined word used correctly? Write *yes* or *no*.

6. <u>Shampoo</u> makes hair dirty.
7. Anna uses a <u>brush</u> to cut her hair.
8. You can <u>trim</u> hair that gets too long.

1. _____
2. _____
3. _____
4. _____
5. _____
6. _____
7. _____
8. _____

FACT FILE

Fashions often seem odd once they are out-of-date. For example, some people once wore long, curled wigs that were powdered white.

Enrichment

19

👪 \âr\ *Pairs*

Players: 2   **You need:** 22 word cards (two for every Basic Word except *where*)

How to play: Each player takes five cards. Player 1 spells the \âr\ sounds shown on one of his or her cards and asks for the matching card. For example, Player 1 might say, "Do you have the *a-i-r* word *hair*?" If a match is made, Player 1 lays down both cards. If not, Player 1 draws a card from the pile, and Player 2 takes a turn. The first player to "go out" wins.

Do you have the a-i-r word hair?

📖 *Writing*
A Hair Scare

Write a story about the worst or the funniest thing that happened when you had a haircut. Did the person cutting it make a mistake? Did you cut your own hair? Try to use words from the unit lists. Be sure to proofread your story.

HAIR STYLES

Make new hair styles! Draw at least three styles that you like. Call that page "Styles to Show That You Care." Then fill a page with the wildest styles you can imagine. Name that page "Styles That Scare!"

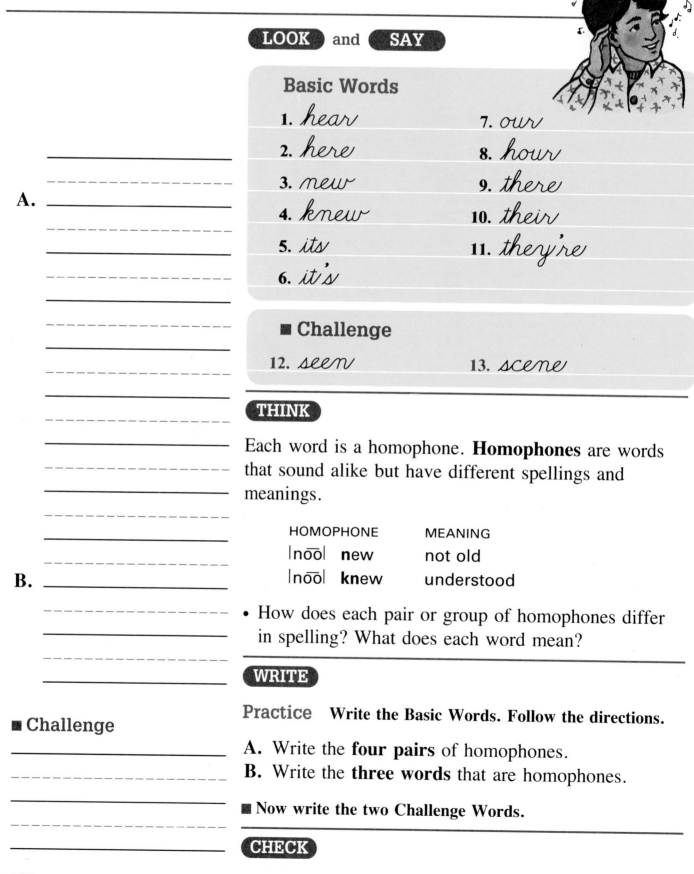

Theme: Using Your Senses

20 Homophones

A. _____

LOOK and SAY

Basic Words

1. *hear*	7. *our*
2. *here*	8. *hour*
3. *new*	9. *there*
4. *knew*	10. *their*
5. *its*	11. *they're*
6. *it's*	

■ Challenge

12. *seen*   13. *scene*

THINK

Each word is a homophone. **Homophones** are words that sound alike but have different spellings and meanings.

HOMOPHONE		MEANING
|nōō|	**new**	not old
|nōō|	**kn**ew	understood

• How does each pair or group of homophones differ in spelling? What does each word mean?

B. _____

WRITE

Practice   **Write the Basic Words. Follow the directions.**

A. Write the **four pairs** of homophones.
B. Write the **three words** that are homophones.

■ Challenge

■ Now write the two Challenge Words.

CHECK

Independent Practice

Context Sentences   Write the Basic Word that completes each sentence.

1. Mom says (its, it's) okay to have a snack.
2. The church bells ring every (hour, our).
3. The car is so clean because it is (knew, new).
4. Come (hear, here) and listen to this record.
5. Jan likes tacos if (they're, their, there) very spicy.
6. My sister and I think of (our, hour) uncle's farm when we smell newly cut grass.
7. Look how the car glows with (its, it's) new coat of paint!
8. Jim, do you (here, hear) those dogs growling?
9. Eliza and Paul always eat (they're, their, there) spinach.
10. Jeffrey (knew, new) that he should be home before dark.
11. Did Missy leave her glasses at the park when she was (their, they're, there)?

■ **Challenge Words**   Write the Challenge Word that completes each sentence. Use your Spelling Dictionary.

12. Have you ever (scene, seen) a rainbow?
13. The first (seen, scene) in that play was so sad that I almost cried.

1. _____
2. _____
3. _____
4. _____
5. _____
6. _____
7. _____
8. _____
9. _____
10. _____
11. _____
12. _____
13. _____

Summing Up

Homophones are words that sound the same but have different spellings and meanings.

Basic

1. hear
2. here
3. new
4. knew
5. its
6. it's
7. our
8. hour
9. there
10. their
11. they're

■ Challenge

12. seen
13. scene

Review

1. eye
2. I

Expanding Vocabulary

Homophones Which shines—a *sun* or a *son*? These two words are homophones.

sun a large star
son a boy

Practice Write the homophone that completes each sentence. Use your Spelling Dictionary.

fair fare pail pale sail sale

1. Lee's face turned ___ with fright.
2. Use this ___ to carry water from the well.
3. Dean rode the merry-go-round at the ___.
4. You must have exact change for the bus ___.
5. That store is having a big ___ next week.
6. It's hard to ___ when there is no wind.

1. _____ 4. _____

2. _____ 5. _____

3. _____ 6. _____

Dictionary

Homophones Look at the dictionary entry below. Notice the ♦ in the last line. This points out the homophone for *it's*.

it's |ĭts| Contraction of "it is" or "it has."
♦ *These sound alike* **it's, its.**

Practice Look up each word in your Spelling Dictionary. Write its homophone.

1. seem   3. know   5. main
2. blue   4. week

1. _____

2. _____

3. _____

4. _____

5. _____

Review: Spelling Spree

Puzzle Play   Write a Basic or Review Word for each clue. Circle the letter that would be in the box.
Example: in this place   _ _ □ _   he(r)e

1. belongs to it   _ □ _
2. belongs to them   _ □ _ _ _
3. what we see with   _ _ □
4. belongs to us   _ _ □
5. not old   _ □ _

Write the letters you circled in order. They will spell a Basic Word that completes this sentence.

6. Sam said that ___ was plenty of chili left.

Proofreading   **7–13.**   Find and cross out seven misspelled Basic or Review Words. Then write each word correctly.

I love to here birds! They started to sing an our ago. There are more birds hear this year. Eye never new they could be so loud! Wow—its as if their cheering!

■ **Challenge Words**   Write four sentences, using each Challenge Word in two sentences. Leave a blank line for each Challenge Word. Write the answers on the back of your paper. Trade papers with a partner.

1. _____

2. _____

3. _____

4. _____

5. _____

6. _____

7. _____

8. _____

9. _____

10. _____

11. _____

12. _____

13. _____

Writing Application: A Description   What is your favorite food? How does it look, smell, and taste? Write a paragraph describing it. Try to use three words from the list on page 128.

20 Spelling Across the Curriculum

Language Arts: *Using Your Senses*

Theme Vocabulary

bumpy
shiny
burnt
squeaky
sour

Using Vocabulary Write the Vocabulary Words to complete the paragraph. Use your Spelling Dictionary.

Today my senses told me that I had a bad day! First, I had __(1)__ toast for breakfast. Then the milk on my cereal was __(2)__. This afternoon I fell off my bike on a __(3)__ dirt road. Now my new shoes don't look __(4)__ anymore, and my bike sounds __(5)__.

1. _____
2. _____
3. _____
4. _____
5. _____
6. _____
7. _____
8. _____

Understanding Vocabulary Write a Vocabulary Word to answer each question.

6. What kind of match will not light?
7. What kind of door needs oil?
8. How does a lemon taste?

FACT FILE

Braille is an alphabet that blind people can read with their fingers. There is a different pattern of tiny bumps for each letter.

Enrichment

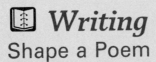 Writing
Shape a Poem

Write a shape poem that uses this form:

noun—
three adjectives (describe the noun)—
verb
three words (to finish sentence).

Copy your poem onto a piece of paper cut in the shape of your noun. Try to use words from the unit lists. Be sure to proofread your poem.

Snowflakes—
soft, white, sparkling—
cover
our new roof.

"Pear Pair" Tree

With your classmates cut out a big tree from construction paper, and tack it on the bulletin board. Next, cut out paper pears. Write the homophones used in this unit on the pears. Pin the pears to the tree in pairs or groups. Add other homophones.

SENSE MOBILES

Draw five pictures of things you see, hear, touch, smell, and taste. Name and describe each picture on the back. Use sense words, such as *a squeaky mouse* or *a shiny penny*. Hang the pictures from string to make a mobile.

21 Compound Words

LOOK and **SAY**

Basic Words

1. airplane
2. inside
3. grandmother
4. sometimes
5. himself
6. nothing
7. birthday
8. herself
9. outside
10. grandfather
11. baseball
12. something

■ Challenge

13. suitcase
14. everybody

THINK

Each word is a compound word. A **compound word** is made up of two or more shorter words.

air + **plane** = airplane
him + **self** = himself

• What two words make up each compound word? How do you say the Elephant Word? How do you say the two words that form the Elephant Word?

WRITE

Practice   Write the twelve Basic Words. Draw a line between the two words that make up each compound word.

■ Now write the two Challenge Words.

CHECK

■ Challenge

Independent Practice

Word Attack   Use Basic Words in these exercises.

1-6. Each word below is part of two compound
words. Write the six compound words.

    1-2. grand

    3-4. self

    5-6. side

Context Sentences   Write the Basic Word that
completes each sentence.

   7. Jay took an ___ instead
of a train to Chicago.

   8. We played a lot of games
at the ___ party.

   9. There is always ___ fun
to do at Uncle Ben's.

 10. Becky saw her favorite ___ team
play at Candlestick Park.

 11. Maria usually goes to her grandparents' house on
Sundays, but ___ she goes to her aunt's.

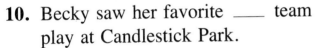
airplane

Elephant Word   Write the Elephant Word to
complete the sentence.

 12. My family will let ___ spoil our trip.

Challenge Words   Write the Challenge Word that
completes each sentence. Use your Spelling Dictionary.

 13. Each person may take only one ___ on the
weekend trip.

 14. The trip leader told ___ to meet at the train
station.

1. _____
2. _____
3. _____
4. _____
5. _____
6. _____
7. _____
8. _____
9. _____
10. _____
11. _____
12. _____
13. _____
14. _____

Summing Up

A **compound word** is made up of two or more
shorter words.

Basic

1. airplane
2. inside
3. grandmother
4. sometimes
5. himself
6. nothing
7. birthday
8. herself
9. outside
10. grandfather
11. baseball
12. something

■ Challenge

13. suitcase
14. everybody

Review

1. someone
2. cannot

Proofreading Marks

¶ Indent
∧ Add something
℘ Take out something
≡ Capitalize
/ Make a small letter

Expanding Vocabulary

Compound Words A compound word has the meanings of the shorter words that form it.

out + side = outside   "the side that is out"

Practice Write a compound word that fits each meaning by matching a word in the left box with a word in the right box.

foot	flag
day	soap

time	print
suds	pole

1. the time of day between sunrise and sunset
2. a pole for a flag
3. the bubbles in soapy water
4. the mark left by a foot

1. _____   3. _____

2. _____   4. _____

Proofreading

Quotation Marks Put quotation marks around a speaker's exact words.

Ed asked, "May I go?"

Practice Proofread this story. Use proofreading marks to correct three misspelled words. Add two missing quotation marks.

Example: "The ~~airplan~~ *airplane* has arrived!" Liza cried.

It was pouring outside. I said, I canot see anything. Then I saw somone. There was my granmother!

Review: Spelling Spree

Compound Clues Write a Basic or Review Word to answer each question.

1. What word means the opposite of *nothing*?
2. What day is the day you become a year older?
3. What is in your backpack if it is empty?
4. What word means the opposite of *inside*?
5. What is a name for your father's father?
6. What does a pilot fly?
7. What word means the opposite of *no one*?
8. What game do you play with a bat?

Compound Words Each word is part of a Basic or Review Word. Write those Basic and Review Words.

9. mother   11. her   13. in
10. can   12. times   14. him

■ **Challenge Words** Write the two sentence beginnings below. Complete the sentences by writing words or names in ABC order. Some answers have been given to get you started. Can you get to *z*?

1. I'm going on a trip, and in my suitcase I'll pack ____. *an apple, a bathing suit*
2. Everyone is coming, including ____. *Ann, Bill*

📖 *Writing Application:* A Telephone Call
You are staying at a friend's home on your little brother's birthday. He is six years old. Call home and talk to him. Write what you say to each other. Use quotation marks. Try to use three words from the list on page 134.

1. _____
2. _____
3. _____
4. _____
5. _____
6. _____
7. _____
8. _____
9. _____
10. _____
11. _____
12. _____
13. _____
14. _____

21   Spelling Across the Curriculum

Social Studies: *Going for a Visit*

Theme Vocabulary

visit
aunt
pajamas
slippers
bathrobe

Using Vocabulary   Write the Vocabulary Words to complete the paragraph. Use your Spelling Dictionary.

My uncle and __(1)__ invited me to __(2)__ them in Chicago. They said, ''Our house gets cold! You will need warm __(3)__ for sleeping.'' I will also take a __(4)__ to wear over my pajamas and __(5)__ for my feet.

Understanding Vocabulary   Write the Vocabulary Word that fits each clue.

6. These special shoes are worn inside the house.
7. You might ride on an airplane to do this.
8. This pair has a top and a bottom.

1. _____
2. _____
3. _____
4. _____
5. _____
6. _____
7. _____
8. _____

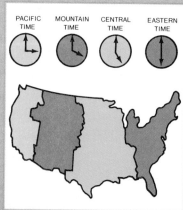

PACIFIC TIME   MOUNTAIN TIME   CENTRAL TIME   EASTERN TIME

FACT FILE

Most of the United States lies in four time zones. At 3:00 P.M. in Oregon, it is 4:00 P.M. in Utah, 5:00 P.M. in Iowa, and 6:00 P.M. in New York.

Enrichment

COMPOUND CUPBOARD

Make a cupboard. First, fold a piece of construction paper in half. Open it flat again. Next, fold both ends of the paper so that they meet in the middle to make doors. Write compound words on shelves inside the cupboard. Decorate your cupboard.

inside

airplane

birthday

Writing
A Great Time

You are on a trip. People at home want to hear about it. Write a letter to your family or a friend. Where are you? Whom are you with? Are you visiting anyone? What have you done? Try to use words from the unit lists. Be sure to proofread your letter.

Visit Water Park

Players: 2–4, a reader
You need: a game board, a spinner, game markers, a list of unit spelling words
How to play: The reader reads a word to a player. The player tries to spell the word correctly. If correct, the player spins the spinner and moves his or her marker. If wrong, the player does not move. The first player to reach Water Park wins.

FINISH

START

Theme: Building a Tree House

22 Words That End with -ed or -ing

LOOK and **SAY**

Basic Words

1. chopped
2. tapping
3. saving
4. cared
5. rubbed
6. fixing
7. smiled
8. joking
9. dropped
10. grinning
11. wrapped
12. patted

■ Challenge

13. propped
14. framed

THINK

Each word has a base word and -ed or -ing. A **base word** is a word to which an ending may be added.

care − e + ed = car**ed**
rub + b + ing = ru**bbing**

• How do *care* and *rub* change when an ending is added? How is the Elephant Word different?

WRITE

Practice Write Basic Words to answer the questions about adding -ed or -ing to base words.

A. Which **four** words drop the final *e*?
B. Which **seven** words double the final consonant?
C. Which **one** word does not change its spelling?

■ Now write the two Challenge Words.

CHECK

A. _____
_____
_____
_____
_____

B. _____
_____
_____
_____
_____

C. _____

■ Challenge
_____
_____

Independent Practice

Word Attack   Use Basic Words in these exercises.

1–4. Write four words by adding *-ed* or *-ing* to each base word.

   1. grin

   2. wrap

   3. care

   4. save

Context Sentences   Write the Basic Word that completes each sentence.

   5. Dad ___ wood for the tree house.

   6. I liked to hear the hammer ___ the nails.

   7. Alice ___ the doorknob until it shined.

   8. Dad shouted when he ___ a hammer out of the window.

   9. Dad ___ me on the back when we finished.

   10. Luis ___ happily when he saw the tree house.

   11. Tim was only ___ when he said he hated trees.

Elephant Word   Write the Elephant Word to complete the sentence.

   12. Mom will be ___ the door today.

Challenge Words   Write the Challenge Word that fits each meaning. Use your Spelling Dictionary.

   13. enclosed   **14.** supported

1. _____

2. _____

3. _____

4. _____

5. _____

6. _____

7. _____

8. _____

9. _____

10. _____

11. _____

12. _____

13. _____

14. _____

Summing Up

When a base word ends with *e*, drop the *e* before adding *-ed* or *-ing*.

When a base word ends with one vowel and one consonant, the consonant is usually doubled before *-ed* or *-ing* is added.

Basic

1. chopped
2. tapping
3. saving
4. cared
5. rubbed
6. fixing
7. smiled
8. joking
9. dropped
10. grinning
11. wrapped
12. patted

■ Challenge

13. propped
14. framed

Review

1. making
2. stopped

Expanding Vocabulary

Easily Confused Words   Some words can be confused if you do not spell them correctly. Look at *tap* and *tape*. How does the spelling of each word change when *-ed* or *-ing* is added?

| tap | ta**pped** | ta**pping** |
| tape | ta**ped** | ta**ping** |

Practice   Write *tapped*, *tapping*, *taped*, or *taping* to complete each sentence.

1. The rain ____ on the window.
2. Amy ____ the picture to the paper.
3. Lester is ____ the tag to the gift.
4. Mr. Gomez is ____ the chalk on the board.

1. _____ 3. _____

2. _____ 4. _____

Dictionary

Base Words   How can you find out how to spell a word that ends with *-ed* or *-ing*? Look up its base word in a dictionary.

pat |păt| *v.* **patted, patting** To touch gently with the open hand: *Don't pat the dog.*

Practice   Write the base word you would look up in a dictionary to find each word below.

1. joking   3. fixing   5. making
2. smiled   4. stopped   6. chopped

1. _____ 3. _____ 5. _____

2. _____ 4. _____ 6. _____

Review: Spelling Spree

Ending Match   Write eight Basic or Review Words by matching the puzzle pieces. Remember to double the final consonant or drop the final *e*.

ing   ed

1. tap   3. drop   5. care   7. joke
2. make   4. grin   6. save   8. wrap

Proofreading   9–14. Find and cross out six misspelled Basic or Review Words. Then write each word correctly.

March 14   *Sam dropped by and saw that I was fiksing my new tree house. He stoped, smild, and pated my back. I told him that Dad had choped and sawed the wood. I had rubed the edges with sandpaper. His praise left me grinning from ear to ear.*

■ **Challenge Words**   Write four riddles. Use each Challenge Word in two riddles. Your answers should rhyme with the Challenge Words.
Example: It rhymes with <u>propped</u> and means "wiped up."   *mopped*

📖 *Writing Application:* A Story   Pretend that you are a squirrel. Suddenly a tree house appears in your tree! Write a story, telling how your life changes. Try to use three words from the list on page 140.

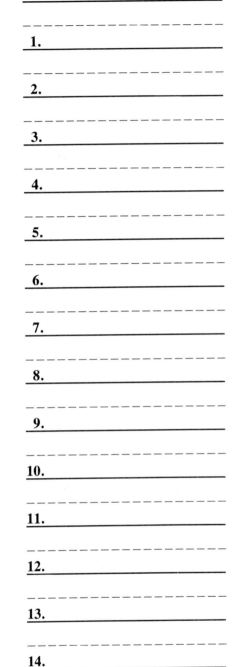

1. _____
2. _____
3. _____
4. _____
5. _____
6. _____
7. _____
8. _____
9. _____
10. _____
11. _____
12. _____
13. _____
14. _____

22 Spelling Across the Curriculum

Industrial Arts: *Building a Tree House*

Theme Vocabulary

build
plan
branches
ladder
boards

Using Vocabulary Write the Vocabulary Words to complete the paragraph. Use your Spelling Dictionary.

Mom has a great __(1)__ to help us __(2)__ a tree house. First, we will choose the biggest __(3)__ of the tree. Then Mom will climb up the __(4)__. I will hand her the tools, nails, and __(5)__. When the house is done, we will paint it.

Understanding Vocabulary Write a Vocabulary Word to answer each clue.

6. Follow this to complete a project.
7. Climb this to reach something high.
8. These parts of a tree are like arms.

1. _____
2. _____
3. _____
4. _____
5. _____
6. _____
7. _____
8. _____

FACT FILE

In the rain forests of Costa Rica, a man named Donald Perry builds platforms that move through the treetops. Here he studies plants, animals, and insects.

Enrichment

📖 *Writing*
Home Sweet Home

There are many kinds of tree houses. Some look like forts or castles. Others look like real homes. Write a paragraph describing your ideal tree house. How would it look? What would be in it? Try to use words from the lists in this unit. Be sure to proofread your paper.

👥 *Alphabet Ladders*

Players: any number
You need: paper, pencils, a list of Basic and Review Words, a timer
How to play: Each player draws a ladder with 14 steps. Starting together, players have 5 minutes to "climb down" by writing a Basic or Review Word on each step. Words must be written in ABC order.

TREE HOUSE PLAN

Draw a plan that shows what your ideal tree house would look like. How big would it be? Would it have a roof? How would it fit in the tree? How would you climb up to it? Label each part of your plan.

23 Changing Final y to i

Theme: Baby Animals

A. _____

B. _____

■ Challenge

_____

LOOK and **SAY**

Basic Words

1. babies
2. puppies
3. cried
4. carried
5. stories
6. dried
7. hurried
8. ponies
9. flies
10. tried
11. parties
12. pennies

■ Challenge

13. canaries   14. libraries

THINK

Each word is made up of a base word and the ending -es or -ed. The spelling of the base word changes when -es or -ed is added.

baby − y + ies = bab**ies**
cry − y + ied = cr**ied**

• Does a consonant or a vowel come before the final y in each base word? How do *baby* and *cry* change when -es or -ed is added?

WRITE

Practice   **Write Basic Words to answer the questions.**

A. Which **seven** words end with -ies?
B. Which **five** words end with -ied?

■ **Now write the two Challenge Words.**

CHECK

Independent Practice

Word Attack Use Basic Words in these exercises.

1-4. Each word below is missing a double consonant.
Write the four words.
1. hu __ __ ied
2. pe __ __ ies
3. ca __ __ ied
4. pu __ __ ies

5-7. Add the ending *-ed* to each base word below.
Write the three new words.
5. cry   7. dry
6. try

Making Inferences Write the Basic Word that
matches each clue.
8. People often read
   these in books.
9. Children often have
   these on their birthdays.
10. These often buzz around
    food at picnics.
11. Children often ride
    these at fairs.
12. These are very young
    children.

■**Challenge Words** Write the Challenge Word that
completes each sentence. Use your Spelling Dictionary.
13. Carlos has two yellow ____ for pets.
14. Anita looked for facts on pet care at two ____.

1. _____
2. _____
3. _____
4. _____
5. _____
6. _____
7. _____
8. _____
9. _____
10. _____
11. _____
12. _____
13. _____
14. _____

Summing Up

When a base word ends with a consonant and *y*,
change the *y* to *i* before adding *-es* or *-ed*.

Basic

1. babies
2. puppies
3. cried
4. carried
5. stories
6. dried
7. hurried
8. ponies
9. flies
10. tried
11. parties
12. pennies

■ **Challenge**

13. canaries
14. libraries

Review

1. lady
2. very

Proofreading Marks

¶ Indent
∧ Add something
ℓ Take out something
≡ Capitalize
/ Make a small letter

Expanding Vocabulary

Words for Animal Sounds   Some words, such as *cried* and *howled*, name special sounds that animals make.

The dogs **cried**.   The wolves **howled**.

Practice   Write the word that best completes each sentence. Use your Spelling Dictionary.

snarled   hissed   cackled   squeaked

1. The hens ——— when I brought their food.
2. The mouse ——— in fear when it saw the cat.
3. The guard dog ——— at the thief.
4. The snakes ——— at the zookeeper.

1. _____   3. _____

2. _____   4. _____

Proofreading

End Marks in Quotations   Put quotation marks around a speaker's exact words. Put the end mark inside the quotation marks.

Alex cried, "Hurry!"   Kate answered, "I am."

Practice   Proofread this story. Use proofreading marks to correct three misspelled words. Add a missing end mark.

Example: I asked, "How many ~~pupies~~ *puppies* are there"?"

I visited a lade and her puppies. She said, "They cryed all night" Doesn't she know that puppies are babys?

Review: Spelling Spree

Alphabet Dash   Write the Basic or Review Word that goes in ABC order between each pair of words.

1. easy, ___, goose
2. gray, ___, ice
3. joke, ___, milk
4. use, ___, wait
5. band, ___, cone
6. cool, ___, cub
7. paint, ___, paste
8. swing, ___, trot

Sentence Pairs   Write the Basic Word that best completes each pair of sentences.

Example: A bee cannot swim. It only ___. *flies*

9. I do not see any big horses. I only see ___.
10. My sisters are not grownups. They are ___.
11. I do not have any dimes. I only have ___.
12. Dad does not sing songs. He tells ___.
13. I do not have grown dogs. I have only ___.
14. We did not wash the dishes. We only ___ them.

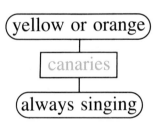

yellow or orange

canaries

always singing

■ **Challenge Words**   Make a cluster for each Challenge Word. Then write at least four sentences, using the Challenge Words and words from the clusters.

📖 *Writing Application:* Creative Writing
Write a story about a baby animal that is separated from its parents and is raised by a different kind of animal. What happens when the baby learns what kind of animal it really is? Try to use three words from the list on page 146.

1. _____
2. _____
3. _____
4. _____
5. _____
6. _____
7. _____
8. _____
9. _____
10. _____
11. _____
12. _____
13. _____
14. _____

23 Spelling Across the Curriculum

Science: *Baby Animals*

Theme Vocabulary

calf
fawn
cub
chick
duckling

Using Vocabulary Write the Vocabulary Words to complete the paragraph. Use your Spelling Dictionary.

The baby and grown-up names for animals are sometimes related. A young chicken is a __(1)__, for example. A baby duck is a __(2)__. The baby and grown-up names for animals may also be very different. A baby bear is a __(3)__, a young bull is a __(4)__, and a baby deer is a __(5)__.

Understanding Vocabulary Is the underlined word used correctly? Write *yes* or *no*.

6. The mother cow looked for its <u>calf</u>.
7. The <u>fawn</u> trotted after the other deer.
8. A bear usually has one <u>chick</u> or twins.

1. _____
2. _____
3. _____
4. _____
5. _____
6. _____
7. _____
8. _____

FACT FILE

A baby kangaroo is a joey. It is less than an inch long when it is born. A joey lives in its mother's pouch for six to eight months.

Enrichment

23

PARENTS' ADVICE

Make a book of advice that father and mother animals might give about baby care. First, make a four-page book by folding a piece of paper in half. Next, draw four parents and their babies, a father or a mother with a baby on each page. Last, write each parent's advice, such as "Do not let your cub eat too many fish," under each picture. Try to use words from the unit lists.

Writing
Babies, Babies!

Puppies and human babies are alike and different. Write a paragraph, telling three ways puppies and babies are the same. Then write another paragraph, telling three ways they are different. Try to use words from the unit lists. Be sure to proofread your paper.

Meet the Family

With your class, make a mural that shows different animals with their babies. First, draw or cut out pictures of the animals. Write their names under the pictures. Then look up facts about each animal, and make a fact card for it. Tape the cards under the pictures.

24 Review: Units 19–23

Unit 19 Vowel + |r| Sounds in *hair* pp. 120–125

bear	chair	where
pear	fair	scare

Remember: The |âr| sounds can have these patterns:
are, as in *care*   **ear**, as in *bear*
air, as in *hair*

Write the words to complete the paragraph.

Bonnie and I went to the county __(1)__ yesterday. I bought an apple and a __(2)__ to eat, and Bonnie bought a fuzzy toy __(3)__. Bonnie saw a strong man who could break a __(4)__ in half with one hand. The most fun was the House of Horrors, __(5)__ we had a really good __(6)__!

1. _____
2. _____
3. _____
4. _____
5. _____
6. _____

Unit 20 Homophones pp. 126–131

its	hear	our
it's	here	hour

Remember: **Homophones** are words that sound the same but have different spellings and meanings.

new knew

Write the word that completes each sentence.
7. If it snows, we will wear (hour, our) boots.
8. My dog really likes (its, it's) bath.
9. Dinner will be ready in an (our, hour).
10. Do you (hear, here) those birds singing?
11. Dad says that (its, it's) going to rain today.
12. Carla will meet us (here, hear) at noon.

7. _____
8. _____
9. _____
10. _____
11. _____
12. _____

Half of the words from each unit are reviewed on these pages.
The rest are reviewed on pages 238–240.

Unit 21   Compound Words   pp. 132–137

| grandmother | himself | nothing |
| outside | birthday | baseball |

Remember: A **compound word** is made up of two or more shorter words.

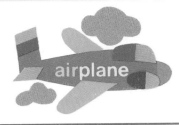

airplane

Write the word that belongs in each group.
13. myself, herself, ___   **14.** soccer, hockey, ___
Write the word that completes each sentence.
15. Debby will have her ___ party tomorrow.
16. The box had ___ in it.
17. Tina is going ___ to water the garden.
18. Jud's ___ is coming to visit on Sunday.

_____

13. _____

14. _____

15. _____

16. _____

17. _____

18. _____

Unit 22   Words with -ed or -ing   pp. 138–143

| cared | tapping | fixing |
| joking | wrapped | smiled |

Remember: The spelling of some base words changes when **-ed** or **-ing** is added.

care − e + ed = car**ed**
tap + p + ing = tap**ping**

s a v i n g
e

Write the word that rhymes with each word below.
19. trapped   **20.** napping
Write four spelling words by adding -ed or -ing to each base word below.
21. smile   **23.** fix
22. joke   **24.** care

_____

19. _____

20. _____

21. _____

22. _____

23. _____

24. _____

Unit 23   Changing Final _y_ to _i_   pp. 144–149

| carried | stories | dried |
| ponies | pennies | tried |

Remember: When a base word ends with a consonant and **y**, change the **y** to **i** before adding **-es** or **-ed**.

Write the word that completes each sentence.
25. We played outside while the wet paint ___.
26. Ilene ___ to open the door, but it was stuck.
Write four spelling words by adding _-es_ or _-ed_ to each base word below.
27. pony   **29.** story
28. carry   **30.** penny

25. _____
26. _____
27. _____
28. _____
29. _____
30. _____

■**Challenge Words   Units 19–23**   pp. 120–149

| libraries | framed | seen |
| everybody | compare | scene |

Write two spelling words by adding _-es_ or _-ed_ to each base word below.
31. frame
32. library
Write the word that completes each sentence.
33. At the Science Fair, the judges will ___ the projects and choose a winner.
34. We have already ___ that movie.
35. An actor forgot his lines in the first ___.
36. Our teacher says that ___ is going on the trip.

31. _____
32. _____
33. _____
34. _____
35. _____
36. _____

Spelling-Meaning Strategy

Word Forms

Knowing the meanings and spellings of pairs of homophones will help you spell the other words in their families. Read these sentences.

> This **week** I will go skiing on the **weekend**.
> "I am **weak** from the flu," Jo said **weakly**.

Think

- How are *week* and *weekend* alike in meaning and spelling?
- How are *weak* and *weakly* alike in meaning and spelling?

Here are words in the *week* and *weak* families.

week	weekly	weak	weakly
weekend	biweekly	weakness	weaker

Apply and Extend

Complete these activities on another piece of paper.

1. Look up the meaning of each word in the Word Box above in your Spelling Dictionary. Write eight sentences, using one word in each sentence.

2. With a partner list words related to *bear* and *bare* and to *son* and *sun*. Then look in your Spelling-Meaning Index beginning on page 268. Add any other words in these families to your list.

Description

These paragraphs describe an oak tree. Which words help you picture the tree in your mind?

A big, old oak tree grew on the bank of a river. During the summer its green leaves hid many of its branches. Other branches were dead and bare. Light gray bark covered most of its trunk. Once the oak had had firm, pale brown wood under its bark, but over the years parts of it had rotted and turned gray. The tree had a few large holes in its trunk, and some of its branches had broken off.

One autumn night, the biggest storm in years shook the old oak tree. Strong winds whipped away many of its yellow and brown leaves. The tree swayed and creaked, and the wind pulled at its roots. Some of the roots that were rotten broke, and the oak tree fell to the riverbank.

from An Oak Tree Dies and a Journey Begins
by Louanne Norris and Howard E. Smith, Jr.

Think and Discuss

1. Which words tell how the tree **looked**? How did it **sound** during the storm?
2. What **details** describe what the big storm did to the old tree?

The Writing Process

The description on page 154 helps you see and hear the oak tree. When you write a description, use **sense words** and **details** that tell how your topic looks, sounds, feels, smells, and tastes.

Assignment: Write a Description

Step One: Prewriting

1. List people and things you can describe, and discuss them with a friend. Choose a topic.
2. Write sense words that describe your topic.

Step Two: Write a First Draft

1. Think about your purpose and your audience.
2. Do not worry about mistakes—just write!

Step Three: Revise

1. Where do you need sense words and details?
2. Use your Thesaurus to find exact words.
3. Read your paper to a partner. Make changes.

Step Four: Proofread

1. Did you use commas with words in a series?
2. Did you correct any misspelled words? Add them to your Notebook for Writing.

Step Five: Publish

1. Copy your description, and add a title.
2. Make a greeting card. Put your description inside the card. Give your card to a friend.

Composition Words

bare
hear
outside
patted
tapping
smiled
dried
cried

Proofreading Marks

¶ Indent
∧ Add something
ℓ Take out something
≡ Capitalize
/ Make a small letter

25 The Prefixes re- and un-

(Theme: A Bad Day)

A. _____

B. _____

Basic Words

1. unfair
2. unhappy
3. rewrite
4. unkind
5. remake
6. untie
7. unlike
8. unclear
9. unhurt
10. retell
11. unwrap
12. reuse

■ Challenge

13. unimportant   14. review

THINK

Each word has a prefix and a base word. A **prefix** is a word part added to the beginning of a base word.

PREFIX		BASE WORD		NEW WORD	MEANING
re	+	write	=	**re**write	to write again
un	+	happy	=	**un**happy	not happy
un	+	tie	=	**un**tie	opposite of *tie*

• What prefixes were added to *write*, *happy*, and *tie*? What do the prefixes mean?

WRITE

Practice   **Write Basic Words to answer the questions.**

A. Which **four** words have the prefix *re-*?
B. Which **eight** words have the prefix *un-*?

■ **Now write the two Challenge Words.**

CHECK

■ Challenge

_____

_____

Independent Practice

Word Attack   Use Basic Words in these exercises.

1. Write the word that ends with a double consonant.

2-5. Write the four words with a long vowel sound spelled with the vowel-consonant-*e* pattern.

Context Sentences   Write the Basic Word that completes each sentence.

6. Joshua tripped over a rock, but he was ___.

7. The baby was ___ until she got her bottle.

8. If your shoe is wet, ___ it and take it off.

9. Dad told Sue that she could ___ her presents.

10. Do not be ___ to animals.

11. Christopher thought that the judge's ruling was ___.

12. Betsy got lost because the directions were very ___.

write

rewrite

■ **Challenge Words**   Write the Challenge Word that fits each meaning. Use your Spelling Dictionary.

13. to study again

14. having little meaning or value

1. _____

2. _____

3. _____

4. _____

5. _____

6. _____

7. _____

8. _____

9. _____

10. _____

11. _____

12. _____

13. _____

14. _____

Summing Up

A **prefix** is a word part added to the beginning of a base word. It adds meaning to the base word.
- The prefix *re-* means "again."
- The prefix *un-* means "not" or "opposite of."

Basic

1. unfair
2. unhappy
3. rewrite
4. unkind
5. remake
6. untie
7. unlike
8. unclear
9. unhurt
10. retell
11. unwrap
12. reuse

■ **Challenge**

13. unimportant
14. review

Review

1. do
2. have

Expanding Vocabulary

Building Words with Prefixes   Different prefixes can be added to a base word to build new words with different meanings.

wrap ''to put a covering on''
unwrap ''to take off a covering''
rewrap ''to wrap again''

Practice   Add *re-* or *un-* to each word below to write a word that fits each meaning.

fold   used   done

1. to fold again
2. not done
3. to be used again
4. done again
5. to open the folds of
6. not used

1. _____
2. _____
3. _____
4. _____
5. _____
6. _____

1. _____
2. _____
3. _____
4. _____
5. _____
6. _____

Dictionary

Syllables   A **syllable** is a word part with one vowel sound. The dictionary uses black dots (·) to separate the syllables of an entry word.

un·hap·py |ŭn hăp′ ē| *adj.* **unhappier, unhappiest**
Not happy; sad.

Practice   Write each word below. Draw a line between the syllables. Use your Spelling Dictionary.

1. picnic
2. almost
3. balloon
4. neighbor
5. outside
6. circus

Review: Spelling Spree

Puzzle Play Write the Basic Word that matches each clue. Circle the letter that would appear in the box. Write the circled letters in order. They will spell something you can do to brighten a bad day.

Example: not fair __ __ ☐ __ __ __   un(f)air

1. to open a present __ __ ☐ __ __ __
2. not bruised __ __ ☐ __ __ __
3. to loosen __ __ __ ☐ __
4. to use again __ __ __ ☐ __
5. to write again __ __ __ __ __ ☐ __
6. to tell again __ __ __ __ __ ☐
7. to make again __ ☐ __ __ __ __

Mystery Word: __ __ __ __ __ __ __

Proofreading **8–14.** Find and cross out seven misspelled Basic or Review Words. Then write each word correctly.

> It is unlik you to be anhappy. Maybe your thoughts are unkleer, but doo not think that life is uncind and unfare. If you hav a bad day, think about something funny, or retell a good joke!

■ **Challenge Words** Write two sentences that tell how to avoid having a bad day. Use a Challenge Word in each sentence.

Writing Application: A Personal Story
Write a short story about a bad day you have had. Try to use three words from the list on page 158.

1. _____
2. _____
3. _____
4. _____
5. _____
6. _____
7. _____
8. _____
9. _____
10. _____
11. _____
12. _____
13. _____
14. _____

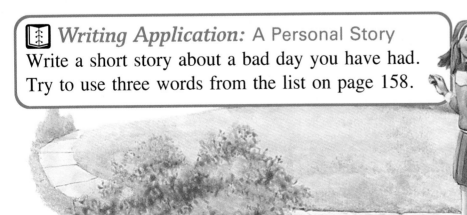

25 Spelling Across the Curriculum

Life Skills: *A Bad Day*

Theme Vocabulary

trouble
oversleep
quarrel
mistake
angry

Using Vocabulary Write the Vocabulary Words to complete the paragraph. Use your Spelling Dictionary.

This morning Lisa's dad thought she might **(1)** , so he woke her. Lisa got **(2)** and started to **(3)** with him. Lisa's dad just smiled and asked, "What's the **(4)** ?"

"I'm just tired," said Lisa. "It was a **(5)** to fight with you." She gave him a hug.

Understanding Vocabulary Write *yes* or *no* to answer each question.

6. If you got up early, did you oversleep?
7. Might people quarrel if they don't agree?
8. Will a perfect paper have a mistake?

1. _____

2. _____

3. _____

4. _____

5. _____

6. _____

7. _____

8. _____

FACT FILE

When people say, "Every cloud has a silver lining," they mean that something good can come out of trouble or bad luck.

Enrichment

👪 *Tick-Tack-Prefix*

Players: 2 or more, 1 caller **You need:** paper, pencils, a list of Basic Words
How to play: Players divide their papers into nine squares and write *re* or *un* in each square. As the caller reads a word, the players write it in a square that has the same prefix. The first player to have three correctly spelled words in a row wins.

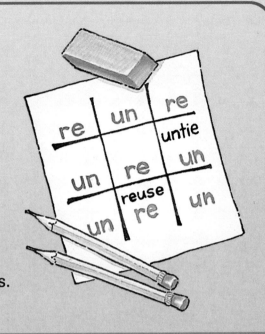

📖 *Writing*
Wise Words

Dear Helpful,

I played a joke on my friends. Now they don't like me. What can I do?

Sincerely,
Sadder but Wiser

Write a letter to Sadder but Wiser. Try to use words from the unit lists. Be sure to proofread your letter.

PREFIX PUZZLE

Write five Basic Words in large letters on a piece of heavy paper. Draw a shape around the words. Then draw ten puzzle pieces so that each prefix and base word is on a separate piece. Cut out the pieces, mix them up, and put the puzzle together.

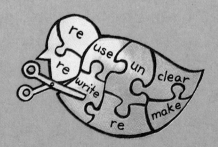

26 The Suffixes -ful, -ly, and -er

A. _____

B. _____

C. _____

■ Challenge

_____

_____

LOOK and SAY

Basic Words

1. teacher
2. friendly
3. useful
4. careful
5. slowly
6. helper
7. quickly
8. farmer
9. hopeful
10. singer
11. thankful
12. sadly

■ Challenge

13. listener   14. calmly

THINK

Each word is made up of a base word and a suffix. A **suffix** is a word part added to the end of a base word.

BASE WORD	SUFFIX	NEW WORD	MEANING
care	+ ful	= care**ful**	full of care
slow	+ ly	= slow**ly**	in a slow way
help	+ er	= help**er**	one who helps

• What three suffixes do you see?

WRITE

Practice   Write Basic Words to answer the questions.

A. Which **four** words have the suffix -*ful*?
B. Which **four** words have the suffix -*ly*?
C. Which **four** words have the suffix -*er*?

■ Now write the two Challenge Words.

CHECK

Independent Practice

Word Attack Use Basic Words in these exercises.

1-3. Write the word that names the person who does each job.
   1. help
   2. sing
   3. farm

4-5. Write the two words with the |ō| sound spelled *ow* or *o*-consonant-*e*.

Word Clues Write the Basic Word that fits each clue.
   6. the opposite of *useless*
   7. the opposite of *careless*
   8. the opposite of *unfriendly*
   9. how people feel at Thanksgiving
   10. the opposite of *slowly*
   11. a person who helps others learn how to read, write, and spell
   12. the opposite of *happily*

■ **Challenge Words** Write the Challenge Word that means the opposite of each word below. Use your Spelling Dictionary.
   13. nervously
   14. speaker

1. _____
2. _____
3. _____
4. _____
5. _____
6. _____
7. _____
8. _____
9. _____
10. _____
11. _____
12. _____
13. _____
14. _____

Summing Up

A **suffix** is a word part added to the end of a base word. It adds meaning to the base word.
• The suffix *-ful* can mean "full of" or "having."
• The suffix *-ly* can mean "in a way that is."
• The suffix *-er* can mean "a person who."

Basic

1. teacher
2. friendly
3. useful
4. careful
5. slowly
6. helper
7. quickly
8. farmer
9. hopeful
10. singer
11. thankful
12. sadly

■ Challenge

13. listener
14. calmly

Review

1. of
2. said

Proofreading Marks

¶ Indent
∧ Add something
℘ Take out something
≡ Capitalize
/ Make a small letter

Expanding Vocabulary

Building Words with Suffixes   You can build words by adding suffixes to a base word. Each suffix adds to the meaning of the base word.

help + ful   = help**ful**   ''full of help''
help + ful + ly = help**fully** ''in a helpful way''

Practice   Add *-ful* or *-fully* to each word to write a word that fits each meaning.

pain   play

1. full of pain   3. full of play
2. in a painful way   4. in a playful way

1. _____   3. _____

2. _____   4. _____

Proofreading

Book Titles   Begin the first, last, and each important word of a book title with a capital letter. Underline the book title.

Tina read The Farmer and the Singer of Tales.

Practice   Proofread Mia's report. Use proofreading marks to correct three misspelled words and a missing capital letter. Add an underline.

Example: Miss Nelson is Back is about a ~~techer~~. *teacher*

Title Miss Nelson Is missing

Author Harry Allard

About the Book   Miss Nelson leaves, and her class kwikly misses her. They hope for the return af their frendly teacher.

Review: Spelling Spree

Hidden Words   Write the Basic or Review Word that is hidden in each group of letters. Do not let the other words fool you.

Example: l a l s l o w l y   *slowly*

1. a s i n g e r e t
2. a f t e a c h e r
3. t h o p e f u l e
4. c o h e l p e r t

5. h o s a i d e s t
6. s t e f a r m e r
7. f u t e t o f
8. s i s a d l y a t

Comparisons   Write the Basic Word that best completes each comparison.

9. Tina can run as ___ as a frightened deer.
10. This tool is as ___ as a lamp in the dark.
11. Mr. Jensen felt as ___ as a person whose life had been saved.
12. That baby is as ___ as a puppy that is wagging its tail.
13. Kim is as ___ as someone carrying eggs.
14. Ginger moves as ___ as a sleepy turtle.

■ **Challenge Words**   Make up four book titles, using each Challenge Word in two titles. Underline the titles, and use capital letters correctly. Then write a sentence describing each book.

📖 *Writing Application:* An Explanation
Write a paragraph telling what you would do if you were a teacher. What would you expect of your students? Try to use three words from the list on page 164.

1. _____
2. _____
3. _____
4. _____
5. _____
6. _____
7. _____
8. _____
9. _____
10. _____
11. _____
12. _____
13. _____
14. _____

26   Spelling Across the Curriculum

Careers: *Teaching*

Theme Vocabulary

students
recess
September
test
learn

Using Vocabulary   Write the Vocabulary Words to complete the paragraph. Use your Spelling Dictionary.

Summer was over, and the month of (1) had started. Mr. Reams hoped that his new (2) would be ready to (3) new ideas. He thought, "I will start slowly and not give a (4) this week." He could hardly wait to see their faces light up when they saw the new swings at (5).

Understanding Vocabulary   Write the Vocabulary Word that belongs in each group.

6. class time, lunch, ____
7. July, August, ____
8. teachers, principal, ____

1. _____
2. _____
3. _____
4. _____
5. _____
6. _____
7. _____
8. _____

FACT FILE

When Sequoya invented an alphabet for the Cherokee language, thousands of Cherokee learned to read and write their language.

Enrichment

👥 *A Classful of Words*

Players: 2 teams, a judge **You need:** a list of Basic and Review Words

How to play: Each team draws a "desk" on the chalkboard for each team member. The judge reads a word to Team 1. A player on Team 1 writes the word on one of the team's "desks." If correct, the word stays on the desk. If wrong, the word is erased. Then Team 2 takes a turn. The first team to write correct words on all of its desks wins.

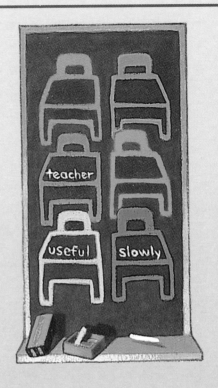

STRING WORDS

Print a spelling word on colored paper. Then trace over the word with glue. Next, lay a piece of string over each letter in the word. Glue it to the paper to make a string word. Do the same for three more words.

📖 *Writing*
Farmer? Baker?

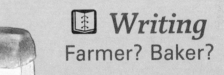

What job would you like when you grow up? Perhaps you have a hobby that could be a job. Write a paragraph telling what your job may be and why you would like it. Try to use words from the unit lists. Be sure to proofread your paper.

27 The VCCV Pattern

(Theme: Invitations)

LOOK and SAY

Basic Words

1. invite
2. Monday
3. enjoy
4. until
5. forget
6. napkin
7. window
8. Sunday
9. garden
10. market
11. basket
12. order

■ Challenge

13. expect
14. wisdom

THINK

Each word has two syllables. Each word also has the vowel-consonant-consonant-vowel (VCCV) pattern. Divide a word with the VCCV pattern between the two consonants to find the syllables. In each syllable look for spelling patterns you have learned.

V C | C V	V C | C V
Mon|day	**for|get**

• Where are *Monday* and *forget* divided into syllables? Why?

WRITE

Practice   Write the twelve Basic Words. Draw a line between the consonants to show the syllables.

■ Now write the two Challenge Words.

CHECK

■ Challenge

Independent Practice

Word Attack   Use Basic Words in these exercises.

1. Write the word that has the |ō| sound.

2. Write the word that has the same first syllable as *under*.

3-4. Write the two words that begin with a capital letter.

5-7. Write the words that include these words.
   5. joy   **6.** get   **7.** nap

Making Inferences   Write the Basic Word that matches each clue.

8. Beans and carrots may grow here.
9. People can buy food in this place.
10. You do this when you send away for T-shirts.
11. You do this when you ask someone to a party.
12. You may use this to carry food to a picnic.

■ **Challenge Words**   Write the Challenge Word that completes each sentence. Use your Spelling Dictionary.
13. Sam will ___ his friends at two o'clock.
14. Andy knows the ___ of saving money for a gift.

1. _____
2. _____
3. _____
4. _____
5. _____
6. _____
7. _____
8. _____
9. _____
10. _____
11. _____
12. _____
13. _____
14. _____

Summing Up

Divide a word with the VCCV pattern between the two consonants to find the syllables. Look for spelling patterns you have learned. Spell the word by syllables.

Basic

1. invite
2. Monday
3. enjoy
4. until
5. forget
6. napkin
7. window
8. Sunday
9. garden
10. market
11. basket
12. order

■ **Challenge**

13. expect
14. wisdom

Review

1. after
2. under

Expanding Vocabulary

Meanings for *order* Do you give orders? Are *1*, *2*, and *3* in order? *Order* has many meanings.

> **or·der** |ôr′dər| *n.*, *pl.* **orders 1.** A grouping of things, one after the other. **2.** A command or rule. **3.** A portion of food in a restaurant.

Practice   **Which meaning of *order* is used in each sentence? Write the meaning.**

1. When Mom gives me an <u>order</u>, I follow it.
2. Kit asked the waiter for an <u>order</u> of rice.
3. Put those words in ABC <u>order</u>.

1. _____

2. _____

3. _____

Dictionary

The Schwa Sound   Say *useful*. The second syllable has a weak vowel sound called the **schwa** sound. The pronunciation key shows this sound as |ə|. The |ə| sound can be spelled with any vowel.

ə   ab**ou**t, sil**e**nt, penc**i**l, lem**o**n, circ**u**s

Practice   **Look at each word and its pronunciation below. Write each word. Then underline the letter that spells the schwa sound.**

1. second |sĕk′ ənd|
2. hopeful |hōp′ fəl|
3. teacher |tē′ chər|

4. stencil |stĕn′ səl|
5. alive |ə līv′|

1. _____

2. _____

3. _____

4. _____

5. _____

Review: Spelling Spree

Classifying Write the Basic Word that names something that belongs in each group of pictures.

1.

2.

3.

4.

5.

Proofreading **6–14.** Find and cross out nine misspelled Basic or Review Words. Then write each word correctly.

Last Munday a new boy came to my school. He was sad untill I decided to invit him to my party on Sanday. I also asked him to help me oder my cake at the market. He was happy aftr that. He also seemed to injoy the party. He left a note undr his present. "I will never forgat my good friend," it said.

■ **Challenge Words** Write four sentences, using each Challenge Word in two sentences.

📖 *Writing Application:* A Letter Pretend that the author of your favorite book lives nearby. Write a short letter to invite the author to talk to your class. Try to use three words from the list on page 170.

1. _____
2. _____
3. _____
4. _____
5. _____
6. _____
7. _____
8. _____
9. _____
10. _____
11. _____
12. _____
13. _____
14. _____

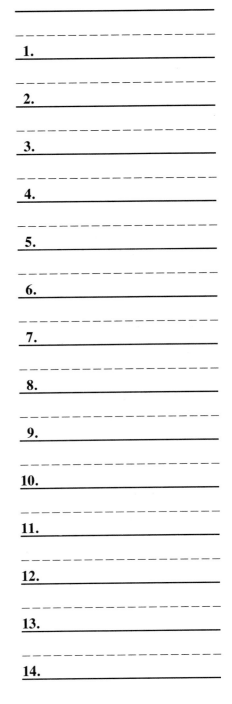

27 Spelling Across the Curriculum

Language Arts: *Invitations*

Theme Vocabulary
Tuesday
Wednesday
Thursday
Friday
Saturday

Using Vocabulary An invitation needs a date. Complete each date by writing the correct Vocabulary Word. Use this calendar.

May

Tuesday	Wednesday	Thursday	Friday	Saturday
3	4	5	6	7

1. ___, May 5
2. ___, May 7
3. ___, May 3
4. ___, May 4
5. ___, May 6

Understanding Vocabulary Write the Vocabulary Word that matches each clue.

6. This day is the day before Thursday.
7. This day comes between Friday and Sunday.
8. This day is the day after Monday.

1. _____
2. _____
3. _____
4. _____
5. _____
6. _____
7. _____
8. _____

FACT FILE

You might see the letters *R.S.V.P.* on an invitation. These letters stand for French words that mean "Please reply."

Enrichment

👥 *Guess That Word*

Players: 4–5   **You need:** 14 cards with a Basic or Review Word on each card

How to play: Place cards face down. Player 1 picks a card. The other players take turns asking questions about the word that can be answered with *yes* or *no*, such as "Does it begin with *m*?" or "Is it a day of the week?" Players who know the word can try to spell it on their next turn. The player who spells the word correctly picks the next card.

📖 *Writing*
A Dream Party

Write plans for your ideal party. Where would it take place? What would you have to eat? What would you do? Try to use words from the unit lists. Be sure to proofread your paper.

YOU'RE INVITED!

Make a party invitation. Fold a piece of paper in half. Draw a picture on the front. Write details about the party inside the invitation. Where and when is the party? What should guests wear?

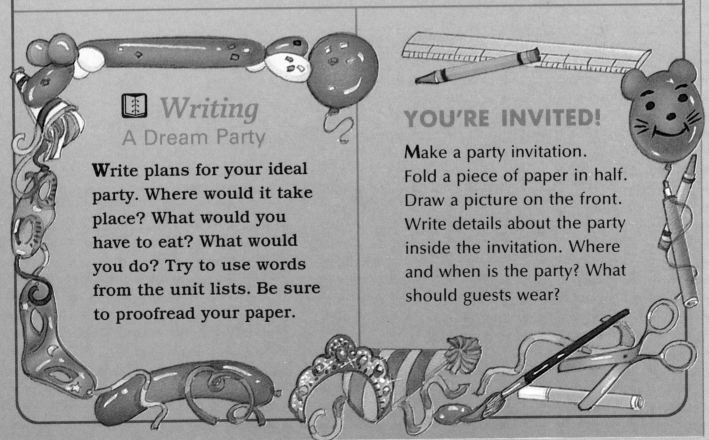

(Theme: Fables)

28 Double Consonants

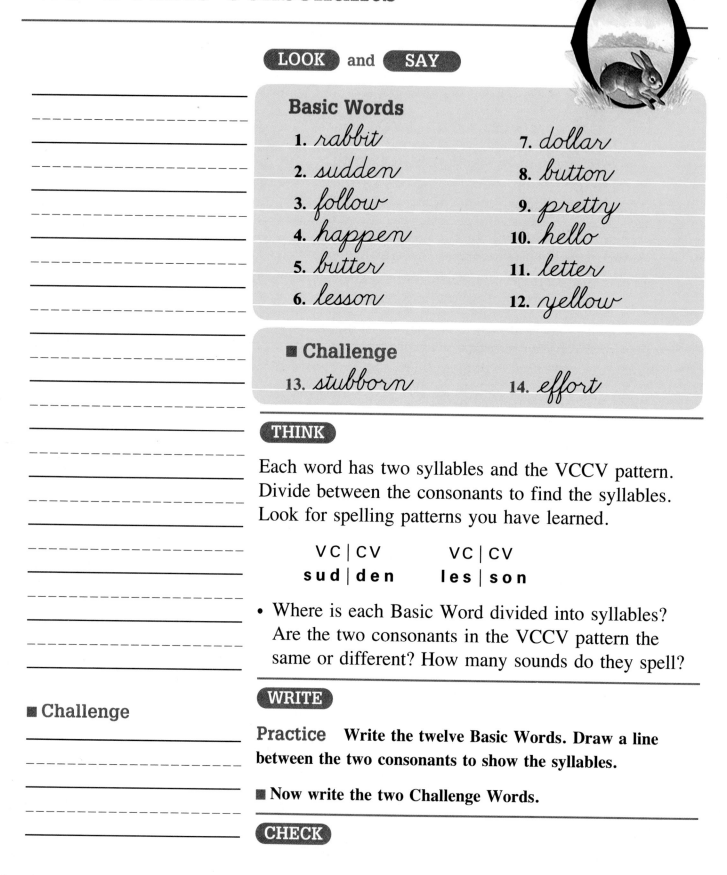

LOOK and SAY

Basic Words

1. rabbit
2. sudden
3. follow
4. happen
5. butter
6. lesson
7. dollar
8. button
9. pretty
10. hello
11. letter
12. yellow

■ Challenge

13. stubborn
14. effort

THINK

Each word has two syllables and the VCCV pattern.
Divide between the consonants to find the syllables.
Look for spelling patterns you have learned.

VC | CV   VC | CV
sud | den   les | son

- Where is each Basic Word divided into syllables?
  Are the two consonants in the VCCV pattern the
  same or different? How many sounds do they spell?

WRITE

Practice Write the twelve Basic Words. Draw a line
between the two consonants to show the syllables.

■ Now write the two Challenge Words.

CHECK

■ Challenge

Independent Practice

Word Attack   Use Basic Words in these exercises.

1-3. Write the three words that have the |ō| sound.

4-8. Write five words by adding a syllable to each syllable below.

    4. sud | ___

    5. ___ | pen

    6. ___ | son

    7. rab | ___

    8. ___ | ty

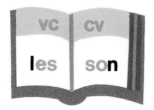

Word Pairs   Write Basic Words to complete each pair of sentences.

    9. You zip up your jacket to close it.
    You ___ your shirt to close it.

  10. *6* is a number.
    A is a ___.

  11. You put gravy on meat.
    You put ___ on toast.

  12. Five nickels are worth one quarter.
    One hundred pennies are worth one ___.

■ **Challenge Words**   Write the Challenge Word that completes each sentence. Use your Spelling Dictionary.

  13. Lori made a special ___ to help her sister.

  14. A mule is often a very ___ animal.

1. _____
2. _____
3. _____
4. _____
5. _____
6. _____
7. _____
8. _____
9. _____
10. _____
11. _____
12. _____
13. _____
14. _____

Summing Up

A VCCV word may have a double consonant. Divide between the consonants to find the syllables. Look for spelling patterns you know. Spell the word by syllables.

Basic

1. rabbit
2. sudden
3. follow
4. happen
5. butter
6. lesson
7. dollar
8. button
9. pretty
10. hello
11. letter
12. yellow

◼ Challenge

13. stubborn
14. effort

Review

1. funny
2. better

Proofreading Marks

¶ Indent
∧ Add something
℮ Take out something
≡ Capitalize
/ Make a small letter

Expanding Vocabulary

Animal Names *Rabbit* is spelled with a double consonant. Do you know these other animal names that are spelled with double consonants?

     lemming   otter   gibbon   opossum

Practice   **Write the animal name above that completes each sentence. Use your Spelling Dictionary.**
1. The web-footed ____ dived into the water.
2. The long-armed ____ is the smallest ape.
3. That plump ____ looks like a mouse.
4. An ____ hangs upside down by its tail.

1. _____   3. _____

2. _____   4. _____

Proofreading

Commas with Places and Dates   Use a comma to separate the names of a city and a state and to separate the month and the day from the year.

     Dallas, Texas   March 30, 1990

Practice   **Proofread this diary entry. Use proofreading marks to correct three misspelled words. Add two missing commas.**

Example: Tad's ~~leter~~ *letter* was dated May 3, 1990.

May 8 1990

Tad sent me a funy letter and a book from Lima Ohio. They cost a doller to mail! I read the story about a rabit.

Review: Spelling Spree

Word Web   1–10. Find ten Basic or Review Words by matching the syllables. One word has been shown. Write the ten words.

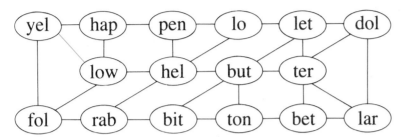

Missing Letters   Each missing letter fits in ABC order between the other two letters. Write the missing letters to spell a Basic or Review Word.

Example: r _ t   n _ p   e _ g   s _ u   *soft*

11. e _ g   t _ v   m _ o   m _ o   x _ z

12. r _ t   t _ v   c _ e   c _ e   d _ f   m _ o

13. k _ m   d _ f   r _ t   r _ t   n _ p   m _ o

14. o _ q   q _ s   d _ f   s _ u   s _ u   x _ z

```
h e l l o
      f
      f
      o
      r
s t u b b o r n
```

■ **Challenge Words**   Make a puzzle. Write the Challenge Words so that they cross. Then add as many Basic or Review Words as you can. Look at the example.

📖 *Writing Application:* Creative Writing
Write a story about a rabbit that learns a lesson when it gets sick from eating too many carrots. Try to use three words from the list on page 176.

1. _____
2. _____
3. _____
4. _____
5. _____
6. _____
7. _____
8. _____
9. _____
10. _____
11. _____
12. _____
13. _____
14. _____

28 Spelling Across the Curriculum

Language Arts: *Fables*

Theme Vocabulary

tortoise
hare
brag
fable
finish

Using Vocabulary Write the Vocabulary Words to complete the paragraph. Use your Spelling Dictionary.

One well-known __(1)__ tells about a furry __(2)__ who liked to __(3)__ about his speed. Then a slow __(4)__ offered to race him. During the race the rabbit ran so far ahead that he took a nap. He awoke just as the turtle crossed the __(5)__ line!

Understanding Vocabulary Is the underlined word used correctly? Write *yes* or *no*.

6. Always start a race at the <u>finish</u> line.
7. It is not nice to <u>brag</u> about winning.
8. Brush your <u>hare</u>, and then tie your shoe.

1. _____
2. _____
3. _____
4. _____
5. _____
6. _____
7. _____
8. _____

FACT FILE

In Aesop's fables animals talk and act like people. Each story teaches a lesson about how or how not to behave.

Enrichment

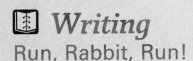 *Writing*

Run, Rabbit, Run!

The hare who lost the race to the tortoise is as foolish as ever. Now he wants to run in a new race. The course goes through a forest and into the mountains, so the hare plans to take a short cut. What will happen to him this time? Write a new fable that tells how the hare learns the lesson "Look before you leap." Try to use words from this unit. Be sure to proofread your story.

SPELLING SHELL

Draw a turtle. Draw 24 boxes to show the pattern on its shell. Write the Basic Words on the shell. Write the first syllable of one word in one box and the second syllable in the next box. Remember to divide each word between the consonants.

 *Perform a Skit*

With a partner write a skit based on "The Tortoise and the Hare." Write what the two main characters say before, during, and after the race. What other characters can you add? Try to use words from the unit lists. Act out your skit for younger students.

29 Spelling the |s| Sound in city

Theme: The City

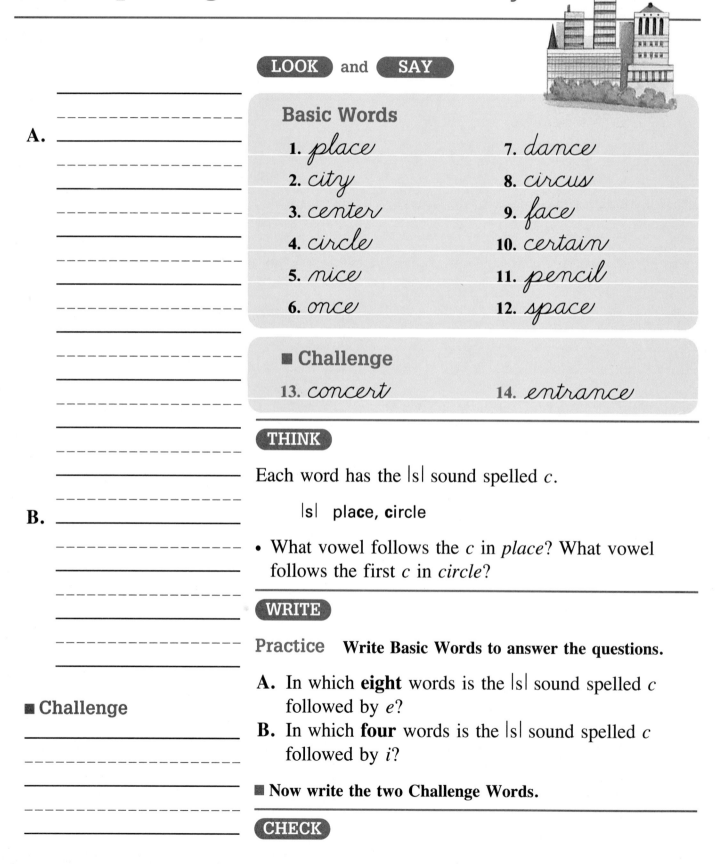

LOOK and **SAY**

Basic Words

1. place
2. city
3. center
4. circle
5. nice
6. once
7. dance
8. circus
9. face
10. certain
11. pencil
12. space

■ Challenge

13. concert
14. entrance

THINK

Each word has the |s| sound spelled *c*.

|s| pla**c**e, **c**ircle

• What vowel follows the *c* in *place*? What vowel follows the first *c* in *circle*?

WRITE

Practice   **Write Basic Words to answer the questions.**

A. In which **eight** words is the |s| sound spelled *c* followed by *e*?

B. In which **four** words is the |s| sound spelled *c* followed by *i*?

■ **Now write the two Challenge Words.**

CHECK

A.

B.

■ Challenge

Independent Practice

Word Attack   Use Basic Words in these exercises.

1. Write the word that starts with the sound you hear at the beginning of *one*.

2. Write the word that rhymes with *ice*.

3-4. Write the two words in which *c* spells the |k| sound.

5-7. Write *place*. Then write two other words that rhyme with *place*.

Context Sentences   Write the Basic Word that completes each sentence.

8. Jim likes the country, and I like the ___.

9. I want to draw that building, so I need a ___.

10. We saw some people sing and ___ in City Park.

11. George lives near here in the ___ of the city.

12. It is Friday, so I am ___ the library is open.

■ **Challenge Words**   Write the Challenge Word that completes each sentence. Use your Spelling Dictionary.

13. The town band has a ___ in the park every week.

14. This store has one ___ on Milk Street and another on Center Street.

1. _____

2. _____

3. _____

4. _____

5. _____

6. _____

7. _____

8. _____

9. _____

10. _____

11. _____

12. _____

13. _____

14. _____

Summing Up

The |s| sound may be spelled *c* when the *c* is followed by *i* or *e*.

Basic

1. place
2. city
3. center
4. circle
5. nice
6. once
7. dance
8. circus
9. face
10. certain
11. pencil
12. space

■ **Challenge**

13. concert
14. entrance

Review

1. same
2. house

Proofreading Marks

¶ Indent
∧ Add something
ℓ Take out something
≡ Capitalize
/ Make a small letter

Expanding Vocabulary

Exact Words for *nice* ''Be nice.'' ''Have a nice day!'' *Nice* has many meanings, such as ''kind'' or ''pleasant.'' Use exact words for *nice*.

Practice **Write the word below that best replaces *nice* in each sentence. Use your Thesaurus.**

helpful   friendly   pleasant

1. We had very <u>nice</u> weather for our picnic.
2. Our teacher is <u>nice</u> when we have problems.
3. My <u>nice</u> neighbor waves whenever I walk by.

1. _____   3. _____

2. _____

Proofreading

Letter Greetings and Closings Begin the first word of a greeting or a closing with a capital letter. Put a comma after a greeting or a closing.

GREETING: Dear Jed,   CLOSING: Your cousin,

Practice **Proofread this letter. Use proofreading marks to correct three misspelled words and a missing capital letter. Add a comma.**

Example: very ~~truely~~ *truly* yours,

dear Mrs. Rossi

I have moved to a new cite. I live in a nice houes in the senter of Salem.

Sincerely yours,
Liza Grodin

Review: Spelling Spree

Hink Pinks   Write a Basic or Review Word that fits each clue and rhymes with the given word.

Example: a wet light ___ **lamp** *damp*

1. a ribbon store   **lace** ___
2. good seasoning   ___ **spice**
3. something you play again   ___ **game**
4. your turn to move to music   ___ **chance**
5. a store in which masks are bought   ___ **place**
6. the contest to reach Mars first   ___ **race**
7. a small animal that stays inside   ___ **mouse**

Name Game   Write the Basic Word hidden in each name. Look for the *c*'s to find the words. Use all small letters in your answers.

Example: Dr. Alf A. Celebrity *face*

8. Miss Pen Cilia
9. Mr. Mercir Cleats
10. Mr. Perci R. Cusa
11. Mrs. Traci T. Yang
12. Mr. Onion C. Eddy
13. Mrs. Lancer Tainer
14. Miss Millicent Errs

■ **Challenge Words**   Look at the Name Game activity. Then write four silly names. Hide each Challenge Word in two names. Trade papers with a partner, and try to find each other's hidden words.

Writing Application: Instructions   Write instructions telling a friend how to get from your house to another place in town. Write your instructions in step-by-step order. Try to use three words from the list on page 182.

1. _____
2. _____
3. _____
4. _____
5. _____
6. _____
7. _____
8. _____
9. _____
10. _____
11. _____
12. _____
13. _____
14. _____

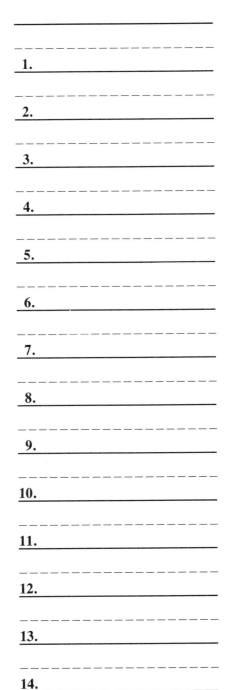

29 Spelling Across the Curriculum

Social Studies: *The City*

Theme Vocabulary

apartment
hotel
subway
taxi
skyscraper

Using Vocabulary Write the Vocabulary Words to complete the paragraph. Use your Spelling Dictionary.

This was Abby's first trip to the city. She made plans as she rode down the street and gazed out the (1) window. First, she would check into her (2) . Next, she would ride the (3) under the city to visit Anne. Anne lived in an (4) on the fiftieth floor of a (5) .

Understanding Vocabulary Write the Vocabulary Word that matches each clue.

6. This is like a train.
7. City visitors stay here.
8. You pay to ride in this kind of car.

1. _____
2. _____
3. _____
4. _____
5. _____
6. _____
7. _____
8. _____

FACT FILE

The Empire State Building in New York City has 102 floors. It was the tallest building in the world from 1931 to 1972.

Enrichment

A CITY IN SPACE

What would a city in space look like? Draw a picture of such a city. Would people live above or below the ground? How would they get air to breathe? How would they move from place to place? Label the buildings and places, such as "Space Center." Try to use words from the unit lists.

📖 *Writing*
Big City Visit

What city would you most like to visit? Write a paragraph explaining your choice. What is special about this city? What would you see and do there? Try to use words from the unit lists. Be sure to proofread your paper.

👨‍👩‍👧 *Our Town*

With your classmates make a guidebook to your town. List places and things that visitors should see and do. Do you know good places to eat? What stores are interesting? Write a short description of each place. Try to use some list words. Staple the pages together, and keep the book where classmates can use it.

30 Review: Units 25–29

Unit 25   The Prefixes re- and un-   pp. 156–161

unfair	rewrite	unhappy
retell	unwrap	reuse

Remember: A **prefix** is a word part added to the beginning of a base word. **Re-** and **un-** are prefixes.

Write the word that means the opposite of each word below.
1. wrap   2. fair   3. happy

Write the word that completes each sentence.
4. Do not throw out that cup. You can ___ it.
5. I did not hear the story. Please ___ it.
6. Mom cannot read your note. Please ___ it.

1. _____
2. _____
3. _____
4. _____
5. _____
6. _____

Unit 26   The Suffixes -ful, -ly, -er   pp. 162–167

useful	teacher	friendly
quickly	hopeful	singer

Remember: A **suffix** is a word part added to the end of a base word. Some words have the suffix **-ful**, **-ly**, or **-er**.

Write the words to complete the paragraph.
   Our __(7)__ invited a famous __(8)__ to perform for our class today. She was very __(9)__, and she taught us many __(10)__ things about writing songs. After class, she had to leave __(11)__, but we are __(12)__ that she will visit us again.

7. _____
8. _____
9. _____
10. _____
11. _____
12. _____

Half of the words from each unit are reviewed on these pages.
The rest are reviewed on pages 241–243.

Unit 27 The VCCV Pattern pp. 168–173

| napkin | enjoy | until |
| garden | basket | window |

Remember: Divide a word with the VCCV pattern between the two consonants to find the syllables.

Write the word that has the same first syllable as each word below.

13. winter   **14.** enter   **15.** garbage

Write the word that completes each sentence.

16. You may need a ___ when you eat that chicken.
17. Doug cannot play catch ___ this afternoon.
18. Shirley uses a ___ to carry her groceries.

13. _____
14. _____
15. _____
16. _____
17. _____
18. _____

Unit 28 Double Consonants pp. 174–179

| sudden | lesson | follow |
| dollar | letter | hello |

Remember: A VCCV word may have double consonants. Divide between the consonants to find the syllables.

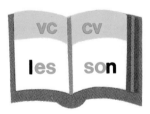

Write the word with the same second syllable as each word below.

19. bitter   **20.** hidden   **21.** pillow

Write the word that belongs in each group.

22. penny, dime, ___   **24.** school, study, ___
23. hi, good morning, ___

19. _____
20. _____
21. _____
22. _____
23. _____
24. _____

30 Review

Unit 29   The |s| Sound in *city*   pp. 180–185

| circle | place | center |
| circus | pencil | dance |

Remember: The |s| sound may be spelled **c** when the **c** is followed by an **i** or an **e**.

Write the word that completes each sentence.

25. Cory and I like to see the clowns at the ___.
26. Clowns often perform at the ___ of the ring.
27. Some clowns juggle, and some clowns ___.
28. That one jumps up and down in ___.
29. Cory brought a ___ to draw a clown.
30. We laughed when the clowns danced in a ___.

25. _____
26. _____
27. _____
28. _____
29. _____
30. _____

■ Challenge Words   Units 25–29   pp. 156–185

| stubborn | listener | unimportant |
| expect | entrance | |

Write the word that has almost the same meaning as each word below.

31. await
32. opening

Write the word that completes each sentence.

33. If I have a problem, I talk to Julie because she is a good ___.
34. Mom cannot make Joshua eat his spinach because he is very ___.
35. Whether or not we wax the car today is ___.

31. _____
32. _____
33. _____
34. _____
35. _____

Spelling-Meaning Strategy

Word Forms

A word may have a sound that is spelled in an unexpected way. Other words in its family usually spell that sound in the same way because they are related in meaning. Read this paragraph.

> I usually **place** my house key on a hook in the kitchen when I come home. I **misplaced** my key on Monday, and I still cannot find it.

Think

- How are *place* and *misplaced* alike in meaning?
- How are *place* and *misplaced* alike in spelling?

Here are words in the *place* family.

place	placing	replace
misplaced	placed	placement

Apply and Extend

Complete these activities on another piece of paper.

1. Look up the meaning of each word in the Word Box above in your Spelling Dictionary. Write six sentences, using one word in each sentence.

2. With a partner list words related to *ice*, *peace*, and *trace*. Then look in your Spelling-Meaning Index beginning on page 268. Add any other words in these families to your list.

Letters

Julius ordered a monster from a mail order company in The Monster in the Mail Box *by Sheila Gordon. Julius might have written the letter below. Whom is Julius writing to and why?*

heading —
38 East Third Street
Tulsa, OK 74103
May 10, 1990

greeting —
Dear Grammie,

body —
Remember the monster I ordered? When it finally came, it was just a rubbery thing that popped right away. I made the company return my money. Then I bought a monster book. The stories and the pictures are very scary.

closing —
Love,

signature —
Julius

Think and Discuss

1. To **whom** did Julius write the letter?
2. What information did Julius tell Grammie?
3. Why would this information interest her?
4. Name and explain the **five parts** of a letter.

The Writing Process

Julius's letter on page 190 told Grammie about the monster. When you write a letter, choose topics that will interest your **reader**.

Assignment: Write a Letter

Step One: Prewriting

1. Choose someone to write to. List topics that would interest him or her. Talk about your ideas with a friend, and choose a topic.
2. Have a friend ask questions about your topic.

Step Two: Write a First Draft

1. Think about your purpose and your audience.
2. Do not worry about mistakes—just write!

Step Three: Revise

1. Would your letter interest your reader?
2. Use your Thesaurus to find exact words.
3. Read your letter to a friend. Make changes.

Step Four: Proofread

1. Did you use commas correctly?
2. Did you include all five letter parts?
3. Did you correct any misspelled words? Add them to your Notebook for Writing.

Step Five: Publish

1. Copy and sign your letter.
2. Address an envelope, and mail your letter.

Composition Words

unlike
quickly
useful
Monday
order
happy
dollar
certain

Proofreading Marks

¶ Indent
∧ Add something
ℓ Take out something
≡ Capitalize
/ Make a small letter

31 Vowel Sounds in tooth and cook

A. _____

B. _____

C. _____

■ Challenge Words
_____
_____

LOOK and **SAY**

Basic Words

1. tooth
2. chew
3. grew
4. cook
5. shoe
6. blue
7. boot
8. flew
9. shook
10. balloon
11. drew
12. spoon

■ Challenge

13. loose   14. crooked

THINK

Each word has the vowel sound in *tooth* or the vowel sound in *cook*. These sounds are shown as |o͞o| and |o͝o|.

|o͞o| **t**ooth, ch**ew** |o͝o| **c**ook

• What are two spelling patterns for the |o͞o| sound? What is one pattern for the |o͝o| sound? How is the |o͞o| sound spelled in the Elephant Words?

WRITE

Practice   Write Basic Words to answer the questions.

A. Which **six** words have |o͞o| or |o͝o| spelled *oo*?
B. Which **four** words have |o͞o| spelled *ew*?
C. Which **two** words have |o͞o| spelled other ways?

■ Now write the two Challenge Words.

CHECK

Independent Practice

Word Attack   Use Basic Words in this exercise.

1-5. Write the five words that have these consonants.

1. gr ____
2. dr ____
3. ch ____
4. fl ____
5. sh ____ k

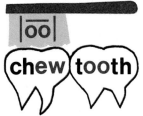

Classifying   Write the Basic Word that belongs in each group.

6. fork, knife, ____
7. firefighter, bus driver, ____
8. kite, paper plane, ____
9. umbrella, raincoat, ____
10. toothbrush, toothpaste, ____

Elephant Words   Write the Elephant Word that completes each sentence.

11. Last week Dr. Valdez painted the walls of his office a light ____.
12. Give Bess time to put on her other sock and ____, and then we will leave.

Challenge Words   Write the Challenge Word that means the opposite of each word. Use your Spelling Dictionary.

13. tight
14. straight

1.
2.
3.
4.
5.
6.
7.
8.
9.
10.
11.
12.
13.
14.

Summing Up

The |oo̅| sound, as in *tooth* or *chew,* may be spelled with the pattern *oo* or *ew.*

The |oŏ| sound, as in *cook,* may be spelled with the pattern *oo.*

Basic

1. tooth
2. chew
3. grew
4. cook
5. shoe
6. blue
7. boot
8. flew
9. shook
10. balloon
11. drew
12. spoon

■ Challenge

13. loose
14. crooked

Review

1. good
2. soon

Proofreading Marks

¶ Indent
∧ Add something
℮ Take out something
≡ Capitalize
/ Make a small letter

Expanding Vocabulary

Compound Words   Some words can be joined to make a compound word.

cook + book = cookbook

Practice   **Write the compound word that fits each meaning. Use a word from each box.**

shoe	blue
cook	tooth

brush	out
lace	bird

1. food cooked outdoors
2. a blue-feathered bird
3. a lace for shoes
4. a brush for teeth

1. _____
2. _____
3. _____
4. _____

Proofreading

Abbreviations   An **abbreviation** is the short form of a word. Begin an abbreviation of a person's title with a capital letter. End it with a period.

Dr. Ross   Mr. Tobin   Ms. Yuan   Mrs. Ramos

Practice   **Proofread this story. Use proofreading marks to correct three misspelled words and a missing capital letter. Add a period.**

Example: I broke a ~~tuth~~ *tooth* at mrs. Logan's house.

I tripped over a shoo and broke a tooth. When dr Cox checked it, he said he would soone make it as gud as new.

Review: Spelling Spree

Word Web 1–7. Find seven Basic and Review Words by matching the letters. Write the words. One word has been shown.

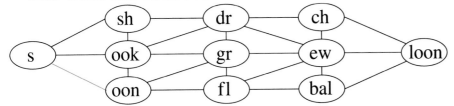

Hink Pinks Write the Basic or Review Word that fits each clue and rhymes with the given word.

Example: worried thief —— **crook** *shook*

8. logs that will burn well —— **wood**
9. paste that is the color of the sky —— **glue**
10. silverware for an astronaut **moon** ——
11. footwear for boating **canoe** ——
12. a small place for fixing food —— **nook**
13. footwear for an owl in the rain **hoot** ——
14. a place to clean your teeth —— **booth**

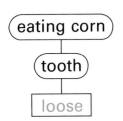

■ **Challenge Words** Make a cluster for each Challenge Word. Then write at least four sentences, using the Challenge Words and other words in the clusters.

📖 *Writing Application:* Creative Writing
Write about a time when you lost a baby tooth. What problems did you have? Try to use three words from the list on page 194.

1. _____
2. _____
3. _____
4. _____
5. _____
6. _____
7. _____
8. _____
9. _____
10. _____
11. _____
12. _____
13. _____
14. _____

31 Spelling Across the Curriculum

Health: *Visiting the Dentist*

Theme Vocabulary

dentist
gums
floss
cavity
x-ray

Using Vocabulary Write the Vocabulary Words to complete the paragraph. Use your Spelling Dictionary.

I had my teeth checked today. Dr. Lee, my __(1)__, took a picture of them. The __(2)__ showed a dark spot on one tooth. For me, having only one __(3)__ is very good. Cleaning between my teeth with dental __(4)__ has worked! When I brush my teeth now, my __(5)__ do not bleed.

Understanding Vocabulary Write the Vocabulary Word that matches each clue.

6. This machine takes pictures of teeth.
7. This person says, ''Open wide.''
8. A dentist fills this kind of hole.

1. _____
2. _____
3. _____
4. _____
5. _____
6. _____
7. _____
8. _____

FACT FILE

Your baby teeth fall out because their roots dissolve. Then permanent teeth can push through the gums and fill empty spaces.

Enrichment

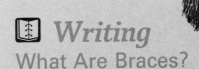 A Toothy Game

Players: 2, a reader **You need:** game markers, a game board of a mouth with the same number of teeth on the top and the bottom, a list of Basic and Review Words

How to play: Each player chooses a row of teeth. The reader reads a spelling word to a player. If the player spells the word correctly, the player moves ahead one tooth. The first player to reach the end of the row wins.

X-RAY VIEW

An x-ray of teeth shows each tooth, its roots, and the jaw, as if you could see through the gums. Draw your own x-ray. Use white chalk on black paper for the teeth, the roots, and the jaw. Leave a dark spot on a tooth to make a cavity. Label the parts of your picture.

Writing
What Are Braces?

Some people wear braces on their teeth. What problems can braces fix? How do they work? How do braces affect eating? Look up facts about braces in the library, and write a short report. Try to use words from the unit lists. Proofread your report.

32 The Vowel Sound in bought

A. _____

B. _____

C. _____

■ Challenge
_____
_____

LOOK and **SAY**

Basic Words

1. caught
2. thought
3. bought
4. laugh
5. through
6. enough
7. fought
8. daughter
9. taught
10. brought
11. ought
12. cough

■ Challenge

13. sought   14. naughty

THINK

Most of the words have the vowel sound in *bought*.
This sound is shown as |ô|.

|ô| b**ough**t, c**augh**t

• What are two spelling patterns for the |ô| sound?
What sounds are spelled with these patterns in the
Elephant Words?

WRITE

Practice   **Write Basic Words to answer the questions.**

A. Which **five** words have the |ô| sound spelled *ough*?
B. Which **three** words have the |ô| sound spelled *augh*?
C. In which **four** words does *ough* or *augh* spell
other sounds?

■ **Now write the two Challenge Words.**

CHECK

Independent Practice

Word Attack   Use Basic Words in this exercise.

1-4. Each word below is missing four letters that spell the |ô| sound. Write the four words correctly.

    1. br _ _ _ _ t

    2. f _ _ _ _ t

    3. b _ _ _ _ t

    4. t _ _ _ _ t

Context Sentences   Write the Basic Word that completes each sentence.

    5. Mr. Pascal's ___ lost her cat Flint last week.

    6. Clara said that she ___ to look for Flint.

    7. I ___ that the Pascals should offer a reward.

    8. Randy saw Flint running along a wall, and he ___ him.

Elephant Words   Write the Elephant Word that completes each sentence.

    9. My dog Blitz is so funny. He makes us ___.

    10. There is ___ dog food to last Blitz all week.

    11. After I walked Blitz in the rain, I began to sneeze and ___.

    12. I hope Blitz will not sneak ___ the fence again.

Challenge Words   Write the Challenge Word that means the same as each clue below. Use your Spelling Dictionary.

    13. bad

    14. looked for

Summing Up

The |ô| sound can be spelled with these patterns:
- *ough*, as in *bought*
- *augh*, as in *caught*

1. ___
2. ___
3. ___
4. ___
5. ___
6. ___
7. ___
8. ___
9. ___
10. ___
11. ___
12. ___
13. ___
14. ___

Basic
1. caught
2. thought
3. bought
4. laugh
5. through
6. enough
7. fought
8. daughter
9. taught
10. brought
11. ought
12. cough

■ **Challenge**
13. sought
14. naughty

Review
1. teeth
2. was

Expanding Vocabulary

Exact Words for *laugh*   Read the sentences.

Hear the crowd **laugh**.   Hear the crowd **roar**.

Roar describes a loud laughing sound more exactly than *laugh*. Try to use exact words.

Practice   **Write the exact word for *laugh* that best fits each sentence. Use your Thesaurus.**

roar   chuckle   giggle   snicker

1. I always blush and <u>laugh</u> when I'm nervous.
2. Do not <u>laugh</u> rudely at someone's mistake.
3. Dad will <u>laugh</u> softly at a funny TV show.
4. My uncles <u>laugh</u> loudly at funny jokes.

1. _____   3. _____

2. _____   4. _____

Dictionary

Spelling Table   How can you look up *cough* if you do not know how to spell the |f| sound? Turn to the **spelling table**, which shows the different ways a sound can be spelled. Check each spelling for |f| until you find *cough*.

SOUND	SPELLINGS	SAMPLE WORDS
|f|	**f, ff, gh**	**f**unny, o**ff**, enou**gh**

Practice   **Write the correct spelling for each word below. Use the spelling table above and your Spelling Dictionary.**

1. ru + |f| + le   **2.** tou + |f| **3.** scar + |f|

1. _____   2. _____   3. _____

Review: Spelling Spree

Code Breaker Some Basic and Review Words are written in the code below. Write the words.

⟨ = augh	☽ = e	∞ = n	↑ = t
● = c	☐ = l	⊗ = ough	▱ = th

Example: ↑ ⊗ *tough*

1. ● ⊗

2. ↑ ⟨ ↑

3. ▱ ⊗ ↑

4. ☐ ⟨

5. ↑ ☽ ☽ ▱

6. ☽ ∞ ⊗

7. ⊗ ↑

8. ● ⟨ ↑

Proofreading **9–14.** Find and cross out six misspelled Basic or Review Words. Then write each word correctly.

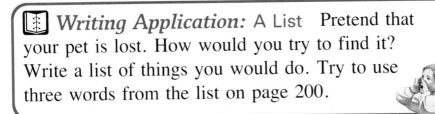

My dauter lost the new dog that she had bout. When she broght him home, he fot with a cat. He wuz last seen running throo the park. If you have caught him, please call 999-1100.

■ **Challenge Words** Make up a code. Write each Challenge Word and five Basic Words in your code. Then write the words correctly on the back of your paper. Have a friend try to decode the words.

 Writing Application: A List Pretend that your pet is lost. How would you try to find it? Write a list of things you would do. Try to use three words from the list on page 200.

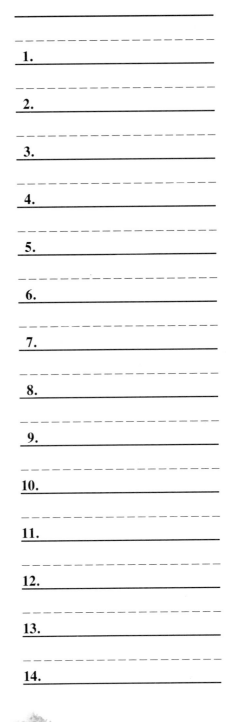

1. _____

2. _____

3. _____

4. _____

5. _____

6. _____

7. _____

8. _____

9. _____

10. _____

11. _____

12. _____

13. _____

14. _____

32 Spelling Across the Curriculum

Life Skills: *A Lost Pet*

Theme Vocabulary

notice
search
reward
worry
collar

Using Vocabulary Write the Vocabulary Words to complete the paragraph. Use your Spelling Dictionary.

My little cat is gone. Will you help me __(1)__ for her? I will put up a __(2)__ offering a five-dollar __(3)__ for finding her. Her name is Fluff. It is printed on her __(4)__. I will __(5)__ about her until she is found.

Understanding Vocabulary Is the underlined word used correctly? Write *yes* or *no*.

6. Doreen put a <u>notice</u> on the bulletin board.
7. Yellow is my favorite <u>collar</u>.
8. Don got a <u>reward</u> for not doing his chores.

1. _____
2. _____
3. _____
4. _____
5. _____
6. _____
7. _____
8. _____

FACT FILE

An ID tag lists a pet's name and its owner's address and phone number. A lost pet that wears an ID tag may be found more quickly.

Enrichment

👥 *Follow the Paw Prints*

Players: 2–4   **You need:** 12 paper paw prints, game markers, a spinner

How to play: Write a sentence that uses a Basic or Review Word on each paw print. Add an instruction, such as *Move ahead two spaces* or *Lose one turn.* Then make a trail with the paw prints. Use the spinner, and move along the trail. As players land on paw prints, they read the sentences and follow the instructions. The first player to reach the end wins.

You bought a new dog. Move ahead two spaces.

HELP FIND ME!

LOST PET POSTER

Make a poster that tells about a lost pet. Draw a picture of the pet, and describe what it looks like. Tell where and when it was lost. Offer a reward. Try to use words from the unit lists.

📖 **Writing**
Find Me!

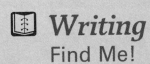

Pretend that you are a lost pet. Write a story that tells what happens to you. What kind of pet are you? How did you get lost? How do you feel? Try to use words from the unit lists. Be sure to proofread your story.

33 Words That End with er or le

(Theme: Seasons)

A. _____

_____

_____

_____

_____

_____

_____

B. _____

_____

_____

_____

_____

_____

■ Challenge

_____

_____

LOOK and **SAY**

Basic Words

1. summer
2. winter
3. little
4. October
🐘5. travel
🐘6. color
7. apple
8. able
9. November
10. ever
11. later
12. purple

■ Challenge

13. thermometer   14. icicle

THINK

Each word ends with a schwa sound + *r* or a schwa sound + *l*. The schwa sound is shown as |ə|.

|ər| summ**er** |əl| litt**le**

• What is one pattern for the |ər| sounds? What is one pattern for the |əl| sounds? How are these sounds spelled in the Elephant Words?

WRITE

Practice   **Write Basic Words to answer the questions.**

A. Which **seven** words end with the |ər| sounds? Remember the Elephant Word.

B. Which **five** words end with the |əl| sounds? Remember the Elephant Word.

■ **Now write the two Challenge Words.**

CHECK

Independent Practice

Word Attack   Use Basic Words in these exercises.

1-2. Write the word that rhymes with each word below.
   1. never
   2. stable

3-4. Write the two words with capital letters.

5-7. Write the three words with double consonants.

Word Pairs   Write the Basic Word that completes each pair of sentences.
   8. It is hot in summer.
      It is cold in ___.
   9. Yellow and blue make green.
      Red and blue make ___.
   10. *Faster* is the opposite of *slower*.
      Earlier is the opposite of ___.

Elephant Words   Write the Elephant Word that fits each clue.
   11. red or blue
   12. to go from city to city

Challenge Words   Write the Challenge Word that completes each sentence. Use your Spelling Dictionary.
   13. Look at the ___ to see how cold it is.
   14. Jennifer used an ___ for her snowman's nose.

1. _____

2. _____

3. _____

4. _____

5. _____

6. _____

7. _____

8. _____

9. _____

10. _____

11. _____

12. _____

13. _____

14. _____

Summing Up

In a word with more than one syllable,
• the final |ər| sounds are often spelled *er*
• the final |əl| sounds can be spelled *le*.

Basic

1. summer
2. winter
3. little
4. October
5. travel
6. color
7. apple
8. able
9. November
10. ever
11. later
12. purple

■ Challenge

13. thermometer
14. icicle

Review

1. flower
2. people

Expanding Vocabulary

Exact Color Words A color can have different shades. These words name two shades of purple.

violet   "bluish purple"
lavender   "light purple"

Use exact words to describe colors.

Practice   Write a color word below to replace each group of underlined words. Use your Thesaurus.

crimson   aqua
navy   beige

1. These <u>dark blue</u> pants are good for hiking.
2. Those apples turn <u>bright red</u> in the fall.
3. The <u>light greenish-blue</u> water looked cool.
4. Reggie has a <u>light yellowish-brown</u> jacket.

1. _____   3. _____

2. _____   4. _____

Dictionary

Stressed Syllables   Say *apple*. Notice that the first syllable is said more strongly, or **stressed**. The dictionary pronunciation shows this syllable in dark print followed by an **accent mark** (′).

ap·ple |ăp′əl| *n., pl.* **apples** A red-skinned fruit.

Practice   Write each word. Circle the stressed syllable. Use your Spelling Dictionary.
Example: later (lat)er

1. little   3. flower
2. forget   4. able

1. _____

2. _____

3. _____

4. _____

Review: Spelling Spree

Puzzle Play Write a Basic or Review Word to fit each clue. Circle the letter that would appear in the box. Write those letters in order to spell two words that name something that stays green all year.

Example: a red fruit _ _ ☐ _ _   ap(p)le

1. a rose ☐ _ _ _ _ _

2. the same as *small* _ ☐ _ _ _ _

3. a color _ _ ☐ _ _ _

4. not *sooner* _ _ ☐ _ _

5. the month after October _ _ _ _ _ _ _ ☐

6. more than one person _ ☐ _ _ _ _

7. a hot season _ _ _ _ ☐ _

Mystery Words: _ _ _ _   _ _ _ _ _

Proofreading 8–14. Find and cross out seven misspelled Basic Words. Then write each word correctly.

> I hope to be abel to go aple picking before wintr. It is aver so much fun! We could travle to a farm in Octber when the leaves change coler. November is too late!

■ **Challenge Words** Make a pictionary. Write each Challenge Word, and draw a picture to show its meaning. Then write a sentence, using the word.

📖 *Writing Application:* A Fashion Guide
Write two paragraphs that tell how people in your town dress in summer and winter. Try to use three words from the list on page 206.

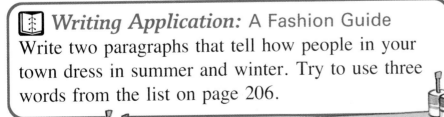

1. _____

2. _____

3. _____

4. _____

5. _____

6. _____

7. _____

8. _____

9. _____

10. _____

11. _____

12. _____

13. _____

14. _____

33   Spelling Across the Curriculum

Science: *Seasons*

Theme Vocabulary

January
February
July
August
December

Using Vocabulary   Write the Vocabulary Words to complete the paragraph. Use your Spelling Dictionary.

   To me, each month is special. The first and last months of the year, __(1)__ and __(2)__, are both cold and wintery. The second month, __(3)__, is the shortest. I like the seventh and eighth months, __(4)__ and __(5)__, when we can go swimming!

Understanding Vocabulary   Write *yes* or *no* to answer each question.

6. Is the first day of the year in July?
7. Is the last day of the year in December?
8. Is August in the winter in the United States?

1. _____
2. _____
3. _____
4. _____
5. _____
6. _____
7. _____
8. _____

FACT FILE

Early Native Americans believed that a warm fall was a gift from a kindly wind god. Warm fall weather is called Indian summer.

Enrichment

WORD TREE

Make an autumn tree. First, draw a tree trunk and branches. Then cut out colored paper leaves. Write words that end with *er* on one color. Write words that end with *le* on another color. Write the Elephant Words on other colors. Glue the leaves to the tree.

📖 *Writing*
A Seasoned Place

What is your favorite outdoor place? Is it a park, a hill, or your back yard? Write two paragraphs describing this place in two different seasons. How is it the same? How is it different? Try to use words from the unit lists. Be sure to proofread your paper.

👪 *Wall of Seasons*

With your classmates, make a seasons mural. First, hang a large piece of paper on one classroom wall. Divide the paper into four parts. Write the name of each season in one part. Then form four groups. Each group should draw or cut out pictures of food, weather, clothes, and other things that go with each season.

34 Words That Begin with a or be

LOOK and **SAY**

A. _____

Basic Words

1. *begin*		7. *alive*
2. *again*		8. *because*
3. *around*		9. *ahead*
4. *before*		10. *between*
5. *away*		11. *behind*
6. *about*		12. *ago*

■ **Challenge**

13. *among*   14. *beyond*

THINK

B. _____

Each word has two syllables. The first syllable has the |ə| sound or the |bĭ| sounds.

|ə| **a**gain |bĭ| **be**fore

• What is one spelling for the |ə| sound when it is the first syllable of a word? What is one spelling for the |bĭ| sounds when they are the first syllable? Is the first or the second syllable stressed in each Basic Word?

WRITE

Practice   **Write Basic Words to answer the questions.**

A. Which **seven** words begin with the |ə| sound?
B. Which **five** words begin with the |bĭ| sounds?

■ Challenge

■ **Now write the two Challenge Words.**

CHECK

Independent Practice

Word Attack   Use Basic Words in these exercises.

1. Write the word with the |ō| sound.

2. Write the word with the |z| sound.

3-4. Write the two words with the |ou| sound, as in *found*.

5-6. Write the two words that have the |ī| sound.

Context Sentences   Write the Basic Word that completes each sentence.

7. My family went ___ on vacation last summer.

8. Just ___ we got to the beach, Dad got lost.

9. "Beach Road should ___ right here," he said.

10. "Go straight ___ for two blocks," a lady said.

11. Finally, we saw Beach Road ___ Plum Street and Marsh Lane.

12. Now we will know where to turn when we come back ___.

|ə| a**way**

|bĭ| be**yond**

■ **Challenge Words**   Write the Challenge Word that completes each sentence. Use your Spelling Dictionary.

13. Look left ___ the library to see the bus stop.

14. Look ___ the branches to find our tree house.

1. _____

2. _____

3. _____

4. _____

5. _____

6. _____

7. _____

8. _____

9. _____

10. _____

11. _____

12. _____

13. _____

14. _____

Summing Up

In a two-syllable word, the unstressed |ə| sound at the beginning of a word may be spelled *a*. The unstressed |bĭ| sounds may be spelled *be*.

Basic

1. begin
2. again
3. around
4. before
5. away
6. about
7. alive
8. because
9. ahead
10. between
11. behind
12. ago

■ Challenge

13. among
14. beyond

Review

1. they
2. want

Proofreading Marks

¶ Indent
∧ Add something
℘ Take out something
≡ Capitalize
/ Make a small letter

Expanding Vocabulary

Two-Syllable Words with *a* or *be* Here are more words that begin with the unstressed syllable *a* or *be*. Can you think of any others?

across   asleep   become   belong

Practice **Write the word above that completes each sentence. Use your Spelling Dictionary.**
1. My colt will ___ a big horse.
2. Chris is ___ in front of the TV.
3. Sally swam ___ the lake today.
4. Grandpa's watch will ___ to me one day.

1. _____   3. _____

2. _____   4. _____

Proofreading

Abbreviations Each day of the week has an abbreviation. It begins with a capital letter and ends with a period. (See page 247 of the Student's Handbook for abbreviations of other days.)

Monday Mon.   Tuesday Tues.

Practice **Proofread these notes. Use proofreading marks to correct three misspelled words and a missing capital letter. Add a period.**

Example: Fri.—Ask Mom ~~abot~~ *about* the school trip.

Mon	tues.
Tell Tim to turn	Ask the class if
left befor Elm St.,	thay want to go to
behind the store.	the museum agan.

Review: Spelling Spree

Syllable Addition Write seven Basic Words by
adding *a* or *be* to the words below.

Example: low *below*

1. go
2. head
3. round
4. hind
5. cause
6. way
7. live

Word Maze **8–14.** Begin at the arrow, and follow
the Word Maze to find seven Basic or Review
Words. Write the words in order.

→ a h o a b o u t a g b e

■ **Challenge Words** Pretend that you see a deer
hiding in the woods. Use both Challenge Words in a
sentence that tells where the deer is. Draw a picture
that shows what you wrote. Label it with your
sentence.

📖 *Writing Application:* Instructions
Write instructions telling a classmate how to go
from your school to your home or to a favorite
place. Try to use three words from the list on
page 212.

1. _____
2. _____
3. _____
4. _____
5. _____
6. _____
7. _____
8. _____
9. _____
10. _____
11. _____
12. _____
13. _____
14. _____

34 Spelling Across the Curriculum

Life Skills: *Following Directions*

Theme Vocabulary

copy
complete
repeat
directions
check

Using Vocabulary   Write the Vocabulary Words to complete the paragraph. Use your Spelling Dictionary.

If you do not know where a place is, ask for __(1)__. Be sure they are __(2)__. Then __(3)__ your memory, and __(4)__ them aloud. If you have a pencil and paper, __(5)__ the information.

Understanding Vocabulary   Write the Vocabulary Word that could be used instead of each direction below.

6. Make another one.
7. Say it again, please.
8. Make sure you are correct.

_____

1. _____

2. _____

3. _____

4. _____

5. _____

6. _____

7. _____

8. _____

FACT FILE

A compass looks like a clock but tells direction, not time. The needle always points north. Knowing this, you can also tell where south, east, and west are.

Enrichment

👥 *Follow the Leader*

Divide your class into two teams. Each student writes a direction that can be followed in the classroom. The directions should use Basic Words, such as *Walk behind Sue's desk*. Players take turns reading their directions to members of the other team. Each player who is given a direction must spell the Basic Word correctly and then follow the direction. A team gets one point when a member gives a correct answer.

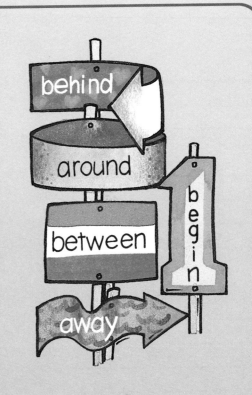

TREASURE MAP

Pretend that you have hidden something in a place near your school or home. Draw a map to help someone find it. Write clues that use words from the unit lists. Use the map to plan a real treasure hunt!

📖 **Writing**
Wrong Turn

Write a funny story about what happened when one person gave another person poor directions. Where was the person trying to go? Where did he or she end up? Try to use words from the unit lists. Be sure to proofread your paper.

35 Contractions

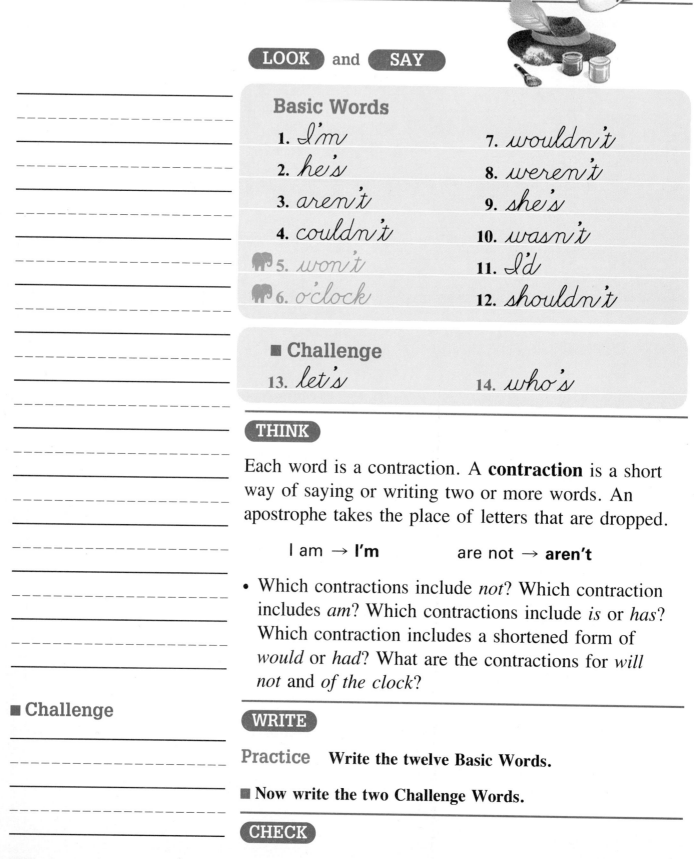

LOOK and SAY

Basic Words

1. I'm
2. he's
3. aren't
4. couldn't
5. won't
6. o'clock
7. wouldn't
8. weren't
9. she's
10. wasn't
11. I'd
12. shouldn't

■ **Challenge**

13. let's
14. who's

THINK

Each word is a contraction. A **contraction** is a short way of saying or writing two or more words. An apostrophe takes the place of letters that are dropped.

I am → **I'm**   are not → **aren't**

• Which contractions include *not*? Which contraction includes *am*? Which contractions include *is* or *has*? Which contraction includes a shortened form of *would* or *had*? What are the contractions for *will not* and *of the clock*?

WRITE

Practice   Write the twelve Basic Words.

■ Now write the two Challenge Words.

CHECK

■ Challenge

Independent Practice

Word Attack   Use Basic Words in these exercises.

1-3. Write the three words that have a silent *l*.

4-5. Write the two words that begin with a capital letter.

Context Sentences   Write the Basic Words that are contractions for the underlined words.

6. There <u>are not</u> many parts in the play.
7. Sue likes machines, so <u>she is</u> doing the lighting.
8. Sid <u>was not</u> here for practice today.
9. The posters <u>were not</u> ready yesterday.
10. Marco is in the play, and <u>he is</u> sure his parents will come to it.

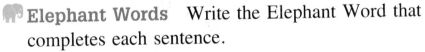

 Elephant Words   Write the Elephant Word that completes each sentence.
11. The play will start at seven ___.
12. The tickets ___ go on sale until Tuesday.

▪ **Challenge Words**   Write the Challenge Words that are contractions for the underlined words. Use your Spelling Dictionary.
13. When everyone is here, <u>let us</u> start practicing.
14. Do you know <u>who is</u> in charge of the music?

1. _____
2. _____
3. _____
4. _____
5. _____
6. _____
7. _____
8. _____
9. _____
10. _____
11. _____
12. _____
13. _____
14. _____

Summing Up

A **contraction** is a short way of saying or writing two or more words. An apostrophe takes the place of one or more letters.

Basic

1. I'm
2. he's
3. aren't
4. couldn't
5. won't
6. o'clock
7. wouldn't
8. weren't
9. she's
10. wasn't
11. I'd
12. shouldn't

■ **Challenge**

13. let's
14. who's

Review

1. can't
2. isn't

Proofreading Marks

¶ Indent
∧ Add
    something
℘ Take out
    something
≡ Capitalize
/ Make a small
    letter

Expanding Vocabulary

Homophones   Some contractions are homophones.

You're sure that **your** aunt is coming today.

You're is a contraction for "you are." *Your* means "belonging to you."

Practice   **Write *your* or *you're* to complete each sentence.**

1. Nita, here are ____ tickets.
2. Cindy, hand me the posters when ____ done.
3. Harry, ____ helping with the lights.
4. Carlos, ____ tape recorder is on the stage.

1. _____   3. _____

2. _____   4. _____

Proofreading

Using *I* and *me*   Use *I* as the subject of a sentence. Use *me* as the object of a verb. Name yourself last when you talk about another person and yourself.

    Al and I are late.   Mom saw you and me.

Practice   **Proofread this note. Use proofreading marks to correct three misspelled words and two places where *I* or *me* is not used correctly.**

Example: Liz ~~wasnt~~ *wasn't* going to meet ~~I~~ *Jan* and ~~Jan~~ *me*.

> Tammy, Dad is'nt home yet. Me
> and you can't ride to the play with
> Jan. She will meet you and I there
> at two oclock. We wont be late.

Review: Spelling Spree

Puzzle Play   Write the Basic or Review Words that are the contractions for the words below. Circle the letters that would appear in the boxes. Write those letters in order. They will spell a mystery word.

Example: I am   _ ' ☐   I'(m)

1. cannot   _☐_ ' _
2. would not   _ _☐_ _ _ _ ' _
3. should not   _ _ _ _ _☐_ ' _
4. is not   ☐_ _ ' _
5. were not   _☐_ _ _ ' _
6. will not   _ _☐ ' _
7. of the clock   _ ' _ _ _☐_
8. are not   _ _☐_ ' _

Mystery Word: _ _ _ _ _ _ _ _

Ending Match   Replace the second piece of each numbered puzzle with a new puzzle piece to make a Basic Word. Write the Basic Words.

⟩'d   ⟩'s   ⊏n't   ⟩'m

9. [he ⟩ has]   11. [was ⊏ not]   13. [I ⟩ am]

10. [could ⊏ not]   12. [I ⟩ had]   14. [she ⟩ is]

■ **Challenge Words**   Write four titles for plays. Use each Challenge Word in two titles. Use capital letters correctly, and underline each title.

 Writing Application: A Play   Choose a story, and rewrite an exciting part as a play. Try to use three words from the list on page 218.

1. _____
2. _____
3. _____
4. _____
5. _____
6. _____
7. _____
8. _____
9. _____
10. _____
11. _____
12. _____
13. _____
14. _____

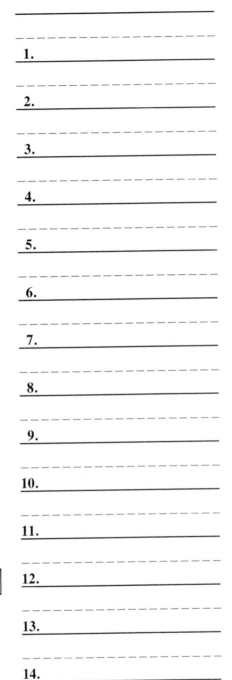

35 Spelling Across the Curriculum

Performing Arts: *Putting on a Play*

Theme Vocabulary

act
cast
skit
make-up
costume

Using Vocabulary   Write the Vocabulary Words to complete the paragraph. Use your Spelling Dictionary.

Some students are performing a short play, or __(1)__ , that Ken wrote about a space trip. The play has one __(2)__ that lasts ten minutes. It is about three astronauts, so the __(3)__ is small. Each actor will wear a shiny silver __(4)__ and put silver __(5)__ on his or her face.

Understanding Vocabulary   Is the underlined word used correctly? Write *yes* or *no*.

6. We are painting the <u>skit</u> for the play.
7. The <u>cast</u> in our play worked very hard.
8. An <u>act</u> is the most important player.

1. _____
2. _____
3. _____
4. _____
5. _____
6. _____
7. _____
8. _____

FACT FILE

A funny play with a happy ending is a comedy. Some comedies are just for fun. Others make you think as well as laugh.

Enrichment

👥 *Make a Match*

Players: 2–4 **You need:** 14 cards with a Basic or Review Word on each; 14 cards with the word or words that make up each Basic or Review Word

How to play: Put the cards face down in rows. Take turns turning over two cards. Keep the cards if they show a contraction and the words that form it. If the cards do not match, turn them face down again. The player with the most cards at the end wins.

📖 *Writing*
What a Play!

Imagine that you have written a play. Write a summary of it for a director. Briefly tell the most important parts of the story. Try to use words from the unit lists. Be sure to proofread your paper.

CONTRACTION MOBILE

Make a contraction mobile. First, write three contractions on cardboard. Next, write the words that make up the contraction on colored paper. Tape them to the matching words on the cardboard. Tie the word groups to a hanger.

I'm

won't
will not

am

36 Review: Units 31–35

Unit 31   Vowel Sounds in *tooth*, *cook*   pp. 192–197

tooth	shoe	blue
flew	balloon	shook

Remember:

|ōō|, as in *tooth* or *chew* → **oo, ew**

|ŏŏ|, as in *cook* → **oo**

Write the word that completes each sentence.

1. Mom ___ my shoulder until I woke up.
2. Molly likes sunny days and clear ___ skies.
3. I watched the flock of birds as they ___ by.
4. Your left ___ needs a little more polish.
5. Brian's loose front ___ fell out today.
6. The party ___ broke with a loud pop.

1. _____
2. _____
3. _____
4. _____
5. _____
6. _____

Unit 32   Vowel Sound in *bought*   pp. 198–203

through	enough	laugh
brought	daughter	cough

Remember: The |ô| sound can have these patterns:

• **ough**, as in *bought*

• **augh**, as in *caught*

Write the word that completes each sentence.

7. Mrs. Levy ___ home a parrot last week.
8. She gave it to her ___ Emma.
9. The parrot was funny. It made Emma ___.
10. It acts as though it can sneeze and ___.
11. One day it tried to fly ___ an open window.
12. It wasn't quick ___. Emma caught it!

7. _____
8. _____
9. _____
10. _____
11. _____
12. _____

Half of the words from each unit are reviewed on these pages.
The rest are reviewed on pages 244–246.

Review 36

Unit 33   Words That End with *er, le*   pp. 204–209

October	travel	color
purple	able	November

Remember:
- final |ər| sounds → **er**
- final |əl| sounds → **le**

Write the word that fits each clue.
13. This is the month before December.
14. You do this with paper and crayons.
15. This word means that you can do something.
16. This is the month after September.
17. Violets may be this color.
18. You do this when you go to a faraway place.

13. _____

14. _____

15. _____

16. _____

17. _____

18. _____

Unit 34   Words That Begin with *a, be*   pp. 210–215

again	before	about
ahead	because	between

Remember: An unstressed first syllable may have one of these patterns:
- |ə| → **a**
- |bĭ| → **be**

Write the word that completes each sentence.
19. I learned all ____ ABC order in school today.
20. I like it ____ it can help me find words fast.
21. *Able* comes ____ *basket* in ABC order.
22. *Market* comes ____ *luck* and *napkin*.
23. *Summer* comes ____ of *travel*.
24. We will talk about ABC order ____ tomorrow.

19. _____

20. _____

21. _____

22. _____

23. _____

24. _____

Unit 35 Contractions pp. 216–221

I'm	won't	o'clock
weren't	she's	shouldn't

Remember: A **contraction** is a short way of saying or writing two or more words. An apostrophe takes the place of one or more letters.

she is

she's

Write a contraction for each group of words.
25. were not **26.** will not **27.** of the clock
Write contractions for the underlined words.
28. We should not wait too long for Emily.
29. Susie says that she is not feeling well.
30. I like to eat a snack while I am reading.

25. _____

26. _____

27. _____

28. _____

29. _____

30. _____

■ Challenge Words Units 31–35 pp. 192–221

loose	naughty	let's
beyond	thermometer	

Write the word that completes each sentence.
31. Dad looked at the ____ and said that it was too cold to go outside.
32. Ben's little brother can be very ____.
33. That toy truck is not working because one wheel is ____.
34. It's very hot today, so ____ go swimming.
35. Our new house is on Perkins Street, just ____ the bakery.

31. _____

32. _____

33. _____

34. _____

35. _____

Word Forms

Words belong to families. The words in a family are spelled alike in some ways. They are also related in meaning. Read this paragraph.

laugh
laughter
laughing

> Mom's **laugh** floated out through the screen onto the porch where I was sitting. Then I heard Dad and Nina's **laughter**. I thought, "Uncle Carl is telling a story."

Think
- How are *laugh* and *laughter* alike in meaning?
- How are *laugh* and *laughter* alike in spelling?

Here are words in the *laugh* family.

laugh	laughing	laughed
laughter	laughingly	laughable

Apply and Extend

Complete these activities on another piece of paper.

1. Look up the meaning of each word in the Word Box above in your Spelling Dictionary. Write six sentences, using one word in each sentence.

2. With a partner list words related to *thought*, *chew*, and *cook*. Then look in your Spelling-Meaning Index beginning on page 268. Add any other words in these families to your list.

Research Report

To stay alive through the cold winter months, some animals save lots of food. Other animals travel to warmer places. What do woodchucks and bears do?

The woodchuck sleeps so deeply that it almost seems dead. Its breathing slows down, and its body becomes cold and hard. If you touched the woodchuck, it wouldn't wake up. The woodchuck might seem dead, but it's really not. Its extra fat keeps it alive during its winter sleep. Its body uses the fat for food.

Bears also sleep in the winter, but not so deeply. They, too, get ready for their long winter sleep by eating a lot. They often sleep in caves. On warm winter days, they may wake up and go outside to look for something to eat. When it gets cold again, they go back to their caves and sleep some more.

from When Winter Comes *by Russell Freedman*

Think and Discuss

1. What **facts** did you learn about how woodchucks and bears spend the winter?
2. What is the **topic sentence** of each paragraph?

The Writing Process

The paragraphs on page 226 include facts about bears and woodchucks. When you write a research report, use **facts** to support your **topic sentences**. Do not use opinions.

Assignment: Write a Research Report

Step One: Prewriting

1. List topics that interest you. Talk about them with a friend, and choose a topic.
2. Write three questions about your topic. Find facts that answer them. Take notes.

Step Two: Write a First Draft

1. Use each question as a topic sentence. Use your notes as supporting details.
2. Do not worry about mistakes—just write!

Step Three: Revise

1. Did you use only facts? Are the facts clear?
2. Use your Thesaurus to find exact words.
3. Read your report to a friend. Make changes.

Step Four: Proofread

1. Did you use commas and end marks correctly?
2. Did you correct any misspelled words? Add them to your Notebook for Writing.

Step Five: Publish

Copy your report. Add a title. Read it aloud.

Composition Words

chew
through
enough
later
able
because
about
shouldn't

Proofreading Marks

⌐ Indent
∧ Add something
℮ Take out something
≡ Capitalize
/ Make a small letter

Student's Handbook

Extra Practice and Review

Cycle 1

Unit 1 Short Vowels pp. 12–17

mix	milk	smell
thick	send	stick

Remember: In most words,
the |ă| sound is spelled **a**,
the |ĕ| sound is spelled **e**,
and the |ĭ| sound is spelled **i**.

Write the word that belongs in each group.
1. stir, blend, ___   3. cream, butter, ___
2. see, taste, ___
Write the word that completes each sentence.
4. While you are away, please ___ me a letter.
5. I keep warm with a ___ blanket.
6. Andy stirred the paint with a ___.

1. ___
2. ___
3. ___
4. ___
5. ___
6. ___

Unit 2 More Short Vowels pp. 18–23

lot	pond	rub
drum	hunt	crop

Remember: In most words,
the |ŏ| sound is spelled **o** and
the |ŭ| sound is spelled **u**.

Write the word that matches each meaning.
7. a small body of water   8. a large amount
Write the word that completes each sentence.
9. Jason beat the ___ as we marched.
10. My cat likes to ___ its back on the fence.
11. A new ___ of tomatoes is ready to be picked.
12. Maria had a treasure ___ at her party.

7. ___
8. ___
9. ___
10. ___
11. ___
12. ___

Cycle 1

Unit 3   Vowel-Consonant-e Pattern   pp. 24–29

| huge | life | wide |
| grade | note | mine |

Remember: A long vowel sound is often spelled vowel-consonant-**e**.

Write the word that belongs in each group.

13. big, large, ___   **14.** school, test, ___

Write the word that completes each sentence.

15. Daria wants to spend her ___ helping others.

16. My dentist says, "Open your mouth ___!"

17. Leave me a ___ if you decide to go out.

18. The workers found gold deep in the ___.

_____
13. _____

_____
14. _____

_____
15. _____

_____
16. _____

_____
17. _____

_____
18. _____

Unit 4   More Long Vowel Spellings   pp. 30–35

| paint | feel | neighbor |
| lay | need | speak |

Remember: In many words, the |ā| sound is spelled **ai** or **ay**. The |ē| sound may be spelled **ea** or **ee**.

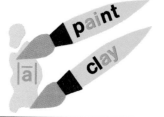

Write the word that rhymes with each word below.

19. seed   **20.** gray

Write the word that matches each clue.

21. You do this when you say something.

22. This is used to color something.

23. This person lives next door to you.

24. You do this when you touch something.

_____
19. _____

_____
20. _____

_____
21. _____

_____
22. _____

_____
23. _____

_____
24. _____

Cycle 1

Unit 5   Spelling the Long *o* Sound   pp. 36–41

float	hold	blow
row	sold	both

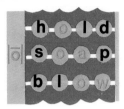

Remember: The |ō| sound is often spelled **oa**, **ow**, or **o**.

Write the word that completes each sentence.

25. Betsy can ___ out ten birthday candles!

26. Can we ___ our boat across the lake?

27. Please ___ the tray with both hands.

28. Those toy ducks will ___ in the bathtub.

29. Zack and Pedro said they can ___ go out.

30. I was sad when we ___ our house and moved.

25. _____

26. _____

27. _____

28. _____

29. _____

30. _____

■ Challenge Words   Units 1–5   pp. 12–41

explode	dodge	crisp
shallow	easel	

Write the word that matches each clue.

31. Artists use this while they work.

32. Balloons filled with too much air may do this.

Write the words to complete the paragraph.

The pond was too **(33)** for swimming, but there were lots of frogs there. I tried to catch one, but it was able to **(34)** me. It leaped from the water and hid among the **(35)**, dry leaves that lay by the shore of the pond.

31. _____

32. _____

33. _____

34. _____

35. _____

Cycle 2

_____

1. _____

2. _____

3. _____

4. _____

5. _____

6. _____

Unit 7   Three-Letter Clusters   pp. 48–53

strong	three	scream
spray	string	stream

Remember: Some words begin with the consonant clusters **scr**, **spr**, **str**, and **thr**.

str**ing**

Write a word that means the same as each word.
1. brook   **2.** yell   **3.** cord
Write the word that completes each sentence.
4. Katie is ___ enough to carry those heavy suitcases.
5. After you wash the car, ___ it with the hose.
6. My ___ cats are named Bingo, Pixie, and Moe.

Unit 8   Spelling the Long *i* Sound   pp. 54–59

sight	child	pie
tie	tight	might

Remember: The /ī/ sound can be spelled with the pattern **igh**, **i**, or **ie**.

Write the word that matches each clue.
7. This has a crust and a filling.
8. This person is very young.
9. This word means the opposite of *loose*.
10. Without this, you cannot see.
11. This word rhymes with *sight* and *tight*.
12. You can wear this around your neck.

_____

7. _____

8. _____

9. _____

10. _____

11. _____

12. _____

Cycle 2

Unit 9   The Vowel Sound in *clown*   pp. 60–65

clown	round	bow
loud	cloud	mouth

Remember: The |ou| sound, as in *clown* and *round*, is often spelled with the pattern **ow** or **ou**.

round
clown

Write the word that rhymes with each word below.
13. south   **14.** gown
Write the word that completes each sentence.
15. After their song, all the singers will ___.
16. The ___ bowl was filled with fruit and nuts.
17. A fluffy white ___ floated past the sun.
18. The pot fell from the shelf with a ___ crash.

13. _____

14. _____

15. _____

16. _____

17. _____

18. _____

Unit 10   The Vowel Sound in *lawn*   pp. 66–71

lawn	raw	talk
wall	cost	also

Remember: These patterns can spell the |ô| sound:
- **aw**, as in *lawn*
- **o**, as in *cloth*
- **a** before **l**, as in *almost*

lawn talk cost
|ô|

Write a word that means the same as each word.
19. uncooked   **21.** speak
20. price   **22.** besides
Write the word that matches each clue.
23. Someone has to mow this.
24. This can divide one room into two.

19. _____

20. _____

21. _____

22. _____

23. _____

24. _____

Cycle 2

Unit 11 Unexpected Patterns pp. 72–77

knee	patch	wrap
match	knock	know

Remember: |n| → **kn**ee
|r| → **wr**ap
|ch| → scra**tch**

Write the word that belongs in each group.

25. tap, bang, ___
27. ankle, hip, ___
26. fix, mend, ___

Write each word by adding the missing letters.

28. ma ___ ___ ___
29. ___ ___ ow
30. ___ ___ ap

25. _____
26. _____
27. _____
28. _____
29. _____
30. _____

■ Challenge Words Units 7–11 pp. 48–77

sprout	lilac	struggle
knuckle	flaw	

Write the word that completes each rhyme.

31. Pencils are perfect for trying to draw,
But erasers are best for correcting a ___.
32. The blossoms will all come out,
After the plants begin to ___.

Write the word that fits each clue.

33. Your thumb has one of these.
34. You do this when something is hard to do.
35. This is both a flower and a color name.

31. _____
32. _____
33. _____
34. _____
35. _____

Cycle 3

Unit 13 Vowel + |r| Sounds pp. 84–89

storm	dark	star
art	smart	ear

Remember: |är| → d**ark**

|îr| → cl**ear**

|ôr| → st**or**m

Write the word that completes each sentence.
1. Sandy likes to paint in ___ class.
2. Carol has a good ___ for music.
3. Tino can act just like a movie ___.
4. Joyce always knows when a ___ is coming.
5. I wore a skirt of a ___ color.
6. When I grow up, I want to be as ___ as Dad.

1. _____
2. _____
3. _____
4. _____
5. _____
6. _____

Unit 14 Vowel + |r| Sounds in *first* pp. 90–95

girl	her	work
bird	hurt	dirt

Remember: The |ûr| sounds can be spelled with the patterns **er, ir, ur,** and **or.**

Write the word that means the opposite of each word below.
7. play   8. boy   9. help

Write the word that completes each sentence.
10. Darrell helps his mother weed ___ garden.
11. Sometimes I wish I could fly like a ___.
12. Dave swept the ___ from the kitchen floor.

7. _____
8. _____
9. _____
10. _____
11. _____
12. _____

Cycle 3

Unit 15   The Vowel Sound in *coin*   pp. 96–101

coin	boy	oil
join	boil	foil

Remember: The |oi| sound, as in *coin* and *boy*, is spelled with the pattern **oi** or **oy**.

Write the word that matches each clue.
13. a child   **14.** something you spend
Write the words to complete the paragraph.
  Would you like to __(15)__ our cooking class? Today we will make chicken with broccoli. First, we cover the chicken with shiny __(16)__. It cooks in the oven without butter or __(17)__! Then we __(18)__ the broccoli.

13. _____

14. _____

15. _____

16. _____

17. _____

18. _____

Unit 16   Spelling the |j| Sound   pp. 102–107

jump	stage	gym
jar	age	page

Remember: The |j| sound can be spelled with **j** or with **g** followed by **e**, **i**, or **y**.

Write the word that matches each clue.
19. Actors perform a play on it.
20. This is part of a book.
21. Frogs and rabbits do this well.
22. You add a year to yours on every birthday.
23. You play indoor sports in this place.
24. You can use this to hold many things.

19. _____

20. _____

21. _____

22. _____

23. _____

24. _____

Cycle 3

Unit 17   The |k| and |kw| Sounds   pp. 108–113

park	queen	skin
quit	crack	quart

Remember: The |k| sound may be spelled **k**, **ck**, or **c**. The |kw| sounds may be spelled with the **qu** pattern.

Write the word that rhymes with each word below.
25. pin   **26.** hit   **27.** mark
Write the word that completes each sentence.
28. Joe bought a ___ of milk at the store.
29. The United States is not ruled by a king or a

___.

30. The plate fell, but it did not ___.

25. _____
26. _____
27. _____
28. _____
29. _____
30. _____

■ **Challenge Words**   Units 13–17   pp. 84–113

courage	freckles	destroy
argue	sturdy	

Write the words to complete the paragraph.
   The girl with the red hair and **(31)** on her nose is a fast runner. She has won many races. Her legs are not long, but they are very **(32)**. People like her because she is fair to other runners and does not **(33)** with the coach. Losing a race does not **(34)** her hopes. She does not win all the time, but she always has the **(35)** to try again.

31. _____
32. _____
33. _____
34. _____
35. _____

Cycle 4

Unit 19 Vowel + |r| Sounds in *hair* pp. 120–125

hair	care	pair
air	bare	share

Remember: The |âr| sounds can have these patterns:

are, as in *care*   **ear**, as in *bear*

air, as in *hair*

|âr|
hair
bear
care

Write the word that matches each clue.

1. This is two of something.
2. This grows on your head.
3. You breathe this.
4. The branches of winter trees may look like this.
5. Babies need lots of this.
6. Two people may do this with one sandwich.

1. _____
2. _____
3. _____
4. _____
5. _____
6. _____

Unit 20 Homophones pp. 126–131

new	there	they're
knew	their	

Remember: Homophones are words that sound the same but have different spellings and meanings.

new **knew**

Write the word that completes each sentence.

7. The twins want (there, their, they're) lunch.
8. Tina (new, knew) the answer to my question.
9. I will be (they're, there, their) at noon.
10. Pat and Jon are glad that (they're, their, there) best friends.
11. Cindy got a (new, knew) bike for her birthday.

7. _____
8. _____
9. _____
10. _____
11. _____

Cycle 4

Unit 21   Compound Words   pp. 132–137

| airplane | inside | sometimes |
| grandfather | something | herself |

Remember: A **compound word** is made up of two or more shorter words.

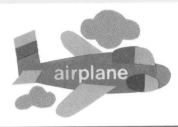

airplane

Write the words to complete the paragraph.

Last week Mom and I went to visit my **(12)**. I flew in an **(13)** for the first time! I could not believe how big the **(14)** of it was! The ride was long, but there was always **(15)** to do. I read, and **(16)** I talked to people. One crew member told me about **(17)** and her flying adventures.

12. _____
13. _____
14. _____
15. _____
16. _____
17. _____

Unit 22   Words with *-ed* or *-ing*   pp. 138–143

| chopped | saving | rubbed |
| dropped | grinning | patted |

Remember: The spelling of some base words changes when **-ed** or **-ing** is added.
rub + b + ed   = ru**bb**ed
save − e + ing = sav**ing**

Write words by changing *-ing* to *-ed*.

18. rubbing   **20.** dropping
19. chopping   **21.** patting

Write the word that completes each sentence.

22. ''Thanks for ____ my cat,'' I said to my neighbor.
23. After Stu told the joke we were all ____.

18. _____
19. _____
20. _____
21. _____
22. _____
23. _____

Cycle 4

Unit 23   Changing Final *y* to *i*   pp. 144–149

babies	puppies	cried
flies	hurried	parties

Remember: When a base word ends with a consonant and **y**, change the **y** to **i** before adding **-es** or **-ed**.

Write the word that completes each sentence.
24. Sandra is going to two ___ this weekend.
25. Tony ___ when he scraped his knee.
Write words by adding *-es* or *-ed* to each base word below.
26. hurry   27. fly   28. baby   29. puppy

___
24. _____

___
25. _____

___
26. _____

___
27. _____

___
28. _____

___
29. _____

■ Challenge Words   Units 19–23   pp. 120–149

canaries	suitcase
propped	flair

Write the word that completes this rhyme.
30. When Mrs. Watson styles my hair,
   She does it with a certain ___.
Write the word that belongs in this group.
31. trunk, overnight bag, ___
Write the word that completes each sentence.
32. Those yellow ___ always sing sweetly in the morning.
33. Dad ___ the ladder against the wall.

___
30. _____

___
31. _____

___
32. _____

___
33. _____

Cycle 5

Unit 25   The Prefixes *re-* and *un-*   pp. 156–161

unkind	remake	untie
unlike	unclear	unhurt

Remember: A **prefix** is a word part added to the beginning of a base word. **Re-** and **un-** are prefixes.

Write the word that means the opposite of each word below.

1. hurt   **2.** clear   **3.** kind   **4.** tie

Write the word that completes each sentence.

5. Aunt Ann was ___ anyone we had ever known.

6. My clay model looked all wrong, so I had to ___ it.

1. _____

2. _____

3. _____

4. _____

5. _____

6. _____

Unit 26   Suffixes *-ful*, *-ly*, *-er*   pp. 162–167

helper	careful	slowly
farmer	sadly	thankful

Remember: A **suffix** is a word part added to the end of a base word. Some words have the suffix **-ful**, **-ly**, or **-er**.

Write the words to complete the paragraph.

Uncle Neil raises cows and chickens. He is a **(7)**. I am his best **(8)**. I do my chores well, but I do them **(9)**. I am always very **(10)** when I gather the eggs. Uncle Neil is always **(11)** for my help. We both wave **(12)** when I have to leave.

7. _____

8. _____

9. _____

10. _____

11. _____

12. _____

Cycle 5

Unit 27   The VCCV Pattern   pp. 168–173

invite	Monday	forget
Sunday	market	order

Remember: Divide a word with the VCCV pattern between the two consonants to find the syllables.

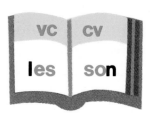

Write the word that has the same first syllable as each word below.

13. margin   **14.** forgive   **15.** inside

Write the word that completes each sentence.

16. My favorite day of the weekend is ___.

17. I go to school every ___.

18. I always ___ rice and beans with my tacos.

13. _____

14. _____

15. _____

16. _____

17. _____

18. _____

Unit 28   Double Consonants   pp. 174–179

rabbit	happen	butter
yellow	button	pretty

Remember: A VCCV word may have double consonants. Divide between the consonants to find the syllables.

les | son

VC | CV

Write the word that belongs in each group.

19. milk, cheese, ___   **21.** zipper, hook, ___

20. fox, deer, ___   **22.** red, blue, ___

Write the word that completes each sentence.

23. I wonder what will ___ at the game.

24. That quilt will look very ___ when it is finished.

19. _____

20. _____

21. _____

22. _____

23. _____

24. _____

Cycle 5

Unit 29   The |s| Sound in *city*   pp. 180–185

city	nice	once
space	certain	face

Remember: The |s| sound may be spelled **c** when the **c** is followed by **i** or **e**.

Write the word that matches each clue.

25. Stars and planets are found in this area.
26. You are this if you are sure about something.
27. You smile and frown with this.
28. This word rhymes with *rice*.
29. Many buildings are found in this place.
30. This word begins many fairy tales.

25. _____
26. _____
27. _____
28. _____
29. _____
30. _____

■ Challenge Words   Units 25–29   pp. 156–185

effort	concert	wisdom
review	calmly	

Write the word that has almost the same meaning as each word below.

31. knowledge
32. check

Write the word that completes each sentence.

33. Albert was very nervous about his piano ____.
34. He made a great ____ to practice every day so that he would not make mistakes.
35. When the big day came, Albert walked ____ on stage and played perfectly.

31. _____
32. _____
33. _____
34. _____
35. _____

Cycle 6

---

1. _____

2. _____

3. _____

4. _____

5. _____

6. _____

Unit 31   Vowel Sounds in *tooth*, *cook*   pp. 192–197

grew	chew	cook
boot	spoon	drew

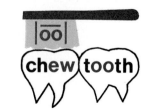

Remember:

|o͞o|, as in *tooth* or *chew* → **oo, ew**

|o͝o|, as in *cook* → **oo**

Write the word that rhymes with each word below.

  1. shoot   **2.** book   **3.** soon

Write the word that completes each sentence.

  4. Dan ___ a picture of his dog on the sidewalk with chalk.

  5. My dog likes to ___ on a bone.

  6. Lily ___ another inch last year.

Unit 32   Vowel Sound in *bought*   pp. 198–203

caught	bought	thought
fought	ought	taught

Remember: The |ô| sound can have these patterns:

- **ough**, as in *bought*
- **augh**, as in *caught*

Write the word that means the opposite of each word below.

  7. sold   **8.** threw   **9.** learned

Write the word that completes each sentence.

  10. The lead runner ___ hard to stay in front.

  11. Sam ___ he should do his homework before bed.

  12. We ___ to leave soon, or we will be late.

7. _____

8. _____

9. _____

10. _____

11. _____

12. _____

Cycle 6

Unit 33   Words That End with *er*, *le*   pp. 204–209

summer	winter	little
ever	later	apple

Remember:
final |ər| sounds → **er**
final |əl| sounds → **le**

Write the word that completes each sentence.
13. Buds turn into ___ green leaves in the spring.
14. The weather is often hot in ___.
15. I like to visit the ___ orchard in the fall.
16. This year we picked more fruit than ___!
17. Tomatoes ripen first, and corn ripens ___.
18. When it is ___ I can go sledding!

13. _____
14. _____
15. _____
16. _____
17. _____
18. _____

Unit 34   Words That Begin with *a*, *be*   pp. 210–215

begin	around	away
alive	ago	behind

Remember: An unstressed
first syllable may have one of
these patterns:

• |ə| → **a**   • |bĭ| → **be**

Write the word that completes each sentence.
19. Two weeks ___ I found a bird on the ground.
20. Its wing was hurt, but it was still ___.
21. I cupped my hands ___ it and picked it up.
22. I put my bag ___ a tree and ran to the vet.
23. She taped its wing so it could ___ to heal.
24. The bird flew ___ when it was better.

19. _____
20. _____
21. _____
22. _____
23. _____
24. _____

Cycle 6

Unit 35 Contractions pp. 216–221

he's	aren't	couldn't
I'd	wasn't	wouldn't

Remember: A **contraction** is a short way of saying or writing two or more words. An apostrophe takes the place of one or more letters.

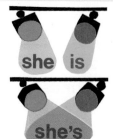

she is

she's

Write a contraction for each group of words.
25. are not   **26.** was not   **27.** he is
Write contractions for the underlined words.
28. <u>I would</u> like to have a sandwich for lunch.
29. Emily said she <u>would not</u> come over today.
30. Carlos <u>could not</u> find his hat this morning.

25. _____
26. _____
27. _____
28. _____
29. _____
30. _____

■ Challenge Words Units 31–35 pp. 192–221

icicle	sought	who's
among	crooked	

Write the words to complete the paragraph.

Once upon a time, there lived a queen who loved winter. One day she said to her subjects, "Search **(31)** the trees on Frozen Mountain. From one branch hangs an **(32)** so cold it will never melt. I will reward anyone **(33)** clever enough to find it." The people **(34)** the treasure day and night. Finally, a young boy found the object hanging from the top of a **(35)** tree.

31. _____
32. _____
33. _____
34. _____
35. _____

Writer's Resources

Capitalization and Punctuation Guide

Abbreviations

	An abbreviation is a short way to write a word. Most abbreviations begin with a capital letter and end with a period.
Titles	Mr. Juan Albano Ms. Leslie Clark Mrs. Frances Wong Dr. Janice Dodd Note: *Miss* is not an abbreviation and does not end with a period.
Days of the week	Sun. *(Sunday)* Thurs. *(Thursday)* Mon. *(Monday)* Fri. *(Friday)* Tues. *(Tuesday)* Sat. *(Saturday)* Wed. *(Wednesday)*
Months of the year	Jan. *(January)* Sept. *(September)* Feb. *(February)* Oct. *(October)* Mar. *(March)* Nov. *(November)* Apr. *(April)* Dec. *(December)* Aug. *(August)* Note: *May, June,* and *July* are not abbreviated.

Quotations

Quotation marks with commas and end marks	***Quotation marks*** **(" ") set off someone's exact words from the rest of the sentence. The first word of a quotation begins with a capital letter. Use a comma to separate the quotation from the rest of the sentence. Put the end mark before the last quotation mark.** Linda said, "We don't know where Donald went."

Capitalization

Rules for capitalization	**Every sentence begins with a capital letter.** What a pretty color the roses are!
	The pronoun *I* is always a capital letter. What should I do next?
	Begin each important word in the names of particular persons, places, or things (proper nouns) with a capital letter. George Herman Ruth New Jersey Liberty Bell
	Titles or their abbreviations when used with a person's name begin with a capital letter. Doctor Lin Mrs. Garcia
	Begin the names of days, months, and holidays with a capital letter. Labor Day is on the first Monday in September.
	The first and last words and all important words in the titles of books begin with a capital letter. Titles of books are underlined. The Hill and the Rock The Bashful Tiger

Punctuation

End marks	**A *period (.)* ends a statement or a command. A *question mark (?)* follows a question. An *exclamation point (!)* follows an exclamation.** The scissors are on my desk. *(statement)* Look up the spelling of that word. *(command)* How is the word spelled? *(question)* This is your best poem so far! *(exclamation)*

Punctuation (continued)

Apostrophe	**Add an apostrophe (') and s to a singular noun to make it show ownership.** doctor's father's grandmother's family's
	For a plural noun that ends in s, add just an apostrophe to show ownership. sisters' families' Smiths' hound dogs'
	Use an apostrophe in contractions in place of missing letters. can't *(cannot)* we're *(we are)* I'm *(I am)*
Comma	**Use commas to separate a series of three or more words.** Rob bought apples, peaches, and grapes.
	Use commas after yes, no, well, and order words when they begin a sentence. First, set the table. No, it is too early.
	Use a comma to separate the month and the day from the year. I was born on June 17, 1951.
	Use a comma between the names of a city and a state. Chicago, Illinois Miami, Florida
	Use a comma after the greeting and after the closing in a letter. Dear Uncle Rudolph, Your nephew,

Friendly Letter

Remember that a letter has five parts.

- The **heading** gives the writer's address and the date.
- The **greeting** says "hello."
- The **body** is the main part. It tells the message.
- The **closing** says "good-by."
- The **signature** tells who wrote the letter.

Use correct letter form when you write to someone. Use capital letters and commas correctly. Study this letter model.

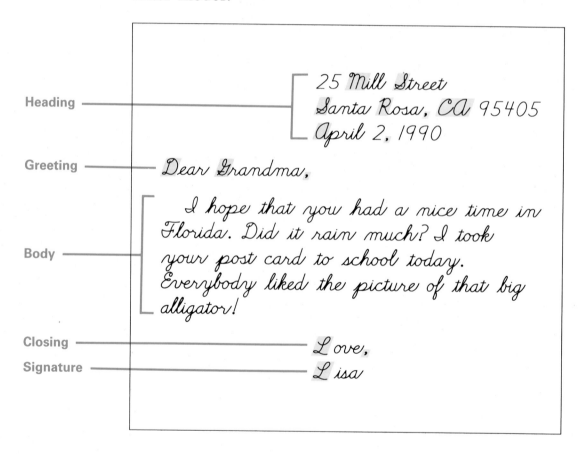

Heading —

25 Mill Street
Santa Rosa, CA 95405
April 2, 1990

Greeting —

Dear Grandma,

Body —

I hope that you had a nice time in Florida. Did it rain much? I took your post card to school today. Everybody liked the picture of that big alligator!

Closing —

Love,

Signature —

Lisa

How to Use This Thesaurus

Use this Thesaurus to make your writing more exact and more interesting. Suppose you write this sentence:

Our town is proud of our *new* hospital.

You decide to replace the word *new* with a more exact word. Turn to your Thesaurus Index for help.

Using the Thesaurus Index   The Thesaurus Index lists all the words in the Thesaurus in alphabetical order. Follow these steps to use the Thesaurus Index:

1. Look up your word in the Thesaurus Index under the letter it begins with. Look up *new* under *N*.
2. Note the main entry word in blue print. Look up the main entry word in the Thesaurus.

main entry word → **new** *adj.*

Suppose you already have the word *fresh* in mind to replace *new*. In the Thesaurus Index you will find

fresh **new** *adj.*

The slanted print means that you will find *fresh* under the main entry word *new* in the Thesaurus.
   The Thesaurus Index also lists antonyms, or opposites, of words. They are shown like this:

old **new** *adj.*

The regular print shows you that *old* is the opposite of the main entry word *new*.

Using the Thesaurus Entry   The main entry words in the Thesaurus are listed in alphabetical order. Study this entry for the main entry word *new*.

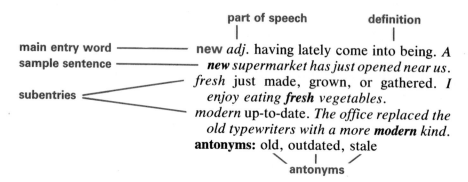

Notice that the entry gives two subentries, or words that you can use in place of *new: fresh* and *modern*. To help you choose one, the Thesaurus gives you
1. a meaning for each subentry, and
2. a sample sentence showing how to use each word.

Now you can choose the best word for your sentence.

Our town is proud of our *modern* hospital.

Practice   Look up each word below in the Thesaurus Index. Write the main entry word for each word.
  1. highway 2. grab 3. hammer 4. ugly 5. soggy

Use the Thesaurus to replace each underlined word. Rewrite each sentence, using the new word you chose.
  6. Aunt Jessie is tall, and she has kind, <u>thin</u> hands.
  7. She is a <u>happy</u> person who is usually smiling.
  8. Aunt Jessie sent me a <u>message</u> last week.
  9. It said, "Come visit, and I will <u>cook</u> chicken."
  10. I can already imagine the <u>smell</u> of this tasty treat.

Thesaurus Index

A

about almost *adv.*
accurate wrong *adj.*
actual real *adj.*
admire like *v.*
adorable pretty *adj.*
adult child *n.*
ailing ill *adj.*
alarm frighten *v.*
almost *adv.*
amend improve *v.*
answer talk *v.*
appreciate like *v.*
approximately
    almost *adv.*
aqua blue *adj.*
area *n.*
argue talk *v.*
arid wet *adj.*
aroma smell *n.*
arrangement order *n.*
assignment job *n.*
attempt try *v.*
attractive pretty *adj.*
authentic real *adj.*

B

baby child *n.*
bake cook *v.*
bang knock *v.*
barbecue cook *v.*
barely very *adv.*
bawl laugh *v.*
beautiful pretty *adj.*
becoming pretty *adj.*
begin end *v.*
beginning last *adj.*
beige brown *adj.*
bellow yell *v.*
better improve *v.*
 big *adj.*

bind fasten *v.*
bird *n.*
blend mix *v.*
blue *adj.*
boil cook *v.*
bony thin *adj.*
boulevard road *n.*
broil cook *v.*
brown *adj.*
bulletin message *n.*
bumpy even *adj.*
business work *n.*
button fasten *v.*

C

calm frighten *v.*
canary bird *n.*
career work *n.*
carrot orange *adj.*
cheap valuable *adj.*
cheerful happy *adj.*
cheerful sad *adj.*
chestnut brown *adj.*
child *n.*
chop cut *v.*
chore job *n.*
chubby thin *adj.*
chuckle laugh *v.*
clasp hold *v.*
clean dirty *adj.*
clip cut *v.*
close fasten *v.*
close near *adj.*
clutch hold *v.*
common usual *adj.*
communication
    message *n.*
complete end *v.*
concluding last *adj.*
connect join *v.*
continue end *v.*
contract grow *v.*

convenient useful *adj.*
cook *v.*
correct wrong *adj.*
costly valuable *adj.*
cradle hold *v.*
criminal wrong *adj.*
crimson red *adj.*
crow bird *n.*
cry laugh *v.*
cut *v.*
cute pretty *adj.*

D

dainty pretty *adj.*
damp wet *adj.*
decrease grow *v.*
delicate soft *adj.*
difficult hard *adj.*
dirty *adj.*
disagreeable nice *adj.*
dislike like *v.*
distant near *adj.*
divide join *v.*
divide mix *v.*
doodle draw *v.*
draw *v.*
drenched wet *adj.*
dripping wet *adj.*
drop grab *v.*
drum knock *v.*
dry wet *adj.*

E

easy hard *adj.*
enchanting pretty *adj.*
end *v.*
endanger save *v.*
enjoy like *v.*
enormous big *adj.*
especially very *adv.*

even adj.
evil wrong adj.
exclaim say v.
expand grow v.
expensive valuable adj.
experiment try v.
extend grow v.
extra very adv.
extraordinary usual adj.
extremely very adv.

F

fair pretty adj.
fair wrong adj.
fake real adj.
false real adj.
false wrong adj.
familiar usual adj.
far near adj.
fasten v.
fat thin adj.
faulty wrong adj.
feeble strong adj.
filthy dirty adj.
final last adj.
finish end v.
first last adj.
fit ill adj.
flat even adj.
fluffy soft adj.
formation order n.
free grab v.
fresh new adj.
friendly nice adj.
frighten v.
fry cook v.

G

genuine real adj.
giggle laugh v.
glad happy adj.

glad sad adj.
gloomy happy adj.
gloomy sad adj.
gold yellow adj.
good wrong adj.
good-looking pretty adj.
gorgeous pretty adj.
gossip talk v.
grab v.
graceful pretty adj.
grasp grab v.
greatly very adv.
grill cook v.
grimy dirty adj.
grow v.
grownup child n.
grubby dirty adj.

H

hack cut v.
hammer knock v.
handsome pretty adj.
handy useful adj.
happen v.
happy adj.
happy sad adj.
hard adj.
hardly very adv.
harm improve v.
hasty quick adj.
hate like v.
healthy ill adj.
help improve v.
helpful nice adj.
helpful useful adj.
highway road n.
hold v.
homely pretty adj.
hop jump v.
howl yell v.
hug hold v.
huge big adj.
hurdle jump v.

hurry v.
hurt improve v.

I

ill adj.
illegal wrong adj.
impractical useful adj.
improve v.
inaccurate wrong adj.
incorrect wrong adj.
inexact wrong adj.
inexpensive valuable adj.
infant child n.

J

job n.
join v.
jolly happy adj.
joyful happy adj.
jump v.
just wrong adj.

K

keep v.
knock v.
knot fasten v.

L

lane road n.
lanky thin adj.
large big adj.
last adj.
laugh v.
lavender purple adj.
lawful wrong adj.
lay put v.
lean thin adj.
leap jump v.
leisurely quick adj.
lemon yellow adj.

letter message *n.*
level even *adj.*
like *v.*
little big *adj.*
location area *n.*
loosen fasten *v.*
lose save *v.*
loud *adj.*
love like *v.*
lovely pretty *adj.*

M

magnificent pretty *adj.*
march walk *v.*
memorandum
   message *n.*
message *n.*
messy dirty *adj.*
mighty strong *adj.*
miserable happy *adj.*
mistaken wrong *adj.*
mix *v.*
modern new *adj.*
moist wet *adj.*
most very *adv.*
multiply grow *v.*

N

nasty nice *adj.*
naughty wrong *adj.*
navy blue *adj.*
near *adj.*
nearly almost *adv.*
neighboring near *adj.*
new *adj.*
nice *adj.*
noisy loud *adj.*
normal usual *adj.*
note message *n.*

O

occupation work *n.*
occur happen *v.*
odor smell *n.*
old new *adj.*
open fasten *v.*
orange *adj.*
order *v.*
ordinary usual *adj.*
outdated new *adj.*
outstanding usual *adj.*
overweight thin *adj.*
owl bird *n.*

P

parched wet *adj.*
patter knock *v.*
pattern order *n.*
peach orange *adj.*
peculiar usual *adj.*
phony real *adj.*
place put *v.*
plain pretty *adj.*
pleasant nice *adj.*
plump thin *adj.*
poach cook *v.*
pounce grab *v.*
pound knock *v.*
powerful strong *adj.*
practical useful *adj.*
precious valuable *adj.*
pretty *adj.*
priceless valuable *adj.*
profession work *n.*
purple *adj.*
put *v.*

Q

quick *adj.*
quiet loud *adj.*
quit end *v.*

R

rap knock *v.*
rare usual *adj.*
real *adj.*
recover save *v.*
red *adj.*
reduce grow *v.*
region area *n.*
release grab *v.*
rescue save *v.*
reserve keep *v.*
retain keep *v.*
right wrong *adj.*
road *n.*
roar laugh *v.*
roaring loud *adj.*
roast cook *v.*
robin bird *n.*
rough even *adj.*
roughly almost *adv.*
ruby red *adj.*
rush hurry *v.*

S

sad *adj.*
sad happy *adj.*
sample try *v.*
save *v.*
save keep *v.*
say *v.*
scamper hurry *v.*
scarcely very *adv.*
scare frighten *v.*
scent smell *n.*
scold talk *v.*
scrawny thin *adj.*
scream yell *v.*
screech yell *v.*
scribble draw *v.*
sea gull bird *n.*
seal fasten *v.*
seize grab *v.*

separate join *v.*
separate mix *v.*
sequence order *n.*
shriek yell *v.*
shrink grow *v.*
sick ill *adj.*
sickly ill *adj.*
silent loud *adj.*
simmer cook *v.*
simple hard *adj.*
sketch draw *v.*
skinny thin *adj.*
slender thin *adj.*
slice cut *v.*
slight thin *adj.*
slim thin *adj.*
slow quick *adj.*
small big *adj.*
smell *n.*
smooth even *adj.*
snatch grab *v.*
snicker laugh *v.*
snip cut *v.*
sob laugh *v.*
soft *adj.*
soft loud *adj.*
soggy wet *adj.*
soiled dirty *adj.*
solid soft *adj.*
soothe frighten *v.*
sopping wet *adj.*
space area *n.*
speedy quick *adj.*
spin twist *v.*
splendid pretty *adj.*
spotless dirty *adj.*
spread grow *v.*
spring jump *v.*
stale new *adj.*
start end *v.*
state say *v.*
steam cook *v.*
stew cook *v.*
stir mix *v.*

stop end *v.*
strange usual *adj.*
street road *n.*
stride walk *v.*
strong *adj.*
stunning pretty *adj.*
sturdy soft *adj.*
swell grow *v.*

T

take place happen *v.*
talk *v.*
tap knock *v.*
task job *n.*
tender soft *adj.*
terrify frighten *v.*
test try *v.*
thin *adj.*
thump knock *v.*
tie fasten *v.*
tiny big *adj.*
toast cook *v.*
toddler child *n.*
tot child *n.*
tough hard *adj.*
tough soft *adj.*
trace draw *v.*
trade work *n.*
tremendous big *adj.*
true real *adj.*
try *v.*
turn twist *v.*
turnpike road *n.*
twirl twist *v.*
twist *v.*

U

ugly pretty *adj.*
undertaking job *n.*
underweight thin *adj.*
unexpected usual *adj.*

unfair wrong *adj.*
unhappy sad *adj.*
unhealthy ill *adj.*
unite join *v.*
unjust wrong *adj.*
unlawful wrong *adj.*
unpleasant nice *adj.*
unwell ill *adj.*
upgrade improve *v.*
useful *adj.*
useless useful *adj.*
usual *adj.*

V

valuable *adj.*
very *adv.*
vicinity area *n.*
violet purple *adj.*

W

walk *v.*
weak strong *adj.*
weep laugh *v.*
well ill *adj.*
wet *adj.*
wicked wrong *adj.*
withhold keep *v.*
work *n.*
worsen improve *v.*
worthless useful *adj.*
worthless valuable *adj.*
wrong *adj.*

Y

yell *v.*
yellow *adj.*
youngster child *n.*

Z

zone area *n.*

Thesaurus

A

almost *adv.* just short of. *Loren is **almost** as old as Carrie.*

about nearly; almost. *It takes Ann **about** ten minutes to walk to school.*

approximately almost exactly. *That basket will hold **approximately** thirty apples.*

nearly almost but not quite. *Joey **nearly** caught the fish, but it got away.*

roughly about. *Both bedrooms are **roughly** the same size.*

area *n.* a surface. *Mom uses one **area** of the yard for her garden.*

location an area where something is placed or found. *The hardware store was moved to a new **location.***

region usually a large area of the earth's surface. *The Antarctic is the **region** around the South Pole.*

space the open area between objects. *Will the sofa fit in this **space,** or will we have to put it somewhere else?*

vicinity a nearby or surrounding area. *This park is mainly used by people who live in the **vicinity.***

zone an area set off from others by a special use. *The speed limit is fifteen miles per hour in a school **zone.***

B

big *adj.* of great size. *It is easy to get lost in a **big** city.*

enormous very big. *Look at that **enormous** elephant!*

huge very big, giant-sized. *It took days to climb the **huge** mountain.*

large bigger than average. *The **large** yard gave us plenty of room to play in.*

tremendous great in size or amount. *The king lived in a **tremendous** castle that had five hundred rooms.*

antonyms: little, small, tiny

bird *n.* a warm-blooded animal that lays eggs. A bird has two wings and a body covered with feathers. *Did you ever wish you could fly like a **bird?***

canary a songbird, often yellow in color, that can be kept as a pet in a cage. *My **canary** likes to perch on my finger.*

crow a large black bird with a harsh, hoarse call. *The **crow** sat on a branch and cawed loudly.*

owl a bird that has a large head, large eyes, and a short hooked bill. Owls usually fly and hunt at night. *An **owl** was sitting on the tree branch in the moonlight.*

robin a North American songbird with a rust-red breast and a dark gray back. *The cheerful chirping of a **robin** told us that spring was coming.*

sea gull a bird that lives on coasts and has long wings. It usually has gray and white feathers and webbed feet. *A **sea gull** circled high above the sailboat.*

blue *adj.* having the color of a clear sky. *On a sunny day, the **blue** boat matched the sky.*

aqua light greenish-blue. *The water near the shore has a lovely **aqua** color.*

navy dark blue. *The highway police wear **navy** uniforms.*

brown *adj.* of the color of wood or soil. *The leaves on the ground had all turned **brown**.*

beige light yellowish-brown. *The **beige** rug will blend with the green and brown furniture in the living room.*

chestnut reddish-brown. *I stroked the pony's **chestnut** mane.*

C

child *n.* a young boy or girl. *Every man, woman, and* **child** *needs exercise to stay fit.*

baby a very young child, infant. *The* **baby** *crawled happily around the playpen and then began shaking its rattle.*

infant a child from the earliest period of life up to about two years of age. *She laid the* **infant** *in a crib.*

toddler a child who has learned to walk but is still unsteady on his or her feet. *The* **toddler** *walked a few steps and then fell down.*

tot a small child. *The clown leaned down and handed the* **tot** *a balloon.*

youngster a young person or child. *"When I was a* **youngster**, *there was no TV," Grandma said.*

antonyms: adult, grownup

Word Bank

cook *v.* to prepare food for eating by using heat.

bake	*roast*
barbecue	*simmer*
boil	*steam*
broil	*stew*
fry	*toast*
poach	

cut *v.* to form, separate, or divide by using a sharp instrument. *Please* **cut** *the rope into six pieces.*

chop to cut up into small pieces. *Dad* **chopped** *a carrot and some potatoes and put them in the soup.*

clip to cut the surface growth of. *Barb* **clipped** *the bushes to make them look neat.*

hack to cut with heavy blows. *Andy* **hacked** *his way through the thick jungle.*

slice to cut into thin, flat pieces. *I* **sliced** *two pieces of bread from the loaf.*

snip to cut with short, quick strokes. *Liza used scissors to* **snip** *the ribbons in half before she made the bows.*

D

dirty *adj.* full of or covered with dirt; not clean. *Don loaded the* **dirty** *laundry into the washing machine.*

filthy extremely dirty. *The walls were so* **filthy** *that you could not tell what color they were.*

grimy covered with heavy dirt. *He scrubbed the grease and soot from his* **grimy** *hands.*

grubby dirty and messy. *We fed the stray dog and washed his* **grubby** *coat.*

messy untidy. *I swept out the* **messy** *closet and put everything in order.*

soiled having become or been made dirty. *The tablecloth was* **soiled** *where someone had spilled gravy.*

antonyms: clean *adj.*, spotless

draw *v.* to make a picture with lines. *Mandy* **drew** *a picture of her apartment building.*

doodle to scribble while thinking about something else. *Molly* **doodled** *on a notepad while she listened to the story.*

scribble to draw carelessly. *I* **scribbled** *some lines with each crayon to try out the different colors.*

sketch to make a rough drawing. *Daniel quickly* **sketched** *the bird before it flew away.*

trace to copy by following lines seen through a sheet of transparent paper. *Louie carefully* **traced** *the sailboat picture in the magazine.*

E

end *v.* to bring to a close. *The president* **ended** *the meeting.*

complete to make or do entirely. *I* **completed** *the work in a day.*

finish to reach the end of. *He* **finished** *the book.*

quit to stop doing. *You will never win if you* **quit** *trying.*

stop to cut off an action: *The fence* **stopped** *me from going farther.*

antonyms: begin, continue, start

even *adj.* without bumps, gaps, or rough parts. *The table wiggled because the floor was not* **even.**

flat having a smooth, even surface. *I need something* **flat** *to write on.*

level having a flat, even surface. *It is easier to walk along* **level** *ground than to walk up and down hills.*

smooth having a surface that is not rough or uneven. *She likes to roller skate where the sidewalk is* **smooth.**

antonyms: bumpy, rough

F

fasten *v.* to attach firmly. *She* **fastened** *the tag to her shirt.*

bind to hold together. *Birds* **bind** *their nests with mud.*

button to fasten or close a garment by slipping small disks through holes. **Button** *your coat, or you will be cold.*

close to shut. *The lid of the trunk would not* **close.**

knot to fasten by tying together one or more pieces of string, rope, or twine. *She* **knotted** *the two pieces of rope together.*

seal to close tightly with glue, wax, or other hardening material. *He* **sealed** *the letter shut so that no one would read it.*

tie to fasten with a cord or rope. *She* **tied** *the box shut with cord.*

antonyms: loosen, open *v.*

frighten *v.* to make or become afraid. *The thunder and lightning* **frightened** *us.*

alarm to make suddenly very worried. *News of the accident* **alarmed** *the family.*

scare to startle or shock. *A loud noise* **scared** *the sleeping cat.*

terrify to frighten greatly. *The spreading forest fire* **terrified** *the animals.*

antonyms: calm *v.*, soothe

G

grab *v.* to take hold of suddenly. *I* **grabbed** *the railing to stop myself from falling.*

grasp to take hold of firmly with the hand. *I* **grasped** *a branch and pulled myself up.*

pounce to seize by swooping. *The cat* **pounced** *on the rubber mouse.*

seize to take hold of suddenly and by force. *The thief* **seized** *the package and ran.*

snatch to grasp quickly. *Gabriel* **snatched** *the ball before his teammate could reach it.*

antonyms: drop *v.*, free *v.*, release

grow *v.* to become larger in size. *My little sister* **grew** *too big for me to pick up.*

expand to make or become larger in size, volume, or amount. *The balloon* **expanded** *until it popped.*

extend to make longer; lengthen. *We plan to* **extend** *our visit from a week to ten days.*

multiply to make or become more in number. *The number of students in this school has* **multiplied** *in the past ten years.*

spread to stretch over a wider area. *As water continued dripping, the puddle* **spread.**

swell to become larger in size or volume as a result of pressure from the inside. *The sponge* **swelled** *as it soaked up water.*

antonyms: contract *v.*, decrease, reduce, shrink

H

happen *v.* to take place, occur. *When did the earthquake **happen**?*

occur to come to pass. *How did the accident **occur**?*

take place to come about. *The wedding will **take place** on board the ship.*

happy *adj.* very satisfied. *I was **happy** to hear the good news.*

cheerful merry, lively. *The **cheerful** song helps him forget his worries.*

glad pleased. *"I would be **glad** to help," said Victor.*

jolly full of fun. *The **jolly** waitress liked making us laugh.*

joyful showing, feeling, or causing great joy or happiness. *The puppy galloped toward its owner with a **joyful** bark.*

antonyms: gloomy, miserable, sad

hard *adj.* difficult to solve, understand, or express. *This book is too **hard** for a first grader.*

difficult hard to make, do, or understand. *Denise practiced the **difficult** dance steps over and over.*

tough difficult to do. *Fixing the rusty old car was going to be a **tough** job.*

antonyms: easy, simple

hold *v.* to have or keep in the arms or hands. *Please **hold** this package for me so that I can unlock the door.*

clasp to hold or hug tightly. *The little girl **clasped** the wriggling puppy.*

clutch to hold tightly with the hands. *She **clutched** the handlebars of her bike as she rode down the street for the first time.*

cradle to hold as if in a small bed for a baby. *I **cradled** the kitten in my arms until it fell asleep.*

hug to put one's arms around and hold closely. *The two friends **hugged** each other when they said good-by.*

hurry *v.* to act or move quickly. *We will miss the bus unless we **hurry**.*

rush to act or move too quickly. *You are likely to make mistakes if you **rush** through your work.*

scamper to run or go hurriedly. *The squirrels **scampered** away when the cat suddenly appeared.*

I

ill *adj.* not healthy. *She stayed home from school because she was **ill**.*

ailing feeling ill or having pain. *My **ailing** uncle will stay with us until he is better.*

sick suffering from an illness. *The vet gave us medicine for our **sick** cat.*

sickly tending to become sick. *My **sickly** brother usually has the flu at least five times every winter.*

unhealthy harmful to one's health. *They often eat **unhealthy** foods, such as candy.*

unwell not well; sick. *"I am sorry to hear that you have been **unwell**," he said.*

antonyms: fit *adj.*, healthy, well *adj.*

improve *v.* to make or become more excellent. *Bonita can **improve** her grades by studying harder.*

amend to change so as to improve. *The law was **amended** to make it more fair.*

better to improve. *The new library will **better** the lives of those who use it.*

help to aid the progress of. *Hard practice has **helped** her piano playing.*

upgrade to raise to a higher rank or level of excellence. *The factory **upgraded** its product by using better materials.*

antonyms: harm, hurt, worsen

J

job *n.* a piece of work. *Building a house is a big **job**.*

assignment a job that has been given to someone. *Katie's **assignment** was to sweep the floors and halls.*

chore a small job, usually done on a regular schedule. *His least favorite **chore** was to put out the garbage every Monday.*

task a piece of work to be done. *Moving that dresser is a **task** for two people.*

undertaking a task that one accepts or attempts. *Fixing a roof can be a dangerous **undertaking**.*

join *v.* to bring or come together. *Let's **join** hands in a circle.*

connect to serve as a way of joining things. *A wire **connects** the lamp with the plug.*

unite to join in action for a certain purpose. *Neighbors from near and far **united** to repair the flood damage.*

antonyms: divide, separate *v.*

jump *v.* to rise up or move through the air by using the leg muscles. *Tom **jumped** as he threw the basketball.*

hop to move with light, quick leaps. *A robin **hopped** along the ground looking for worms.*

hurdle to jump over. *Debby **hurdled** a low stone wall and kept running.*

leap to jump quickly or suddenly. *I **leaped** to the left when I saw the bicycle coming.*

spring to move upward or forward in one quick motion. *The deer easily **sprang** across the brook.*

K

keep *v.* to have and not give up. *Did Rob give you that watch to **keep?***

reserve to set aside for a special purpose. *I **reserve** my warmest and most comfortable boots for winter hiking.*

retain to continue to have. *The company moved, but it **retained** most of its long-time employees.*

save to keep from wasting or spending. *She will **save** her money this week.*

withhold to refuse to give. *The boss **withheld** their pay checks until the job was completely finished.*

Word Bank

knock *v.* to make a noise by hitting a hard surface.

bang	*pound*
drum	*rap*
hammer	*tap*
patter	*thump*

L

last *adj.* coming, being, or placed after all others. *The **last** person to leave must remember to lock the door.*

concluding bringing or coming to an end; finishing. *The teacher said a few **concluding** words and then let the class go.*

final coming at the end. *After the **final** act, all the actors came out to take a bow.*

antonyms: beginning, first

laugh *v.* to smile and make sounds to show amusement or scorn. *That funny TV program always makes me **laugh**.*

chuckle to laugh quietly. *She **chuckled** to herself as she read the comic strip.*

giggle to laugh nervously. *We **giggled** with excitement as Mom opened the gift.*

roar to laugh very loudly. *The audience **roared** when the clown picked up the strong man.*

snicker to laugh in a mean or sly way. *It is unkind to **snicker** when a classmate gives the wrong answer.*

antonyms: bawl, cry *v.*, sob *v.*, weep

like *v.* to be fond of. *He **likes** to hike in the mountains.*

admire to look at with great pleasure. *Everyone **admired** her beautiful hair.*

appreciate to know the worth or quality of. *She **appreciated** the careful drawings.*

enjoy to get pleasure from. *We **enjoyed** the cool weather.*

love to have strong, warm feelings for. *Eddy **loves** his new puppy.*

antonyms: dislike *v.*, hate *v.*

loud *adj.* having a large amount of sound. *The window slammed shut with a **loud** bang.*

noisy making or filled with loud or unpleasant sound. *They had to shout to be heard in the **noisy** factory.*

roaring making a loud, deep sound. *The **roaring** engine drowned out the radio.*

antonyms: quiet *adj.*, silent, soft

M

message *n.* words that are sent from one person or group to another. *He wrote a brief **message** on the post card.*

bulletin a short announcement on a matter of public interest. *The TV program was interrupted by a special news **bulletin.***

communication a message sent by speech, signals, or writing. *The ship sent a **communication** to shore by radio.*

letter a written message to someone that is usually sent by mail in an envelope. *My sister sent me a **letter** full of news about summer camp.*

memorandum a written communication that is sent between members or offices of a business. *The company president sent a **memorandum** to all the office managers.*

note a short letter or message. *I wrote my uncle a **note** to thank him for the gift.*

mix *v.* to combine or blend. ***Mix** the peanuts and raisins in a bowl.*

blend to combine completely. *To make the color orange, **blend** red and yellow.*

stir to mix by using repeated circular motions. ***Stir** the soup as you heat it.*

antonyms: divide *v.*, separate *v.*

N

near *adj.* close in distance or time. *We will choose a winner in the **near** future.*

close near in space, time, or relationship. *Yoko is a **close** friend of mine.*

neighboring living near or located close by; bordering. *People from all the **neighboring** towns came to Greenville for the circus.*

antonyms: distant, far

new *adj.* having lately come into being. *A **new** supermarket has just opened near us.*

fresh just made, grown, or gathered. *I enjoy eating **fresh** vegetables.*

modern up-to-date. *The office replaced the old typewriters with a more **modern** kind.*

antonyms: old, outdated, stale

nice *adj.* kind, pleasant, agreeable. *The boy in the picture has a **nice** smile.*

friendly showing friendship. *Some **friendly** children asked her to join their game.*

helpful providing aid. *The police officer was **helpful** when we got lost.*

pleasant giving pleasure; agreeable. *We enjoyed the **pleasant** scent of the pine trees.*

antonyms: disagreeable, nasty, unpleasant

O

orange *adj.* of a reddish-yellow color. *The **orange** curtains made the room look like a bright sunset.*

carrot of a bright orange color named for the vegetable. *He has **carrot**-red hair.*

peach of a yellowish-pink color named for the fruit. *Her **peach** dress matched the glow in her cheeks.*

order *n.* a grouping of things one after another. *The students' names were called in ABC **order**.*

arrangement the way things are placed in relation to each other. *We planned the seating **arrangement** for the dinner party.*

formation a particular arrangement. *Wild geese fly in a V-shaped **formation**.*

pattern a group of things or events that forms a regular arrangement. *He did not like to change the **pattern** of his daily duties.*

sequence the following of one thing after another in a regular, fixed way. *The seasons always follow each other in the same **sequence**.*

P

Word Bank

pretty *adj.* pleasing to the eye or ear.

adorable	*gorgeous*
attractive	*graceful*
beautiful	*handsome*
cute	*lovely*
dainty	*magnificent*
enchanting	*splendid*
fair	*stunning*
good-looking	

antonyms: homely, plain, ugly

purple *adj.* of a color between blue and red. *The king wore a robe of **purple** velvet.*

lavender light purple. *The flower had pale **lavender** blossoms.*

violet bluish-purple. ***Violet** clouds streaked the sky at sunset.*

put *v.* to cause to be in a certain place. ***Put** the spoons in the drawer.*

lay to put or set down. *He **lays** his coat on the bed.*

place to put in a particular place or order. *She **placed** a bowl of fruit in the center of the table.*

Q

quick *adj.* very fast; rapid. *The frog disappeared into the pond with one **quick** leap.*

hasty done too quickly to be correct or wise; rash. *Someday Manuel may be sorry about his **hasty** decision.*

speedy moving or happening quickly. *The **speedy** horse soon galloped out of sight.*

antonyms: leisurely, slow

R

real *adj.* not artificial or made up. *Those silk flowers look just like **real** ones.*

actual really existing or happening. *I have seen pictures of rainbows, but I have never seen an **actual** rainbow.*

authentic worthy of belief; true. *The book gave an **authentic** picture of life in the Wild West.*

genuine not false; real or pure. *He examined the pearls carefully to make sure that they were **genuine**.*

true being in agreement with fact or reality. *Is it **true** that bees make honey?*

antonyms: fake, false, phony

red *adj.* having the color of strawberries. *Stop signs are usually **red**.*

crimson bright red. *The American flag has **crimson** and white stripes.*

ruby deep red. *The **ruby**-colored flowers were beautiful in the sunlight.*

road *n.* an open way for vehicles, persons, or animals to pass along or through. *This **road** will take you to the next town.*

boulevard a broad street, often with trees and grass planted in the center or along the sides. *Shoppers enjoyed strolling along the shady **boulevard.***

highway a main public road. *Which **highway** is the fastest route between St. Paul and Minneapolis?*

lane a narrow path or road between fences, hedges, or walls. *We walked along the **lane** between the cornfield and the wheat field.*

street a road in a city or town. *The post office and the town hall are on this **street.***

turnpike a wide highway that drivers pay a toll to use. *Cars on the **turnpike** slowed as they neared the toll booths.*

S

sad *adj.* feeling or causing sorrow. *The teacher's illness was **sad** news for the class.*

gloomy sad and discouraged. *The losing team felt **gloomy**.*

unhappy without joy or pleasure. *She tried to forget the **unhappy** summer.*

antonyms: cheerful, glad, happy

save *v.* to keep from danger or harm. *She grabbed the railing and **saved** herself from falling on the ice.*

recover to get something back; to regain. *The police **recovered** the lost truck.*

rescue to remove from a dangerous place. *I **rescued** my cat from the tree.*

antonyms: endanger, lose

say *v.* to make known or put across in words. *What did your brother **say** in the letter?*

exclaim to cry out or say suddenly. *"That's mine!" **exclaimed** the child.*

state to say in a very clear, exact way. *The rule **states** that the pool closes at 5:00 P.M.*

smell *n.* what the nose senses. *The **smell** of smoke warns us of fire.*

aroma a pleasant smell. *The **aroma** of Aunt Carrie's cooking made us all hungry.*

odor a strong smell. *The **odor** of moth balls clung to the coat.*

scent a light smell. *The woman had left, but the **scent** of her perfume remained.*

soft *adj.* not hard or firm. *The **soft** cheese spread smoothly.*

delicate very easily broken or torn. *A slight tug will snap the **delicate** chain.*

fluffy having hair, feathers, or material that stands up in a soft pile. *I want a warm **fluffy** bathrobe for winter.*

tender easily bruised or hurt. *Her **tender** hands were sore from pulling weeds.*

antonyms: solid, sturdy, tough

strong *adj.* having much power, energy, or strength. *A **strong** wind made the treetops sway.*

mighty having or showing great power, strength, or force. *All the animals in the forest feared the **mighty** mountain lion.*

powerful having power, authority, or influence. *The **powerful** king ruled over every city, town, and village in the land.*

antonyms: feeble, weak

T

talk *v.* to say words. *Carmen and I **talked** on the phone last night.*

answer to say, write, or do something in reply or in reply to. *"Yes, I would enjoy going to your party," Terry **answered**.*

argue to disagree. *Jane and Michael **argued** about which movie to see.*

gossip to repeat talk that is often not true. *That silly boy likes to **gossip** about people he does not even know.*

scold to speak angrily to for doing something bad. *I **scolded** my cat for scratching the chair.*

How thin is thin?

thin *adj.* having little fat on the body.

1. thin:
   lanky
   lean
   slender
   slim

2. thinner:
   slight
   underweight

3. very thin:
   bony
   scrawny
   skinny

antonyms: chubby, fat, overweight, plump

---

try *v.* to put to use for the purpose of judging. *If you like apples, **try** these.*

attempt to make an effort. *The student pilot **attempted** his first landing today.*

experiment to do a number of tests to learn or prove something. *She **experimented** to find out which colors looked best in her design.*

sample to test by trying a small part. ***Sample** a dish before you serve it to guests.*

test to use in order to discover any problems. ***Test** the brakes and the horn to be sure that they work.*

twist *v.* to move in a winding path. *The road **twisted** through the mountains.*

spin to move very quickly and continuously around a center. *The ice skater **spun** on one foot like a top.*

turn to move or cause to move around a center; rotate. ***Turn** the cap to the right to open the jar.*

twirl to cause to move quickly around a center. *The cowhand **twirled** the lasso and then threw it.*

U

useful *adj.* being of use or service; helpful. *The car and the telephone have turned out to be very **useful** inventions.*

convenient suited to one's needs or purpose. *It is **convenient** to have a supermarket nearby.*

handy useful, convenient, serving many purposes. *The rope that I took on the camping trip turned out to be very **handy**.*

helpful providing what is needed or useful. *A map can be very **helpful** when you are lost.*

practical having or serving a useful purpose. *Would you rather receive a **practical** gift or one that is just for fun?*

antonyms: impractical, useless, worthless

usual *adj.* happening regularly or all of the time. *Her **usual** breakfast is toast and orange juice.*

common found or occurring often. *Squirrels are **common** in many parts of the United States.*

familiar well-known. *Jason played several **familiar** songs, and everyone sang along.*

normal of the usual or regular kind. *We had the **normal** amount of rain this spring.*

ordinary not unusual in any way. *A visit from my aunt turns an **ordinary** day into a special event.*

antonyms: extraordinary, outstanding, peculiar, rare, strange, unexpected

V

valuable *adj.* worth a lot of money. *Land that contains oil is very **valuable**.*

costly of high price or value. *The queen wore a **costly** diamond necklace and earrings.*

(continued)

very

valuable (continued)

expensive having a high price. *Nina has been saving her money for a year to buy an* **expensive** *bike.*

precious having very great value. *The crown contained diamonds, rubies, and other* **precious** *gems.*

priceless too valuable to be given a price. *A museum guard watched over the* **priceless** *paintings.*

antonyms: cheap, inexpensive, worthless

very *adv.* to a high degree. *We were* **very** *tired after a hard day's work.*

especially more than usually. *All my friends are nice, but Ginny is* **especially** *kind.*

extra unusually; especially. *Last week the weather was* **extra** *hot, even for summer.*

extremely to a very high degree. *Dinosaurs were* **extremely** *large animals.*

greatly very much, to a large degree. *That artist's work has been* **greatly** *admired for centuries.*

most to a high degree. *"This has been a* **most** *delightful evening," said the guest.*

antonyms: barely, hardly, scarcely

W

walk *v.* to move on foot at an easy and steady pace. *I had to* **walk** *home when my bike broke.*

march to walk to an even beat. *The soldiers* **marched** *in the parade.*

stride to walk with long steps. *John* **strode** *to the chalkboard, sure of his answer.*

wet *adj.* being covered or soaked with water. *I wiped the table with a* **wet** *cloth.*

damp slightly wet. *His feet left footprints in the* **damp** *sand.*

drenched wet through and through. *Take this umbrella, or you will get* **drenched**!

dripping being so wet that drops fall. *I wiped my* **dripping** *forehead after running in the hot sun.*

moist slightly wet. *In the morning the grass is* **moist** *with dew.*

soggy soaked with moisture. *Her sneakers were* **soggy** *from walking in the rain.*

sopping thoroughly soaked. *He pulled his* **sopping** *hat from the puddle and squeezed out the water.*

antonyms: arid, dry, parched

work *n.* a way by which a person earns money. *Michael is looking for gardening* **work**.

business a person's occupation, trade, or work. *Mrs. Roth is in the* **business** *of selling houses.*

career a profession that a person follows as a life's work. *My father began his* **career** *as a firefighter when he was twenty.*

occupation a profession, business, or job. *Working as an airline pilot is an interesting* **occupation**.

profession a job that requires training and special study. *Her college courses will prepare her for the teaching* **profession.**

trade an occupation, especially one requiring special skill with the hands. *My aunt chose carpentry as her* **trade** *because she likes working with wood.*

Shades of Meaning

wrong *adj.*

1. not correct:

false	*incorrect*
faulty	*inexact*
inaccurate	*mistaken*

2. bad:

criminal	*unfair*
evil	*unjust*
illegal	*unlawful*
naughty	*wicked*

antonyms: **1.** accurate, correct, right
2. fair, good, just, lawful

Y

yell *v.* to cry out loudly. ***Yell*** *for help.*

bellow to shout in a deep, loud voice. *"Who goes there?" the giant **bellowed**.*

howl to make a long, wailing cry. *He **howled** with pain when he stubbed his toe.*

scream to make a long, loud, piercing cry or sound. *The child **screamed** when the dog ran away with his ball.*

screech to make a high, harsh cry or sound. *"Pretty Polly," the parrot **screeched**.*

shriek to make a loud, shrill sound. *She **shrieked** in fright when the window suddenly slammed shut.*

yellow *adj.* having the color of the sun. ***Yellow*** *tulips lined the sidewalk in front of the apartment building.*

gold having a deep yellow color. *Wheat turns a **gold** color when it is ripe.*

lemon having the color of ripe lemons. *The **lemon**-yellow walls seemed to fill the room with sunshine.*

Spelling-Meaning Index

able, ability, abler, ablest, ably, disable, unable

age, aged, ageless, ages, aging

air, aired, airing, airless

airplane, airplanes

apple, apples

art, artful, artist, artistic, artists, arts

---

baby, babied, babies, babyhood, babying, babyish

balloon, ballooned, ballooning, balloons

bare, bareback, bared, barefoot, barehanded, bareheaded, barely, bareness, barer, bares, barest, baring

baseball, baseballs

basket, basketful, basketry, baskets

bear, bear hug, bearish, bearishly, bears, bearskin, grizzly bear, polar bear

begin, beginner, beginning, begins

bird, birds

birthday, birthdays

blow, blower, blowing, blown, blows

blue, blueness, bluer, blues, bluest

boil, boiled, boiler, boiling, boils

boot, booted, bootie, boots

bow¹, bows

bow², bowed, bowing, bows.

boy, boyhood, boyish, boys

bright, brighten, brightener, brighter, brightest, brightly, brightness

butter, buttered, buttering, butters, buttery, unbuttered

button, buttoned, buttoning, buttons, unbutton

---

care, cared, careful, carefully, careless, carelessly, cares, caring

carry, carriage, carried, carrier, carries, carrying

center, centered, centering, centers, central

certain, certainly, certainty

chair, chairs

chew, chewable, chewed, chewing, chews, chewy

child, childhood, childish, childishly, childishness, childless, childlessness, childlike, children

chop, chopped, chopper, chopping, chops

circle, circled, circles, circling

circus, circuses

city, cities

class, classes

clay, clayish, clays

clear, cleared, clearer, clearest, clearing, clearly, clearness, clears, unclear

cloth, clothe, clothes, clothing, cloths

cloud, clouded, cloudiness, clouding, clouds, cloudy

clown, clowned, clowning, clowns

coach, coached, coaches, coaching

coin, coins

color, colored, colorful, colorfully, coloring, colorless, colors

come, become, comes, coming, incoming

cook, cooked, cooker, cookery, cooking, cooks, cookie, precooked, overcooked, uncooked, undercooked

cost, costing, costly, costs

cough, coughed, coughing, coughs

count, account, countable, counted, counter, counting, countless, counts, miscount, recount, uncounted

crack, cracked, cracking, cracks, cracker

crop, crops

crowd, crowded, crowding, crowds

crown, crowned, crowning, crowns

cry, cried, cries, crying

cube, cubes, cubic

dance, danceable, danced, dancer, dances, dancing

dark, darken, darker, darkest, darkly, darkness

daughter, daughters

die, died, dies, dying

dirt, dirtily, dirtiness, dirty

do, doer, does, doing, redo, undo

dollar, dollars

door, doors

drop, dropped, dropper, dropping, droplet, drops

drum, drummed, drummer, drumming, drums

dry, dried, drier, driest, drying, dryer, dryness

ear, earful, ears

eight, eighteen, eighth, eightieth, eights, eighty

face, faced, faceless, faces, facing

fair¹, fairer, fairest, fairly, fairness, unfair, unfairly, unfairness

fair², fairs

farm, farmed, farmer, farming, farms

feel, feeler, feeling, feels, unfeeling

fight, fighter, fighting, fights

fix, fixable, fixed, fixer, fixes, fixing

float, floatable, floated, floating, floats

fly¹, flier, flies, flying

fly², flies

foil¹, foiled, foiler, foiling, foils

foil², foils

follow, followed, follower, following, follows

forget, forgettable, forgetful, forgetfully, forgetfulness, forgets, forgetting, unforgettable

four, fours, fourteen, fourth

friend, befriend, friendless, friendliness, friendly, friends, unfriendly

front, fronted, frontier, fronting, fronts

garden, gardened, gardener, gardening, gardens

giraffe, giraffes

girl, girlhood, girlish, girlishly, girls

grade, graded, grader, grades, grading

grandfather, grandfatherly, grandfathers

grandmother, grandmotherly, grandmothers

grin, grinned, grinning, grins

ground, grounded, grounding, grounds

hair, hairless, hairs, hairy

happen, happened, happening, happens

happy, happier, happiest, happily, happiness, unhappy

head, headed, heading, headless, heads

hear, heard, hearer, hearing, hears

hello, helloed, helloes, helloing

help, helped, helper, helpful, helpfully, helpfulness, helping, helpless, helplessly, helplessness

her, hers, herself

him, himself

hold, holder, holding, holds

hope, hoped, hopeful, hopefully, hopes, hopefulness, hoping, hopeless, hopelessly, hopelessness

hour, hourly, hours

huge, hugely, hugeness, huger, hugest

hunt, hunted, hunter, hunting, hunts

hurry, hurried, hurriedly, hurriedness, hurries, hurrying, unhurried

hurt, hurtful, hurting, hurts, unhurt

ice, iced, ices, icier, iciest, iciness, icing, icy

inside, insider, insides

invite, invitation, invited, invites, inviting

it, its

jar, jarful, jars

join, joined, joiner, joining, joins, joint, rejoin

joke, joked, joker, jokes, joking, jokingly

joy, enjoy, enjoyable, enjoyably, enjoyment, joyful, joyfully, joyfulness, joyless, joylessly, joylessness, joyous, joyously, joyousness, joys

judge, judged, judges, judgeship, judging, judgment

jump, jumped, jumper, jumping, jumps, jumpy

kind, kinder, kindest, kindliness, kindly, kindness, unkind

knee, kneel, knees

knife, knives

knock, knocked, knocker, knocking, knocks

knot, knots, knotted, knotting, knotty

know, knowable, knowing, knowingly, knowledge, known, knows, unknown

large, enlarge, enlargement, largely, largeness, larger, largest

last, lastly

late, lately, lateness, later, latest

laugh, laughable, laughably, laughed, laughing, laughingly, laughs, laughter

law, lawful, lawfully, lawfulness, lawless, lawlessly, lawlessness, laws, lawyer, outlaw, outlawed, unlawful, unlawfully

lawn, lawns

lay, layer, layered, layering, laying, lays

leave, leaves, leaving

lesson, lessons

letter, lettered, letterer, lettering, letters

lie, lies, lying

life, lifeless, lifelike, lives

like, liken, likeness, likewise, unlike

little, littler, littlest

loud, aloud, louder, loudest, loudly, loudness

love, lovable, lovableness, lovably, loved, loveless, loveliness, lovely, lover, loves, loving, lovingly

luck, luckily, luckiness, luckless, lucky, unlucky

make, maker, makes, making, remake

market, marketed, marketing, markets

match[1], matchable, matched, matcher, matches, matching, matchless

match[2], matches

milk, milked, milker, milkiness, milking, milks, milky

mind, mindful, mindfully, mindfulness, mindless, mindlessly, mindlessness, minds, remind, reminder, unmindful

mine, mined, miner, mines, mining

mix, mixable, mixed, mixer, mixes, mixing, mixture, unmixed

most, mostly

mouth, mouthed, mouthful, mouthing, mouths

napkin, napkins

near, neared, nearer, nearest, nearing, nearly, nearness, nears

need, needed, needful, needing, needless, needs, needy

neighbor, neighbored, neighborhood, neighboring, neighborly, neighbors

new, anew, newer, newest, newly, newness, renew

nice, nicely, niceness, nicer, nicest

noise, noiseless, noises, noisily, noisiness, noisy

north, northerly, northern, northerner

note, noted, notes, noting

nothing, nothingness

oil, oiled, oiliness, oiling, oils, oily

orange, orangeade, oranges

order, disorder, ordered, ordering, orderly, orders, reorder

our, ours, ourselves

outside, outsider

own, owned, owner, ownership, owning, owns

page, paged, pages, paging

paint, painted, painter, painting, paints, repaint

pair, paired, pairing, pairs
park, parked, parking, parks
party, partied, parties, partying
pat, pats, patted, patting
patch, patchable, patched, patches,
  patching, patchy
pay, payable, payer, paying, payment, pays,
  repay, repayment
peace, peaceable, peaceably, peaceful,
  peacefully, peacefulness
pear, pears
pencil, penciled, penciling, pencils
penny, pennies, penniless, pennilessness
picnic, picnicked, picnicker, picnicking,
  picnics
pie, pies
place, displace, misplace, misplaced,
  placed, placement, places, placing,
  replace
point, pointed, pointer, pointing, points,
  pointy
pond, ponds
pony, ponies
pretty, prettier, prettiest, prettily,
  prettiness
puppy, puppies
purple, purpled, purples, purpling,
  purplish

quart, quarts, quarter, quarterly,
  quartered, quartering, quartet
queen, queenlike, queenly, queens
quick, quicken, quicker, quickest, quickly,
  quickness
quit, quits, quitter, quitting

rabbit, rabbits
raw, rawer, rawest, rawness
round, around, rounded, rounder,
  roundest, rounding, roundness, rounds
row, rowed, rower, rowing, rows
rub, rubbed, rubbing, rubs

sad, sadden, sadder, saddest, sadly,
  sadness
save, saved, saver, saves, saving, savings

scare, scared, scares, scaring, scary
school, preschool, preschooler, schooled,
  schooling, schools, unschooled
scratch, scratched, scratches, scratching,
  scratchy
scream, screamed, screaming, screams
screen, screened, screening, screens
second[1], seconds
second[2], secondary, seconded, seconding,
  secondly, seconds
seem, seemed, seeming, seemingly, seems
send, sender, sending, sends, sent
serve, servant, served, server, serves,
  service, serving
sew, sewed, sewing, sewn, sews
share, shared, sharer, shares, sharing
shoe, shoeing, shoeless, shoes
shut, shuts, shutter, shutting
sight, sighted, sighting, sightless, sights
sing, singable, singer, singing, sings
skin, skinned, skinning, skins, skinny
slow, slowed, slower, slowest, slowing,
  slowly, slowness, slows
smart, smarten, smarter, smartest,
  smartly, smartness
smell, smelled, smelling, smells, smelly
smile, smiled, smiles, smiling
smoke, smoked, smokes, smokiness,
  smoking, smokeless, smoky
soap, soaped, soaping, soaps, soapy
sock, socks
soft, soften, softer, softest, softly, softness
soil, soils
sold, resold, unsold
son, grandson, son-in-law, sons, stepson
sound, sounded, sounding, soundless,
  soundlessly, soundproof, sounds
space, spaced, spaces, spacing
speak, speakable, speaker, speaking,
  speaks
spoil, spoiled, spoiling, spoils, unspoiled
spoon, spooned, spoonful, spooning,
  spoons
spray, sprayed, sprayer, spraying, sprays
spread, spreadable, spreading, spreads
spring, springlike, springs

squeeze, squeezable, squeezed, squeezer, squeezes, squeezing

stage, staged, stages, staging

star, starless, starlet, starred, starring, starry, stars

stick, sticker, stickers, stickier, stickiest, stickily, stickiness, sticking, sticks, sticky, unstick

story, stories

storm, stormed, storming, storms, stormy

straight, straighten, straightener, straighter, straightest

straw, straws

stream, streams

street, streets

string, restring, stringing, strings, stringy

strong, stronger, strongest, strongly

sudden, suddenly, suddenness

summer, summers, summery

sun, sunbeam, sunburn, sunburst, sundial, sundown, sunflower, sunglasses, sunless, sunlight, sunnier, sunniest, sunny, sunrise, sunset, sunshine, suntan

---

talk, talkative, talked, talker, talking, talks

tap, tapped, tapper, tapping, taps

teach, reteach, teacher, teaches, teaching

tell, retell, teller, telling, tells

thank, thanked, thankful, thankfully, thankfulness, thanking, thankless, thanks

their, theirs

thick, thicken, thickener, thickening, thicker, thickest, thicket, thickly, thickness

thin, thinly, thinned, thinner, thinness, thinnest, thinning, thins

third, thirdly, thirds

thought, rethought, thoughtful, thoughtfully, thoughtfulness, thoughtless, thoughtlessly, thoughtlessness

three, threefold, threes, threesome

throw, thrower, throwing, thrown, throws

tie, retie, tied, ties, tying, untie

tight, tighten, tighter, tightest, tightly, tightness

tooth, toothed, toothing, toothless, toothy

toy, toys

trace, retrace, traceable, traced, traceless, tracer, traces, tracing

travel, traveled, traveler, traveling, travelogue, travels

try, trial, tried, tries, trying, untried

turn, turned, turning, turns, unturned

---

use, misuse, reuse, reusable, usable, usage, used, useful, usefully, usefulness, useless, uselessly, uselessness, user, uses, using

---

walk, walked, walker, walking, walks

wall, walled, walling, walls

watch, watched, watcher, watches, watchful, watchfulness, watching

weak, weaken, weaker, weakest, weakling, weakly, weakness

week, biweekly, weekday, weekend, weekender, weekly, weeknight, weeks

weigh, weighed, weigher, weighing, weighs, weight, weights

wide, widely, widen, wideness, wider, widest, width

wild, wilder, wildest, wildly, wildness

window, windows

winter, winters, wintry

word, reword, worded, wordiness, wording, wordless, words, wordy

work, rework, workable, worked, worker, working, works

wrap, wrapped, wrapper, wrapping, wraps, unwrap

write, rewrite, writer, writes, writing, written

wrong, wronged, wrongful, wronging, wrongs

---

yellow, yellowed, yellowing, yellowish, yellows, yellowy

Spelling Dictionary

Spelling Table

This Spelling Table shows many of the letter combinations that spell the same sounds in different words. Use it to look up words you cannot spell.

Sounds	Spellings	Sample Words
|ă|	a, au	bat, have, laugh
|ā|	a, ai, ay, ea, eigh, ey	tale, later, rain, pay, great, eight, they
|âr|	air, are, ear, eir, ere	fair, care, bear, their, where
|ä|	a, al	father, calm
|är|	ar	art
|b|	b, bb	bus, rabbit
|ch|	ch, tch	chin, match
|d|	d, dd	dark, sudden
|ĕ|	a, ai, e, ea, ie	any, said, went, head, friend
|ē|	e, ea, ee, ey, y	these, we, beast, tree, honey, lady
|f|	f, ff, gh	funny, off, enough
|g|	g, gg	get, egg
|h|	h, wh	hat, who
|hw|	wh	when
|ĭ|	e, ee, i, ui, y	before, been, mix, give, build, gym
|ī|	i, ie, igh, uy, y	time, mind, pie, fight, buy, try
|îr|	ear, ere	near, here
|j|	dge, g, ge, j	judge, gym, age, jet
|k|	c, ch, ck, k	picnic, school, stick, keep
|kw|	qu	quick
|l|	l, ll	last, all
|m|	m, mm	mop, summer
|n|	kn, n, nn	knee, nine, penny
|ng|	n, ng	think, ring
|ŏ|	a, o	was, pond

Sounds	Spellings	Sample Words
|ō|	ew, o, oa, oe, ough, ow	sew, most, hope, float, toe, though, row
|ô|	a, al, aw, o, ough	wall, talk, lawn, soft, brought
|ôr|	oor, or, ore	door, storm, store
|oi|	oi, oy	join, toy
|ou|	ou, ow	loud, now
|ŏŏ|	oo, ou	good, could
|ōō|	ew, o, oe, oo, ou, ough, ue	flew, do, shoe, spoon, you, through, blue
|p|	p, pp	paint, happen
|r|	r, wr	rub, write
|s|	c, s, ss	city, same, grass
|sh|	s, sh	sure, sheep
|t|	ed, t, tt	fixed, tall, kitten
|*th*|	th	they
|th|	th	thin, teeth
|ŭ|	o, oe, u	front, come, does, sun
|yōō|	u	use
|ûr|	ear, er, ir, or, ur	learn, herd, girl, word, turn
|v|	f, v	of, very
|w|	o, w	one, way
|y|	y	yes
|z|	s, z	please, zoo
|zh|	s	usual
|ə|	a, e, i, o, u	about, silent, pencil, lemon, circus

How to Use a Dictionary

Finding an Entry Word

Guide Words

The word you want to find in a dictionary is listed in ABC order. To find it quickly, turn to the part of the dictionary that has words with the same first letter. Use the guide words at the top of each page for help. Guide words name the first entry word and the last entry word on each page.

Base Words

To find a word ending in **-ed** or **-ing,** you usually must look up its base word. To find **chewed** or **chewing,** for example, look up the base word **chew.**

Reading an Entry

Read the dictionary entry below. Look carefully at each part of the entry.

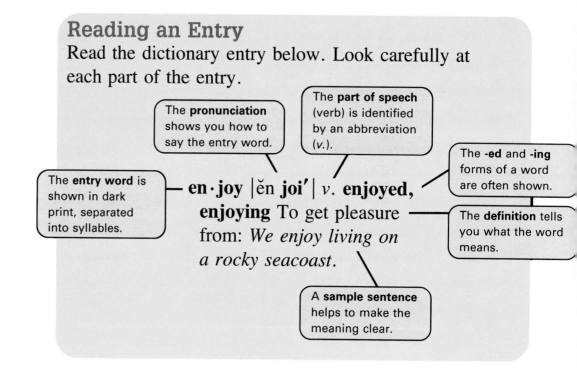

The **pronunciation** shows you how to say the entry word.

The **part of speech** (verb) is identified by an abbreviation (*v.*).

The **-ed** and **-ing** forms of a word are often shown.

The **entry word** is shown in dark print, separated into syllables.

en·joy |ĕn joi′| *v.* **enjoyed, enjoying** To get pleasure from: *We enjoy living on a rocky seacoast.*

The **definition** tells you what the word means.

A **sample sentence** helps to make the meaning clear.

Spelling Dictionary

A

a·ble |ā′ bəl| *adj.* **abler, ablest** Having what is needed to do something: *I will be able to see you tomorrow.*

a·bout |ə bout′| *prep.* Concerned with: *That book is about pets.*

ac·ro·bat |ăk′ rə băt′| *n., pl.* **acrobats** A person who can do stunts such as swinging from a trapeze or walking on a tightrope: *An acrobat rode a little bicycle across the tightrope.*

a·cross |ə krôs′| *prep.* To the other side of: *They rode bicycles across the park.*

act |ăkt| *n., pl.* **acts** One of the main parts of a play: *The first act takes place in a factory.*

a·dult |ə dŭlt′| or |ăd′ ŭlt′| *n., pl.* **adults** A person who is fully grown; grown-up. *Tickets for adults cost $3.00.*

af·ter |ăf′ tər| *prep.* Behind in place or order: *The clowns came after the elephants in the parade.* *conj.* Following the time that: *We can eat after we get home.*

a·gain |ə gĕn′| *adv.* Once more: *If you don't win this time, try again.*

age |āj| *n., pl.* **ages** The length of time someone or something has been alive: *Pablo's age is eight.*

a·go |ə gō′| *adj. and adv.* Before the present time: *They moved to Chicago five years ago.*

a·head |ə hĕd′| *adj. and adv.* In, at, or toward the front: *We moved ahead in line.*

air |âr| *n., pl.* **airs 1.** The colorless, odorless, tasteless mixture of gases that surrounds the earth: *We breathe air.* **2.** The open space above the earth: *The batter hit the ball high into the air.*

air·plane |âr′ plān′| *n., pl.* **airplanes** A vehicle with wings that can fly through the air. Airplanes are driven by propellers or jet engines.

Pronunciation Key

ă	pat	ŏ	pot	û	fur	
ā	pay	ō	go	*th*	the	
â	care	ô	paw, for	th	thin	
ä	father	oi	oil	hw	which	
ĕ	pet	o͞o	book	zh	usual	
ē	be	o͞o	boot	ə	ago, item	
ĭ	pit	yo͞o	cute		pencil, atom	
ī	ice	ou	out		circus	
î	near	ŭ	cut	ər	butter	

Abbreviation Key

n.	noun	*prep.*	preposition
v.	verb	*interj.*	interjection
adj.	adjective	*sing.*	singular
adv.	adverb	*pl.*	plural
pron.	pronoun	*p.*	past
conj.	conjunction	*p. part.*	past participle

a·live |ə līv′| *adj.* Living: *My grandfather is dead, but my grandmother is still alive.*

al·most |ôl′ mōst′| *adv.* Nearly; just short of: *The muffins are almost done.*

al·so |ôl′ sō| *adv.* Besides; too: *My watch tells time and gives the date also.*

a·mong |ə mŭng′| *prep.* In or through the middle of: *A tall apartment building stood among the low houses.*

an·gry |ăng′ grē| *adj.* **angrier, angriest** Feeling or showing that one is strongly displeased: *You say that you aren't angry, but your frown looks angry.*

an·i·mal |ăn′ ə məl| *n., pl.* **animals** A living being that is not a plant. Most animals move around and eat food: *People, horses, fish, and ants are all animals.*

an·y |ĕn′ ē| *adj.* One or some out of three or more: *Take any books that you want to read.*

a·part·ment |ə pärt′ mənt| *n., pl.* **apartments** One or more rooms used as a place to live: *Bill and his parents live in a two-bedroom apartment.*

ap·ple |ăp′ əl| *n., pl.* **apples** A red-skinned fruit.

A·pril |ā′ prəl| *n.* The fourth month of the year. April has 30 days.

a·pron |ā′ prən| *n., pl.* **aprons** A piece of clothing worn over the front of the body to protect the clothes underneath: *Meg wore an apron to keep her dress clean.*

are |är| *v.* **1.** Second person singular present tense of **be:** *You are my friend.* **2.** First, second, and third person plural present tense of **be:** *They are my grandparents.*

aren't |ärnt| Contraction of "are not:" *They aren't here yet.*

ar·gue |är′ gyōō| *v.* **argued, arguing** To discuss something with someone who has different ideas; disagree: *They argued about what color to paint the room.*

a·round |ə round′| *prep.* In a circle surrounding: *I wore a belt around my waist.*

art |ärt| *n., pl.* **arts** An activity, such as painting, in which something beautiful is made.

a·sleep |ə slēp′| *adj.* Not awake: *The baby is asleep in her crib.*

Au·gust |ô′ gəst| *n.* The eighth month of the year. August has 31 days.

aunt |ănt| or |änt| *n., pl.* **aunts** The sister of one's father or mother.

au·tumn |ô′ təm| *n., pl.* **autumns** The season of the year between summer and winter when many crops are harvested; fall.

a·way |ə wā′| *adv.* At or to a distance: *The lake is two miles away.*

B

ba·by |bā′ bē| *n., pl.* **babies** A very young child; infant. A baby grows up to be an adult.

bait |bāt| *n.* Food placed on a hook or in a trap to attract and catch fish, birds, or other animals: *We used worms as bait to catch fish.*

bal·loon |bə lōōn′| *n., pl.* **balloons** A small, bright-colored rubber bag that floats when filled with air or another gas.

band·age |băn′ dĭj| *n., pl.* **bandages** A strip of cloth used to cover and protect a cut or an injury: *We put a bandage on the puppy's scraped leg.*

bare |bâr| *adj.* **barer, barest** Without clothing or covering; naked: *The sand tickled my bare feet.*
♦ These sound alike **bare, bear.**

base |bās| *n., pl.* **bases** One of the four corners of a baseball diamond that a runner must touch to score a run: *She hit the baseball and ran to first base.*

base·ball |bās′ bôl′| *n., pl.* **baseballs** A game played with a bat and ball by two teams of nine players each. Baseball is played on a field with four bases. A run is scored when a player is able to touch all the bases while his or her team is at bat.

bas·ket |băs′ kĭt| *n., pl.* **baskets** A container made of woven grasses or strips of wood often used to carry things.

bath·robe |băth′ rōb′| or |bäth′ rōb′| *n., pl.* **bathrobes** A loose piece of clothing worn as a covering: *John put on his bathrobe and slippers.*

batter |băt′ ər| *n., pl.* **batters** A beaten mixture of flour, eggs, and milk or water that becomes solid when cooked. Batter is used to make pancakes and breads: *Let's mix the batter for pancakes.*

be |bē| *v.* To have a quality: *Jake and Pablo are always truthful.*

bear |bâr| *n., pl.* **bears** A large animal with a shaggy coat and a very short tail. Bears eat mainly fruit and insects.

♦ *These sound alike* **bear, bare.**

ă	pat	ŏ	pot	û	fur
ā	pay	ō	go	*th*	the
â	care	ô	paw, for	th	thin
ä	father	oi	oil	hw	which
ĕ	pet	ōo	book	zh	usual
ē	be	ōo	boot	ə	ago, item
ĭ	pit	yōo	cute		pencil, atom
ī	ice	ou	out		circus
î	near	ŭ	cut	ər	butter

be•cause |bĭ kôz′| *conj.* For the reason that: *I left because I was sick.*

be•come |bĭ kŭm′| *v.* **became, become, becoming** To grow or come to be: *It became cold when the sun set.*

been |bĭn| *v.* Past participle of **be:** *Anthony and I had already been at the bus station for an hour before Dad arrived.*

be•fore |bĭ fôr′| *adv.* Earlier: *Class ends at noon, not before. prep.* Ahead of; earlier than: *The dog got home before me.*

be•gin |bĭ gĭn′| *v.* **began, begun, beginning 1.** To start to do: *I began taking piano lessons last year.* **2.** To have as a starting point: *Proper nouns begin with capital letters.*

be•hind |bĭ hīnd′| *prep.* To or at the back of: *The apple trees are behind the barn. adv.* In the place or situation being left: *My friends stayed behind.*

be•long |bĭ lông′| *v.* **belonged, belonging** To be owned by: *That sweater belongs to Mary.*

bet•ter |bĕt′ ər| *adj.* Comparative of **good:** *This car is better than that one. adv.* Comparative of **well:** *My dog behaves better than Carla's does.*

be•tween |bĭ twēn′| *prep.* In the space separating: *A few trees stand between the house and the road.*

be•ware |bĭ wâr′| *v.* To be careful; look out: *Beware of the ice. It is slippery.*

be•yond |bĭ yŏnd′| *prep.* On or to the far side of: *The forest is beyond the lake.*

bird |bûrd| *n., pl.* **birds** A warm-blooded animal that lays eggs. A bird has two wings and a body covered with feathers.

birth•day |bûrth′ dā′| *n., pl.* **birthdays** The day of a person's birth.

bi•week•ly |bī wēk′ lē| *adv.* Once every two weeks: *I have a music lesson biweekly.*

black |blăk| *adj.* Of the darkest of all colors; the opposite of white.

blaze |blāz| *n., pl.* **blazes** A brightly burning fire: *The blaze destroyed two stores.*

bleach•ers |blē′ chərz| *pl. n.* Seats in rows placed one above another for people watching a sports event: *Three hundred fans sat in the bleachers watching the baseball game.*

blew |blōo| *v.* Past tense of **blow:** *A breeze blew the leaves all over the yard.*

♦ *These sound alike* **blew, blue.**

blood |blŭd| *n.* The liquid that the heart moves through the body. Blood carries oxygen to all parts of the body and carries away waste materials.

blow |blō| *v.* **blew, blown, blowing** To shape by pushing air into: *Can you blow a bubble?*

blue |blōo| *adj.* Having the color of a clear sky.

♦ *These sound alike* **blue, blew.**

board |bôrd| *n., pl.* **boards** A piece of sawed lumber; plank: *We nailed boards together to make a bookcase.*

boil |boil| *v.* **boiled, boiling** To cook in a very hot liquid: *Mom boiled the potatoes for twenty minutes.*

boot |bo͞ot| *n., pl.* **boots** A covering for the foot or shoe. A boot usually covers the ankle and often part of the leg: *Wear your boots when it's raining.*

both |bōth| *pron.* The one as well as the other; the two alike: *I talked to both of them. adj.* The two; the one as well as the other: *Both sides of the valley are steep.*

bought |bôt| *v.* Past tense and past participle of **buy**: *My little sister sold her tricycle and bought a bicycle.*

bounce |bouns| *v.* **bounced, bouncing 1.** To spring back after hitting a surface: *The ball bounced off the wall.* **2.** To cause to hit a surface and spring back: *I bounced a ball on the sidewalk.*

bow¹ |bō| *n., pl.* **bows** A weapon for shooting arrows.

bow² |bou| *v.* **bowed, bowing** To bend the body, head, or knee to show agreement or respect: *He bowed when he met the king. n., pl.* **bows** A bending of the body or head to show respect or thanks: *The jugglers took a bow at the end of the act.*

bow³ |bou| *n., pl.* **bows** The front part of a ship or a boat.

boy |boi| *n., pl.* **boys** A young male person: *The boy helped the girl carry a large box.*

brag |brăg| *v.* **bragged, bragging** To speak with too much pride about oneself: *She bragged about her grades until no one would listen anymore.*

branch |brănch| *n., pl.* **branches** A part that grows out from a trunk or stem of a plant: *The lowest branch of the tree is covered with buds.*

bread |brĕd| *n., pl.* **breads** A food made from flour that is mixed with water or milk, kneaded, and baked: *Use two slices of bread to make a sandwich.*

breathe |brēth| *v.* **breathed, breathing** To take air into the lungs and force it out: *Runners need to breathe deeply.*

bright |brīt| *adj.* **brighter, brightest** Giving off or filled with a lot of light; shining: *The bright sun lit up the meadow.*

bright·en |brīt'n| *v.* **brightened, brightening** To give off or fill with light; to make brighter: *Sunlight brightened the room.*

bright·ly |brīt' lē| *adv.* In a shining way: *The sun shone brightly on the water.*

bright·ness |brīt' nĭs| *n.* The quality of being bright: *The brightness of the headlights shone through the night.*

bring |brĭng| *v.* **brought, bringing** To take with oneself: *Bring the books home.*

broth·er |brŭth' ər| *n., pl.* **brothers** A boy or man having the same mother and father as another person.

brought |brôt| *v.* Past tense and past participle of **bring**: *She brought her homework with her.*

brush |brŭsh| *n., pl.* **brushes** A tool for taking care of the hair. A brush is made of bristles or wire fastened to a hard back or a short handle.

build |bĭld| *v.* **built, building** To make by putting together parts; construct: *Carpenters build houses and stores.*

bum·ble·bee |bŭm' bəl bē'| *n., pl.* **bumblebees** A large, black and yellow bee that flies with a humming sound.

bump·y |bŭm' pē| *adj.* **bumpier, bumpiest** Causing jerks and jolts: *He tripped on the bumpy sidewalk.*

burn |bûrn| *v.* **burned** *or* **burnt, burning 1.** To be or set on fire: *The logs burned in the fireplace.* **2.** To be or cause to be hurt by heat or fire: *I burned my fingers with a match.*

burnt |bûrnt| *v.* A past tense and past participle of **burn:** *The pizza was burnt, so we couldn't eat it.*

but·ter |bŭt′ ər| *n., pl.* **butters** A soft, yellowish fatty food that is made from milk or cream.

but·ton |bŭt′ n| *n., pl.* **buttons 1.** A disk used to fasten together parts of a piece of clothing. **2.** A part that looks like a button: *I pushed the button to turn on the light. v.* **buttoned, buttoning** To fasten or close with buttons: *Don't forget to button your coat.*

buy |bī| *v.* **bought, buying** To get by paying for: *We bought the car that Mickey was selling. n., pl.* **buys** Something bought at a lower price than usual; bargain: *The coat was a good buy.*

buzz |bŭz| *v.* **buzzed, buzzing** To make a low, humming sound like that of a bee: *The alarm clock buzzed.*

ă	pat	ŏ	pot	û	fur
ā	pay	ō	go	*th*	the
â	care	ô	paw, for	th	thin
ä	father	oi	oil	hw	which
ĕ	pet	o͝o	book	zh	usual
ē	be	o͞o	boot	ə	ago, item
ĭ	pit	yo͞o	cute		pencil, atom
ī	ice	ou	out		circus
î	near	ŭ	cut	ər	butter

C

cack·le |kăk′ əl| *v.* **cackled, cackling** To make a shrill sound, such as a hen makes.

calf |kăf| *n., pl.* **calves** A young cow or bull.

calm·ly |käm′ lē| *adv.* Not excitedly; without being nervous.

can |kăn| *helping v.* **1.** Have the knowledge or skill to: *You can skate well.* **2.** Be able to: *I can lift those books.*

ca·nar·y |kə nâr′ ē| *n., pl.* **canaries** A songbird, often yellow in color, that can be kept as a pet in a cage.

can·not |kăn′ ŏt| or |kă nŏt′| *v.* Can not: *Sue has lost her money and cannot find it.*

can't |kănt| Contraction of "can not": *I can't untie this knot.*

care |kâr| *n., pl.* **cares** The responsibility of keeping well and safe: *Are you in the doctor's care? v.* **cared, caring** To keep well and safe: *I know how to care for a puppy.*

care·ful |kâr′ fəl| *adj.* Taking the necessary care; not careless: *She is careful when she crosses the street.*

car·ry |kăr′ ē| *v.* **carried, carrying 1.** To take from one place to another: *Dad carried the groceries into the house.* **2.** To hold up the weight of; support: *These posts carry the weight of the porch roof.*

cast |kăst| *n., pl.* **casts** The actors in a play or a movie: *The cast took a bow at the end of the play.*

catch |kăch| *v.* **caught, catching 1.** To get hold of or grasp something that is moving: *I'll throw the ball, and you catch it.* **2.** To come upon suddenly; surprise: *The wolf caught the deer in a small meadow.*

caught |kôt| *v.* Past tense and past participle of **catch:** *She caught the ball that he threw.*

cav·i·ty |kăv′ ĭ tē| *n., pl.* **cavities** A hole: *The dentist filled the cavity in my tooth.*

cen·ter |sĕn′ tər| *n., pl.* **centers** The middle position, part, or place: *Put the vase of flowers in the center of the table.*

cer·tain |sûr′ tn| *adj.* Having no doubt; sure: *Are you certain that you left the book on the bus?*

chair |châr| *n., pl.* **chairs** A piece of furniture made for sitting on. A chair has a seat, a back, and usually four legs. Some chairs have arms.

char·coal |chär′ kōl′| *n., pl.* **charcoals** A black material made of carbon. Charcoal is made by heating wood or other plant or animal material. Charcoal is often used for cooking outdoors.

check | contest

---

check |chĕk| *v.* **checked, checking** To test, to make sure something is correct; review: *Check your answers after doing the arithmetic problems.*

chew |choo| *v.* **chewed, chewing** To crush or wear away with the teeth: *Always chew your food well.*

chick |chĭk| *n., pl.* **chicks** A young chicken or bird.

child |chīld| *n., pl.* **children** A young boy or girl: *I'm a child now, but I will grow up to be an adult.*

chop |chŏp| *v.* **chopped, chopping** To cut by hitting with a heavy, sharp tool, such as an ax: *I chopped the wood into pieces.*

cir·cle |sûr′ kəl| *n., pl.* **circles** Something that is more or less round: *There is a circle of children around the clown.*

cir·cus |sûr′ kəs| *n., pl.* **circuses** A colorful traveling show with acrobats, clowns, and trained animals.

cit·y |sĭt′ ē| *n., pl.* **cities** A place where many people live close to one another. Cities are larger than towns.

class |klăs| *n., pl.* **classes** 1. A group of students who learn together at the same time: *Mr. Raymond teaches my class.* 2. The time that such a class meets: *No talking is allowed during class.*

clay |klā| *n., pl.* **clays** A firm kind of earth made up of small pieces. Clay is soft when wet, and it can be formed into shapes: *We used clay to make pots in art class.*

clear |klîr| *adj.* **clearer, clearest** 1. Free from clouds, mist, or dust: *Today the sky was clear.* 2. Free from anything that makes it hard to see through: *We could see fish in the clear water.*

cloth |klôth| *n., pl.* **cloths** 1. Material made by weaving together threads of cotton, wool, silk, linen, or manmade fibers. 2. A piece of cloth used for a special purpose, such as a tablecloth or a washcloth.

cloud |kloud| *n., pl.* **clouds** A white or gray object in the sky made up of tiny drops of water or ice floating high in the air: *A rain cloud drifted toward us.*

clown |kloun| *n., pl.* **clowns** A performer in a circus who does tricks or funny stunts.

coach |kōch| *n., pl.* **coaches** A person who trains or teaches athletes, teams, or performers: *The baseball coach showed Tammy how to hold the bat.*

coat |kōt| *n., pl.* **coats** A piece of clothing with sleeves, usually worn outdoors. It is worn over other clothing.

coin |koin| *n., pl.* **coins** A piece of metal used as money, such as a penny or a dime.

cold |kōld| *adj.* **colder, coldest** 1. Being at a low temperature: *The water was cold.* 2. Chilly: *I was cold without my coat.*

col·lar |kŏl′ ər| *n., pl.* **collars** The part of a piece of clothing that fits around the neck. 2. A leather or metal band for the neck of an animal: *Attach the dog's leash to its collar.*

col·or |kŭl′ ər| *n., pl.* **colors** A tint other than black or white: *This picture includes all the colors of the rainbow.* *v.* **colored, coloring** To give color to: *Color the truck red with a crayon.*

come |kŭm| *v.* **came, come, coming** 1. To move toward the speaker or toward a place: *The children came home quickly when they were called for dinner.* 2. To reach a particular condition: *The plants came to life after we watered them.*

com·pare |kəm pâr′| *v.* **compared, comparing** To study in order to see how things are the same or different: *We compared bees and spiders.*

com·plete |kəm plēt′| *adj.* Having all that is necessary: *A complete chess set has 32 pieces and a board.*

con·cert |kŏn′ sûrt| *n., pl.* **concerts** A musical performance given by one or more musicians.

con·test |kŏn′ tĕst′| *n., pl.* **contests** A struggle between two or more people to win, usually for a prize: *Jan won the spelling contest and received a blue ribbon.*

cook |kŏŏk| *n., pl.* **cooks** A person who prepares food: *The cook put the meat in the oven.*

ă	pat	ŏ	pot	û	fur
ā	pay	ō	go	*th*	**the**
â	care	ô	paw, for	th	thin
ä	father	oi	oil	hw	which
ĕ	pet	ŏŏ	book	zh	usual
ē	be	ōō	boot	ə	ago, item
ĭ	pit	yōō	cute		pencil, atom
ī	ice	ou	out		circus
î	near	ŭ	cut	ər	butter

cool |kōol| *adj.* **cooler, coolest** Somewhat cold: *It was a cool fall day.*

cop•y |kŏp´ ē| *v.* **copied, copying** To make something that is exactly like something else: *I copied the address so I would not forget it.*

cost |kôst| *n., pl.* **costs** The amount paid for something; price: *The cost of the tickets was $15.00.* *v.* **cost, costing** To have as a price: *The tickets cost $15.00 each.*

cos•tume |kŏs´ tōōm´| or |kôs´ tyōōm´| *n., pl.* **costumes** Clothes worn by a person playing a part in a play or movie: *We wore dog costumes in the school play.*

cough |kôf| *v.* **coughed, coughing** To force air from the lungs with a sudden sharp noise: *The smoky campfire made Jan cough.*

could |kŏŏd| or |kəd| *v.* Past tense of **can:** *He could watch the baseball game on television if he wanted to.*

could•n't |kŏŏd´ nt| Contraction of "could not:" *They couldn't find their boots.*

count |kount| *v.* **counted, counting 1.** To find the total of; add up: *Count your change.* **2.** To name numbers in order: *We counted from 1 to 10.*

cour•age |kûr´ ĭj| *n.* Bravery: *The firefighter showed courage when she saved a child from the burning house.*

crack |krăk| *v.* **cracked, cracking 1.** To break with a sudden sharp sound: *We cracked the ice.* **2.** To break without splitting into parts: *The mirror cracked.*

cray•on |krā´ ŏn´| or |krā´ ən| *n., pl.* **crayons** A coloring stick: *She drew a bird with her blue crayon.*

crisp |krĭsp| *adj.* **crisper, crispest** Firm but breaks easily; not soggy: *The crisp celery made a crunching sound when we ate it.*

crook•ed |krŏŏk´ ĭd| *adj.* Not straight.

crop |krŏp| *n., pl.* **crops** A plant that is grown and harvested: *Corn and wheat are important farm crops.*

crowd |kroud| *n., pl.* **crowds** A large number of people gathered together: *A crowd waited for the train.*

crown |kroun| *n., pl.* **crowns 1.** A head covering, often made of gold and jewels. A crown is worn by a king or queen. **2.** The top part: *We climbed toward the crown of the hill.*

crumb |krŭm| *n., pl.* **crumbs** A tiny piece of food, especially of bread or cake.

cry |krī| *v.* **cried, crying 1.** To shed tears; weep: *We cried at the end of the sad story.* **2.** To make a special sound or call, as an animal does.

cub |kŭb| *n., pl.* **cubs** A young bear, wolf, or lion.

cube |kyōōb| *n., pl.* **cubes 1.** A solid shape that has six square faces of equal size. **2.** Something having this shape: *Put the ice cubes in your water.*

cup |kŭp| *n., pl.* **cups** A measurement equal to sixteen tablespoons or half a pint.

D

dai·sy |dā′ zē| *n., pl.* **daisies** A plant that has flowers with narrow white, yellow, or pink petals around a yellow center: *We picked a bunch of daisies.*

damp |dămp| *adj.* **damper, dampest** Slightly wet; moist: *The clothes were not quite dry; they were still damp.*

dance |dăns| *v.* **danced, dancing** To move in time to music. *n., pl.* **dances** A set of steps and motions, usually performed to music: *I learned a new square dance.*

dark |därk| *adj.* **darker, darkest** Of a deep shade close to black or brown: *Your eyes are a dark color. n.* Lack of light: *Cats' eyes adjust quickly to the dark.*

daugh·ter |dô′ tər| *n., pl.* **daughters** A female child: *Mrs. Harris has two daughters and one son.*

day |dā| *n., pl.* **days** The time of light between sunrise and sunset.

De·cem·ber |dĭ sĕm′ bər| *n.* The twelfth month of the year. December has 31 days.

de·light |dĭ līt′| *n., pl.* **delights 1.** Great pleasure: *The baby laughed with delight.* **2.** Something that gives pleasure: *The birthday party was a delight.*

den·tist |dĕn′ tĭst| *n., pl.* **dentists** A person who takes care of teeth: *The dentist showed me how to floss my teeth.*

de·stroy |dĭ stroi′| *v.* **destroyed, destroying** To ruin completely: *The fire destroyed several homes.*

die |dī| *v.* **died, dying** To stop living; become dead: *The flowers died in the spring snowstorm.*

di·rec·tion |dĭ rĕk′ shən| *n., pl.* **directions** An instruction or order: *Follow the directions on the package.*

dirt |dûrt| *n.* **1.** Earth or soil. **2.** Something filthy, such as mud.

dish |dĭsh| *n., pl.* **dishes 1.** A flat or shallow container for holding food. **2.** Food prepared in a certain way: *Soup is my favorite dish in the winter.*

do |dōō| *v.* **did, done, doing, does 1.** To carry out an action: *I don't know what to do.* **2.** To act or behave: *Do as I say.*

dodge |dŏj| *v.* **dodged, dodging 1.** To move quickly to the side: *The quarterback dodged and ran for a touchdown.* **2.** To keep away from someone or something by moving quickly: *I dodged the snowballs thrown at me.*

does |dŭz| *v.* Third person singular present tense of **do:** *How does Chris do his homework so quickly?*

dol·lar |dŏl′ ər| *n., pl.* **dollars** A unit of money equal to 100 cents.

door |dôr| *n., pl.* **doors** A movable panel at the entrance to a room, building, or vehicle: *Who is at the back door?*

draw |drô| *v.* **drew, drawn, drawing** To make a picture with lines; sketch.

drew |drōō| *v.* Past tense of **draw:** *She drew a picture of her family.*

drop |drŏp| *n., pl.* **drops** A small bit of liquid in a round mass: *A drop of sweat ran down my face. v.* **dropped, dropping 1.** To fall or let fall in drops. **2.** To fall or let fall: *I dropped a dish on the floor.*

drum |drŭm| *n., pl.* **drums** A musical instrument that is hollow and has a thin layer of material stretched across one or both ends: *She plays the drum in our marching band.*

dry |drī| *v.* **dried, drying** To make or become free from water or moisture: *Jill dried the wet puppy with a towel.*

dry·er |drī′ ər| *n., pl.* **dryers** A device that removes moisture: *Use a hair dryer and brush to style your hair.*

duck·ling |dŭk′ lĭng| *n., pl.* **ducklings** A young duck.

E

ă	pat	ŏ	pot	û	fur
ā	pay	ō	go	*th*	the
â	care	ô	paw, for	th	thin
ä	father	oi	oil	hw	which
ĕ	pet	ōō	book	zh	usual
ē	be	ōō	boot	ə	ago, item
ĭ	pit	yōō	cute		pencil, atom
ī	ice	ou	out		circus
î	near	ŭ	cut	ər	butter

ear |îr| *n., pl.* **ears 1.** The part of the body with which people and animals hear. **2.** The sense of hearing: *The sound of music is pleasant to the ear.*

ear·ly |ûr′ lē| *adv.* **earlier, earliest** Before the usual or expected time: *The plane landed earlier than planned.*

ea·sel |ē′ zəl| *n., pl.* **easels** A stand for holding a painting: *The artist placed her picture on an easel.*

ef·fort |ĕf′ ərt| *n., pl.* **efforts** A sincere attempt; try: *Please make an effort to arrive on time.*

eight |āt| *n., pl.* **eights** A number, written 8, that is equal to the sum of 7 + 1. *adj.* Being one more than seven.

el·e·phant |ĕl′ ə fənt| *n., pl.* **elephants** A very large land animal with a long, bendable trunk and long, curved tusks: *Elephants are the biggest land animals.*

emp·ty |ĕmp′ tē| *adj.* Having nothing inside: *Fill the empty jar with orange juice.*

en·joy |ĕn joi′| *v.* **enjoyed, enjoying** To get pleasure from: *We enjoy living on a rocky seacoast.*

en·joy·a·ble |ĕn joi′ ə bəl| *adj.* Giving joy or happiness: *We had an enjoyable trip to the zoo.*

en·joy·ment |ĕn joi′ mənt| *n., pl.* **enjoyments** The act or condition of enjoying something: *Luis gets great enjoyment from his stamp collection.*

e·nough |ĭ nŭf′| *adj.* Being as much or as many as needed: *There is enough food for everybody. adv.* To or in the amount needed: *You know them well enough to believe what they say.*

en·trance |ĕn′ trəns| *n., pl.* **entrances** A door or opening: *We used the back entrance to the theater.*

-er A suffix that forms nouns. The suffix "-er" means "a person who": *teacher.*

es·cape |ĭ skāp′| *v.* **escaped, escaping** To get free; to get away from: *The dogs escaped by jumping over the fence.*

ev·er |ĕv′ ər| *adv.* In any way: *How could I ever forget that day?*

eve·ry·bod·y |ĕv′ rē bŏd′ ē| *pron.* Every person; everyone: *Everybody makes a mistake sometime.*

ex·pect |ĭk spĕkt′| *v.* **expected, expecting** To look for as likely to happen or appear; await: *The farmers expect an early frost this year.*

ex·plode |ĭk splōd′| *v.* **exploded, exploding** To burst with a loud noise; blow up: *Suddenly the gas tank exploded.*

eye |ī| *n., pl.* **eyes** The organ of sight in people and animals: *I wear glasses because my left eye is weak.*

♦ *These sound alike* **eye, I.**

F

fa·ble |fā′ bəl| *n., pl.* **fables** A story that is meant to teach a lesson. A fable often has animal characters that speak and act like human beings.

face |fās| *n., pl.* **faces** The front part of the head from the forehead to the chin.

fair |fâr| *n., pl.* **fairs** A showing of farm and home products, often together with entertainment, such as a Ferris wheel.
♦ *These sound alike* **fair, fare.**

fare |fâr| *n., pl.* **fares** The money a person must pay to travel on a plane, train, or bus.
♦ *These sound alike* **fare, fair.**

farm·er |fär′ mər| *n., pl.* **farmers** A person who raises crops or animals on a farm: *The farmer fed his chickens, cows, pigs, and ducks.*

fawn |fôn| *n., pl.* **fawns** A young deer.

Feb·ru·ar·y |fĕb′ rōō ĕr′ ē| or |fĕb′ yōō ĕr′ ē| *n.* The second month of the year. February has 28 days except in leap year when it has 29.

feel |fēl| *v.* **felt, feeling 1.** To notice by using the sense of touch: *I feel leaves brushing against my cheek.* **2.** To notice being in a certain condition: *I feel sleepy.*

field |fēld| *n., pl.* **fields 1.** A broad area of open or cleared land. **2.** An area of land where a crop is grown or a special activity is done: *They practiced kicking on the football field.*

fight |fīt| *n., pl.* **fights 1.** A meeting between animals, persons, or groups in which each side, using bodies or weapons, tries to hurt the other: *One dog bit the other during the fight.* **2.** An angry disagreement; argument: *They had a fight about whose turn it was.* *v.* **fought, fighting** A hard struggle or effort: *I was so tired that I had to fight to stay awake.*

find |fīnd| *v.* **found, finding** To look for and discover: *Please help me find my pen.*

fin·ish |fĭn′ ĭsh| *n., pl.* **finishes** The end: *The finish of the race was exciting.*

first |fîrst| *adj.* Coming before all others: *The first house on the block is nicer than the last one.* *adv.* Before all others: *I'll go first, and you follow.*

fish·ing rod |fĭsh′ ĭng rŏd| *n., pl.* **fishing rods** A long, slender rod or stick with a hook, a line, and often a reel, used for catching fish: *I caught two fish with my fishing rod.*

fix |fĭks| *v.* **fixed, fixing** To repair.

flair |flâr| *n., pl.* **flairs** A natural talent: *She has a flair for painting with bright colors.*

flaw |flô| *n., pl.* **flaws** A mistake: *There was a flaw in the beautiful vase, so Mom returned it.*

flew |flōō| *v.* Past tense of **fly**[1]: *The plane flew over the ocean.*

float |flōt| *v.* **floated, floating** To be held up in or at the top of water or air: *Balloons floated in the air.*

floss |flôs| *n., pl.* **flosses** A strong thread used to clean between the teeth: *She uses a toothbrush, toothpaste, and floss to clean her teeth.*

flour |flour| *n., pl.* **flours** A fine powder made by grinding wheat or another grain. Flour is used for making bread and muffins: *You need eggs, milk, and flour to make pancakes.*

flow·er |flou′ ər| *n., pl.* **flowers** A plant that usually has colorful petals: *Roses and daisies are flowers.*

fly¹ |flī| *v.* **flew, flown, flying** To move through the air with wings.

fly² |flī| *n., pl.* **flies** An insect, such as the common housefly, that has a single pair of thin, clear wings.

fog |fôg| *n., pl.* **fogs** A cloud of water droplets floating near the ground: *There was so much fog that we could hardly see the road.*

foil¹ |foil| *v.* **foiled, foiling** To keep from success: *The alarm foiled the thief.*

foil² |foil| *n., pl.* **foils** A thin sheet of metal: *Wrap the meat in foil.*

fold |fōld| *v.* **folded, folding** To bend or double over so that one part lies over another: *I have to fold the clothes in the dryer and put them away.*

fol·low |fŏl′ ō| *v.* **followed, following 1.** To go or come after: *The ducklings followed their mother to the pond.* **2.** To take the same path as: *I followed the trail for a mile.* **3.** To come after in order or time: *Night follows day.*

foot |foŏt| *n., pl.* **feet** The part of the leg of a person or an animal on which it stands or walks.

for·est |fôr′ ĭst| *n., pl.* **forests** A large growth of trees: *Many wild animals live in the forest.*

for·get |fər gĕt′| *v.* **forgot, forgotten** *or* **forgot, forgetting** To be unable to remember: *I forgot my friend's new address.*

fought |fôt| *v.* Past tense and past participle of **fight**: *My dog was hurt when it fought with another dog.*

ă	pat	ŏ	pot	û	fur
ā	pay	ō	go	*th*	the
â	care	ô	paw, for	th	thin
ä	father	oi	oil	hw	which
ĕ	pet	oŏ	book	zh	usual
ē	be	ōō	boot	ə	ago, item
ĭ	pit	yōō	cute		pencil, atom
ī	ice	ou	out		circus
î	near	ŭ	cut	ər	butter

fourth |fôrth| *adj.* Coming after the third: *Tuesday is the third day of the week, and Wednesday is the fourth day.*

frame |frām| *v.* **framed, framing** To enclose in or as if in a frame: *A border of tulips framed the garden.*

freck·le |frĕk′ əl| *n., pl.* **freckles** A small brown spot on the skin: *Antonio has freckles on his arms.*

freeze |frēz| *v.* **froze, frozen, freezing** To hurt or to kill by cold: *This snow will freeze the flowers.*

Fri·day |frī′ dē| *or* |frī′ dā| *n., pl.* **Fridays** The sixth day of the week.

friend |frĕnd| *n., pl.* **friends** A person one knows, likes, and enjoys being with.

friend·ly |frĕnd′ lē| *adj.* **friendlier, friendliest 1.** Showing friendship; not unfriendly: *My new neighbor gave me a friendly smile.* **2.** Liking to meet and to talk with others: *A friendly guide asked us if we needed more directions.*

front |frŭnt| *n., pl.* **fronts** The area directly ahead of the forward part: *The front of the theater is on Main Street. adj.* In or facing the forward part: *The front door is locked.*

frown |froun| *v.* **frowned, frowning** To wrinkle the forehead to show that one is unhappy or puzzled: *Mom frowned at the mess.*

-ful A suffix that forms adjectives. The suffix "-ful" means "full of" or "having": *beautiful.*

full |foŏl| *adj.* **fuller, fullest** Holding as much as possible; filled: *Water ran down the side of the full bucket.*

fun•ny |fŭn′ ē| *adj.* **funnier, funniest**
1. Causing amusement or laughter.
2. Strange; odd: *I heard a funny noise.*

G

gal•lon |găl′ ən| *n., pl.* **gallons** A measurement equal to four quarts: *Tina bought a gallon of milk at the store.*

gar•den |gär′ dn| *n., pl.* **gardens** A piece of land where flowers, vegetables, or fruit are grown.

gib•bon |gĭb′ ən| *n., pl.* **gibbons** A small ape of southeastern Asia. Gibbons live in trees and swing from branch to branch with their long arms.

gi•raffe |jĭ răf′| *n., pl.* **giraffes** A tall African animal with short horns, very long neck and legs, and a tan coat with brown spots.

girl |gûrl| *n., pl.* **girls** A young female person: *The girl greeted her friends.*

give |gĭv| *v.* **gave, given, giving** **1.** To make a gift of: *My sister gave me a new watch.* **2.** To pay: *Sid will give me fifteen dollars for my old bike.*

glad |glăd| *adj.* **gladder, gladdest** **1.** Bringing joy or pleasure: *The letter brought glad news.* **2.** Pleased; happy: *We were glad to be home again.*

go |gō| *v.* **went, gone, going, goes** To move away from a place; leave.

gog•gles |gŏg′ əlz| *pl. n.* A pair of glasses worn to protect the eyes against water, dust, wind, or sparks: *The welder wore goggles when he used a blowtorch.*

good |good| *adj.* **better, best** **1.** Suitable for a particular use: *Crayons are good for drawing.* **2.** Not weakened or damaged: *The old dog's hearing is still good.*

grade |grād| *n., pl.* **grades** **1.** A class or year in a school: *The twins will enter the fourth grade next fall.* **2.** A mark showing what kind of work a student does: *I got a good grade in science.*

grand•fa•ther |grănd′ fä′ thər| *n., pl.* **grandfathers** The father of one's father or mother.

grand•moth•er |grănd′ mŭth′ ər| *n., pl.* **grandmothers** The mother of one's father or mother.

green |grēn| *n., pl.* **greens** The color of most plant leaves and growing grass. *adj.* **greener, greenest** Of the color green.

grew |groo| *v.* Past tense of **grow**: *The puppies grew into large dogs.*

grill |grĭl| *n., pl.* **grills** A cooking device on which food, such as meat or fish, may be broiled: *We cooked hamburgers on the grill.*

grin |grĭn| *v.* **grinned, grinning** To smile: *The child grinned with delight at the birthday present.*

ground |ground| *n., pl.* **grounds** The solid surface of the earth; land: *We sat on a blanket on the ground.*

grow |grō| *v.* **grew, grown, growing** To become larger in size: *Our class studied how plants grow.*

gum |gŭm| *n., pl.* **gums** The firm flesh that is around the teeth: *Using dental floss will help keep your gums healthy.*

gym |jĭm| *n., pl.* **gyms** A room for indoor sports and exercise: *Sharon, Louise, Lee, and I sometimes play basketball or volleyball in the gym after school.*

H

hair |hâr| *n., pl.* **hairs** A covering of fine, thin strands that grow from the skin: *Lou has curly red hair.*
♦ *These sound alike* **hair, hare.**

ham•bur•ger |hăm′ bûr gər| *n., pl.* **hamburgers** A patty of fried or broiled ground beef, usually served in a roll or bun: *Dad cooked hamburgers for dinner.*

hap•pen |hăp′ ən| *v.* **happened, happening** To take place; occur: *Tell me everything that happened today.*

hard |härd| *adj.* and *adv.* **harder, hardest 1.** Not bending when pushed; firm: *The steel blade is hard.* **2.** Having much force: *I suddenly felt a hard wind on my back, and it almost knocked me over.*

hare |hâr| *n., pl.* **hares** An animal that looks like a rabbit, but has longer ears and larger back feet.

♦ *These sound alike* **hare, hair.**

ă	pat	ŏ	pot	û	fur
ā	pay	ō	go	*th*	*the*
â	care	ô	paw, for	th	thin
ä	father	oi	oil	hw	which
ĕ	pet	o͝o	book	zh	usual
ē	be	o͞o	boot	ə	ago, item
ĭ	pit	yo͞o	cute		pencil, atom
ī	ice	ou	out		circus
î	near	ŭ	cut	ər	butter

have |hăv| *v.* **had, having, has 1.** To own: *I have a bicycle.* **2.** To contain: *A year has 365 days.* **3.** To hold in one's mind: *I have my doubts.* **4.** To go through; to experience: *I have a cold.*

head |hĕd| *n., pl.* **heads** The top part of the body, containing the brain, eyes, ears, nose, mouth, and jaws.

hear |hîr| *v.* **heard, hearing** To take in sounds through the ear: *We heard a dog barking.*

♦ *These sound alike* **hear, here.**

heat |hēt| *n., pl.* **heats** The condition of being hot; warmth: *I could feel the heat of the sun on my back.*

hel•lo |hĕ lō′| or |hə lō′| or |hĕl′ ō| *interj.* A word used as a greeting.

help |hĕlp| *v.* **helped, helping 1.** To give or do what is needed or useful: *I helped my parents with the dishes.* **2.** To give relief from: *This medicine will help your cold.*

help•er |hĕlp′ ər| *n., pl.* **helpers** Someone or something that helps: *My dad needs a helper at the gas station.*

her |hûr| *pron.* The objective case of **she:** *Do you see her? adj.* Relating or belonging to her: *Where did she put her hat?*

here |hîr| *adv.* At or in this place: *Put the package here.*

♦ *These sound alike* **here, hear.**

her•self |hər sĕlf′| *pron.* Her own self: *She blamed herself.*

he's |hēz| Contraction of "he is" or "he has": *He's my best friend.*

him•self |hĭm sĕlf′| *pron.* His own self: *He found himself in a strange place.*

hiss |hĭs| *v.* **hissed, hissing** A sound like a long *s,* such as a snake makes.

hive |hīv| *n., pl.* **hives** A home for honeybees: *The beekeeper has dozens of hives filled with honeybees.*

hold |hōld| *v.* **held, holding** To have or keep in the arms or hands without dropping: *The baby is learning to hold a cup.*

home run |hōm′ rŭn′| *n., pl.* **home runs** A hit in baseball that allows the batter to touch all bases and score a run: *The fans cheered when he hit a home run.*

hon•ey |hŭn′ ē| *n., pl.* **honeys** A sweet thick liquid that bees make from flowers and use as food: *Mom usually uses honey instead of sugar to sweeten foods.*

hook |ho͝ok| *n., pl.* **hooks** A bent object, often made of metal, that is used to catch, hold, or pull something: *A fish bit the hook at the end of my fishing line.*

hope |hōp| *v.* **hoped, hoping** To wish and at the same time expect that the wish will come true: *He hopes that he will do well on the test.*

hopeful | joyous

hope•ful |hōp′ fəl| *adj.* Feeling or showing hope.

ho•tel |hō tĕl′| *n., pl.* **hotels** A house or building where travelers pay to live and eat: *Dad stays in a hotel when he goes away on business.*

hour |our| *n., pl.* **hours** A unit of time that is equal to 60 minutes: *There are 24 hours in a day.*
  ◆ *These sound alike* **hour, our.**

house |hous| *n., pl.* **houses** A building people live in: *We moved into our new house.*

huge |hyōoj| *adj.* **huger, hugest** Very big; enormous.

hunt |hŭnt| *v.* **hunted, hunting** To make a careful search: *Help me hunt for my glasses. n., pl.* **hunts** A careful search: *The hunt for my lost keys was a success.*

hur•ry |hûr′ ē| *v.* **hurried, hurrying 1.** To act or move quickly; rush: *Do not hurry through your work.* **2.** To take, send, or move quickly: *The doctor hurried the patient to the hospital.*

hurt |hûrt| *v.* **hurt, hurting 1.** To cause pain or injury to: *I fell and hurt my wrist.* **2.** To have a bad effect on: *The dogs can't hurt that old couch.*

I

I |ī| *pron.* The person who is the speaker or writer: *I like cats a lot, but cats don't seem to like me.*
  ◆ *These sound alike* **I, eye.**

i•ci•cle |ī′ sĭ kəl| *n., pl.* **icicles** A thin, pointed, hanging piece of ice.

I'd |īd| Contraction of "I had," "I would," or "I should": *I'd rather leave now, not later.*

I'm |īm| Contraction of "I am": *I'm ready to go.*

in•sect |ĭn′ sĕkt′| *n., pl.* **insects** An animal that has six legs, a body with three main parts, and usually wings. Flies, bees, grasshoppers, and butterflies are insects.

in•side |ĭn′ sīd′| or |ĭn sīd′| *adj.* Inner or interior: *This jacket has an inside pocket. adv.* **1.** Into; within: *I'm staying inside because of my cold.* **2.** On the inner side: *I scrubbed the tub inside and out until it was clean.*

in•vite |ĭn vīt′| *v.* **invited, inviting** To ask someone to come somewhere to do something: *How many guests did you invite to the party?*

is•n't |ĭz′ ənt| Contraction of "is not": *That isn't my dog.*

its |ĭts| *adj.* Belonging to it: *Everything was in its place.*
  ◆ *These sound alike* **its, it's.**

it's |ĭts| Contraction of "it is" or "it has": *It's raining.*
  ◆ *These sound alike* **it's, its.**

J

Jan•u•ar•y |jăn′ yōo ĕr′ ē| *n.* The first month of the year. January has 31 days.

jar |jär| *n., pl.* **jars** A container with a wide opening. Jars are usually made of glass, pottery, or plastic.

jeans |jēnz| *pl. n.* Pants usually made of a strong blue cloth.

job |jŏb| *n., pl.* **jobs** A piece of work; task: *Who gets the job of sweeping the floor?*

join |join| *v.* **joined, joining 1.** To enter into the company of: *Please join us for lunch.* **2.** To become a member of: *I would like to join the club.*

joke |jōk| *v.* **joked, joking** To say or do something funny: *I was only joking when I said that.*

joy |joi| *n., pl.* **joys 1.** A feeling of great happiness or delight: *We felt joy at being with our family again.* **2.** A cause of joy: *It was a joy to see Mom feeling better.*

joy•ful |joi′ fəl| *adj.* Feeling, showing, or causing joy: *Grandpa's birthday was a joyful family event.*

joy•ous |joi′ əs| *adj.* Joyful.

judge |jŭj| *n., pl.* **judges 1.** A person who listens to and decides about cases in a court of law. **2.** A person who decides the winner of a contest or race. *v.* **judged, judging** To decide; to settle a contest or a problem: *Craig will judge the art contest.*

jug‧gler |jŭg′ lər| *n., pl.* **jugglers** A person who tosses things into the air and catches them to entertain people: *The juggler tossed four balls and a plate into the air.*

Ju‧ly |jo͞o lī′| *n.* The seventh month of the year. July has 31 days.

jump |jŭmp| *v.* **jumped, jumping** To rise up or move through the air by using the legs; leap: *Grasshoppers can jump very high.*

June |jo͞on| *n.* The sixth month of the year. Summer begins in June.

K

knee |nē| *n., pl.* **knees** The place where the thigh bone and lower leg bone come together: *The dancer bent his knee and then straightened his leg.*

knew |no͞o| or |nyo͞o| *v.* Past tense of **know:** *I knew how to solve the problem.*
♦ *These sound alike* **knew, new.**

knife |nīf| *n., pl.* **knives** A sharp blade attached to a handle. A knife is used for cutting or carving.

knock |nŏk| *v.* **knocked, knocking** To make a loud noise by hitting a hard surface; rap: *I knocked and knocked, but nobody came to the door.*

knot |nŏt| *n., pl.* **knots 1.** A fastening made by tying together pieces of string, rope, or twine. **2.** A tightly twisted clump; tangle: *The dog's fur is full of knots. v.* **knotted, knotting** To tie or fasten in a knot: *I knotted my shoelaces together.*

know |nō| *v.* **knew, known, knowing 1.** To understand or have the facts about: *Do you know what causes thunder?* **2.** To be sure: *I know that I am right.*
♦ *These sound alike* **know, no.**

ă	pat	ŏ	pot	û	fur
ā	pay	ō	go	th	the
â	care	ô	paw, for	th	thin
ä	father	oi	oil	hw	which
ĕ	pet	o͞o	book	zh	usual
ē	be	o͞o	boot	ə	ago, item
ĭ	pit	yo͞o	cute		pencil, atom
ī	ice	ou	out		circus
î	near	ŭ	cut	ər	butter

knuck‧le |nŭk′ əl| *n., pl.* **knuckles** The place where the bones of the finger or thumb come together.

L

lad‧der |lăd′ ər| *n., pl.* **ladders** A device for climbing, made of two long side pieces joined by short rods used as steps: *We climbed up the ladder to the attic.*

la‧dy |lā′ dē| *n., pl.* **ladies** A woman: *A lady on the bus gave us directions.*

lane |lān| *n., pl.* **lanes** A set route through water or air for swimmers, ships, or planes: *The swimmer in the third lane of the pool won the race.*

large |lärj| *adj.* **larger, largest** Bigger than average: *The zoo has large animals, such as hippos and giraffes.*

last |lăst| *adj.* Coming, being, or placed after all others; final: *We won the last game of the season. We had won a game at last.*

late |lāt| *adj.* **later, latest** Coming after the proper time: *We were late for school. adv.* **later, latest** After the proper time: *The train arrived later than expected.*

laugh |lăf| *v.* **laughed, laughing** To smile and make sounds to show amusement or scorn. *n., pl.* **laughs** The act or sound of laughing.

laugh·a·ble |lăf′ ə bəl| *adj.* Likely to cause laughter or amusement: *The sack race was a laughable event.*

laugh·ing·ly |lăf′ ĭng lē′| *adv.* Jokingly: *Paula laughingly said that I swim like a stone fish.*

laugh·ter |lăf′ tər| *n.* The act or sound of laughing: *The baby's laughter told us that he was happy.*

laun·dry |lôn′ drē| *n., pl.* **laundries** Clothing that must be washed or that has just been washed.

law |lô| *n., pl.* **laws** A rule that tells people what they must or must not do: *It is against the law to drive without a license.*

lawn |lôn| *n., pl.* **lawns** A piece of ground, often near a house or in a park, planted with grass.

lay |lā| *v.* **laid, laying** **1.** To put or set down: *You can lay your books on my desk.* **2.** To put in place: *We helped lay new tiles in the bathroom.*

learn |lûrn| *v.* **learned** *or* **learnt, learning** To get knowledge of something by studying or being taught it: *The third graders are learning Spanish.*

least |lēst| *adv.* In the smallest or lowest degree: *I like tennis best and baseball least.* *n.* The smallest amount or degree: *The least you can do is offer to help.*

leave |lēv| *v.* **left, leaving** **1.** To go away from; go: *Are you leaving this afternoon?* **2.** To let stay behind: *I will leave your book on the desk.* **3.** To have remaining: *Four from seven leaves three.*

left¹ |lĕft| *n.* The side from which a person begins to read a line of English; the side or direction opposite the right: *The number 9 is on the left of a clock's face.*

left² |lĕft| *v.* Past tense and past participle of **leave:** *After dinner some dishes were left on the table.*

lem·ming |lĕm′ ĭng| *n., pl.* **lemmings** A short-tailed animal that lives in northern regions. The lemming is related to the mouse.

les·son |lĕs′ ən| *n., pl.* **lessons** Something to be learned or taught: *Janet goes to her skating lesson every Saturday.*

let's |lĕts| Contraction of "let us": *Let's play this game.*

let·ter |lĕt′ ər| *n., pl.* **letters** **1.** A written mark that stands for a sound and is used to spell words. There are 26 letters in the English alphabet. **2.** A written message to someone that is usually sent by mail in an envelope.

li·brar·y |lī′ brĕr′ ē| *n., pl.* **libraries** A place where books, magazines, records, and other reference materials are kept for reading and borrowing.

lie¹ |lī| *v.* **lay, lain, lying** To be in a flat or resting position: *I lay down under an elm tree.*

lie² |lī| *n., pl.* **lies** A statement that is not the truth; fib.

life |līf| *n., pl.* **lives** **1.** The fact of being alive or staying alive: *I risked my life to save the drowning child.* **2.** The time between birth and death; lifetime: *Uncle Louis spent his life helping other people.*

li·lac |lī′ lək| *n., pl.* **lilacs** A shrub that has purple or white flowers.

lis·ten |lĭs′ ən| *v.* **listened, listening** **1.** To try to hear something: *If you listen, you can hear the ocean.* **2.** To pay attention: *Now listen to me!*

lis·ten·er |lĭs′ ən ər| *n., pl.* **listeners** Someone who listens.

lit·tle |lĭt′ l| *adj.* **littler** *or* **less, littlest** *or* **least** Small: *Dolls look like little people.*

load |lōd| *n., pl.* **loads** An amount of work to be done: *We have a load of dry cleaning to do.*

loose |lo͞os| *adj.* **looser, loosest** Not tight: *I put on a loose sweater.*

lot |lŏt| *n., pl.* **lots** A large number or amount: *I have a lot of work to do.*

loud |loud| *adj.* and *adv.* **louder, loudest** Having a large amount of sound; noisy: *We heard a loud radio. adv.* In a loud manner: *Speak louder.*

love |lŭv| *v.* **loved, loving** To have warm feelings for; lacking hate: *The mother loved her baby.*

luck |lŭk| *n.* The chance happening of good or bad events; fortune: *We had good luck selling our books at the yard sale.*

-ly A suffix that forms adverbs. The suffix "-ly" means "in a way that is": *quickly.*

ă	pat	ŏ	pot	û	fur
ā	pay	ō	go	*th*	the
â	care	ô	paw, for	th	thin
ä	father	oi	oil	hw	which
ĕ	pet	o͞o	book	zh	usual
ē	be	o͞o	boot	ə	ago, item
ĭ	pit	yo͞o	cute		pencil, atom
ī	ice	ou	out		circus
î	near	ŭ	cut	ər	butter

M

main |mān| *adj.* Most important: *Look for the main idea in each paragraph.*
◆ These sound alike **main, mane.**

make |māk| *v.* **made, making** To form, shape, or put together: *I made a shirt.*

make-up *or* **make·up** |māk′ ŭp′| *n., pl.* **make-ups** *or* **makeups** Materials put on the face or body for a play: *The make-up made the boy look like an old man.*

mane |mān| *n., pl.* **manes** The long heavy hair growing from the neck and the head of an animal, such as a horse.
◆ These sound alike **mane, main.**

March |märch| *n.* The third month of the year. March has 31 days.

mark·er |mär′ kər| *n., pl.* **markers** Something used to draw marks or to color: *I used markers to make signs for the fair.*

mar·ket |mär′ kĭt| *n., pl.* **markets** A store that sells food: *I bought lamb chops at the meat market.*

match¹ |măch| *v.* **matched, matching** To be alike: *The two colors match exactly.*

match² |măch| *n., pl.* **matches** A strip of wood or cardboard covered at one end with something that catches fire when it is rubbed on a rough surface.

may |mā| *helping v., past tense* **might** Used to show or express a request for permission: *May I take a swim?*

May |mā| *n.* The fifth month of the year. May has 31 days.

med·al |mĕd′l| *n., pl.* **medals** A small, flat piece of metal with a design. A medal may be given for an action or an accomplishment: *Frank won the jumping medal.*

meet |mēt| *n., pl.* **meets** A gathering for sports contests: *The school held a track meet.*

might |mīt| *v.* Past tense of **may:** *We might have gone swimming, but it rained.*

milk |mĭlk| *n.* A whitish liquid from cows that is used as food by human beings.

mind |mīnd| *n., pl.* **minds** The part of a human being that thinks, feels, understands, and remembers: *You use your mind to do arithmetic.*

mine¹ |mīn| *n., pl.* **mines** An underground tunnel from which minerals such as iron or gold can be taken: *He needed a shovel and a helmet to work in the coal mine.*

mine² |mīn| *pron.* The one or ones that belong to me: *The red scarf on the chair is mine.*

mis·place |mĭs plās′| *v.* **misplaced, misplacing** **1.** To put in the wrong place: *I misplaced my math book this morning.* **2.** To lose: *I misplaced my keys.*

mis·take |mĭ stāk′| *n., pl.* **mistakes** Something that is done incorrectly: *I fixed the mistake that I made in math.*

mitt |mĭt| *n., pl.* **mitts** A large, padded leather glove that is worn to protect the hand when catching a baseball: *Sid jumped and caught the baseball in his mitt.*

mix |mĭks| *v.* **mixed, mixing** To combine or blend: *Mix the flour, water, and eggs to make batter.*

moist |moist| *adj.* **moister, moistest** Slightly wet; damp: *That plant grows best in moist soil.*

Mon·day |mŭn′ dē| or |mŭn′ dā| *n., pl.* **Mondays** The second day of the week.

mos·qui·to |mə skē′ tō| *n., pl.* **mosquitoes** *or* **mosquitos** A small flying bug that sucks blood from animals and people.

most |mōst| *adj.* **1.** Greatest, as in number or size: *The player with the most points won the game.* **2.** The majority of: *Most birds can fly.* *n.* The greatest number or quantity: *Most of the houses in our neighborhood are old.* *adv.* In the greatest degree or size: *The roller coaster is the most exciting ride.*

mouth |mouth| *n., pl.* **mouths** The opening through which an animal takes in food. The human mouth is part of the face and contains the teeth and tongue.

move·ment |moov′ mənt| *n., pl.* **movements** The act or process of moving or changing position: *The player snatched up the ball in a quick movement.*

much |mŭch| *adj.* **more, most** Great in quantity, degree, or extent; a lot of: *We put much work into this project.* *adv.* **more, most** To a great degree or extent: *The test was much harder than I thought.*

mu·sic |myoo′ zĭk| *n.* Sounds that have rhythm, melody, and harmony: *Dad and Mom danced to the music on the radio.*

N

nap·kin |năp′ kĭn| *n., pl.* **napkins** A piece of cloth or soft paper used while eating to protect the clothes or to wipe the mouth and fingers.

naugh·ty |nô′ tē| *adj.* **naughtier, naughtiest** Behaving in a disobedient way; bad: *Brian was naughty because he stayed at the park too long.*

near |nîr| *adv.* To, at, or within a short distance or time: *The deer ran off as we came near.* *prep.* Close to: *Stay near me when we cross the street.*

need |nēd| *n., pl.* **needs** A lack of something that is necessary or wanted: *Their crops are in need of water.* *v.* **needed, needing** **1.** To have to: *I need to return the book today.* **2.** To have need of: *This toaster needs repair.*

neigh·bor |nā′ bər| *n., pl.* **neighbors** A person who lives next door to or near another.

new |noo| or |nyoo| *adj.* **newer, newest** Having lately come into being; not old: *The new supermarket just opened.*
 ♦ *These sound alike* **new, knew.**

nib·ble |nĭb′ əl| *v.* **nibbled, nibbling** **1.** To eat with small, quick bites. **2.** To bite at gently: *The puppy nibbled my toes.*

nice |nīs| *adj.* **nicer, nicest** Kind; pleasant; agreeable: *What a nice thing to say!*

night |nīt| *n., pl.* **nights** The time between sunset and sunrise, especially the hours of darkness.

no |nō| *adv.* Not so: *No, I'm not going.* *adj.* Not any.
 ◆ *These sound alike* **no, know.**

noise |noiz| *n., pl.* **noises** **1.** A loud or unpleasant sound. **2.** Sound of any kind: *The only noise was the wind in the pines.*

no one |nō′ wŭn′| *pron.* Nobody; not anyone: *I thought someone was at the door, but no one was.*

north |nôrth| *n.* The direction to the right of a person who faces the sunset: *Polar bears live in the north, where ice and snow cover the ground most of the year.*

note |nōt| *n., pl.* **notes** A short letter: *My parents sent a note to my teacher, explaining why I had been absent.*

noth·ing |nŭth′ ĭng| *pron.* **1.** Not anything: *I bought nothing, but Tim bought something for two dollars.* **2.** Someone or something of little or no importance or interest: *There's nothing on television tonight.*

no·tice |nō′ tĭs| *n., pl.* **notices** A printed announcement: *The notice said that the game was on Saturday.*

No·vem·ber |nō vĕm′ bər| *n.* The eleventh month of the year. November has 30 days.

O

o'clock |ə klŏk′| *adv.* Of or according to the clock: *When the bell rings, it will be 11 o'clock.*

Oc·to·ber |ŏk tō′ bər| *n.* The tenth month of the year. October has 31 days. Halloween is in October.

oc·to·pus |ŏk′ tə pəs| *n., pl.* **octopuses** A sea animal that has a large head, a soft, rounded body, and eight long arms. The undersides of the arms have sucking disks used for holding.

of |ŭv| or |ŏv| *prep.* **1.** Belonging to or connected with: *The walls of the room are white.* **2.** From the group making up: *Four*

ă	pat	ŏ	pot	û	fur
ā	pay	ō	go	*th*	**the**
â	care	ô	paw, for	th	**thin**
ä	father	oi	oil	hw	**which**
ĕ	pet	ŏŏ	book	zh	usual
ē	be	ōō	boot	ə	ago, item
ĭ	pit	yōō	cute		pencil, atom
ī	ice	ou	out		circus
î	near	ŭ	cut	ər	butter

of the students are here. **3.** Made from: *We built the house of wood.*

oil |oil| *n., pl.* **oils** A greasy, usually liquid substance that burns easily and does not mix with water. Oils are used as fuel and food. They help parts of machines move easily: *Mom added a quart of oil to the truck engine.*

once |wŭns| *adv.* **1.** One time only: *We feed our dog once a day.* **2.** At a time in the past: *Once upon a time, a boy lived in a forest.*

o·pos·sum |ə pŏs′ əm| *n., pl.* **opossums** A furry animal that lives mostly in trees and carries its young in its pouch. The opossum can hang by its tail.

or·ange |ôr′ ĭnj| *n., pl.* **oranges** **1.** A round, juicy fruit with a reddish-yellow skin. Oranges grow in warm places. **2.** A reddish-yellow color.

or·der |ôr′ dər| *n., pl.* **orders** **1.** A grouping of things, one after another. **2.** A command or rule. **3.** A portion of food in a restaurant. **4.** A request for items to be sent: *The teacher placed an order for 20 arithmetic books.* *v.* **ordered, ordering** To place an order for: *We ordered a new washing machine.*

ot·ter |ŏt′ ər| *n., pl.* **otters** An animal with webbed feet that lives in or near water. Otters have thick dark-brown fur and are good swimmers.

ought |ôt| *helping v.* Used to show: **1.** Duty: *We ought to try to help them.* **2.** What is likely: *Dinner ought to be ready by this time.*

our |our| *adj.* Belonging to us: *Our car is being repaired.*
♦ *These sound alike* **our, hour.**

out |out| *adv.* **1.** Away from the inside or center: *I went out for fresh air.* **2.** Away from work, home, or the usual place: *My parents went out for the evening.*

out•side |out sīd′| *or* |out′ sīd′| *adj.* Of, relating to, or located on the outer surface: *We came in through the outside door.* *adv.* Away from the inside: *The children went outside to play.*

ov•en |ŭv′ ən| *n., pl.* **ovens** An enclosed space, as in a stove, used for baking, heating, or drying: *We bake muffins in the oven.*

o•ver•sleep |ō′ vər slēp′| *v.* **overslept, oversleeping** To sleep longer than planned: *I missed the bus this morning because I overslept.*

own |ōn| *adj.* Of or belonging to oneself or itself: *The typewriter came with its own carrying case.* *v.* **owned, owning** To have or possess: *Do your parents own a compact car or a truck?*

P

page |pāj| *n., pl.* **pages** One side of a printed or written sheet of paper, as in a book or newspaper: *Turn to page 24 in your spelling book.*

paid |pād| *v.* Past tense and past participle of **pay:** *Dad paid all the bills.*

pail |pāl| *n., pl.* **pails** A bucket.
♦ *These sound alike* **pail, pale.**

paint |pānt| *n., pl.* **paints** Coloring matter put on surfaces to protect or decorate them. *v.* **painted, painting** To cover or decorate with color: *We painted the porch brown and white.*

pair |pâr| *n., pl.* **pairs** Two matched things that are usually used together: *I lost a pair of running shoes.*
♦ *These sound alike* **pair, pear.**

pa•ja•mas |pə jä′ məz| *or* |pə jăm′ əz| *pl. n.* A loose jacket and pants for sleeping: *Please put on your pajamas, and get ready for bed.*

pale |pāl| *adj.* **paler, palest** Having skin that is a lighter color than usual.
♦ *These sound alike* **pale, pail.**

park |pärk| *n., pl.* **parks** An area of land used for recreation: *We play in the park.* *v.* **parked, parking** To stop and leave a car for a time: *Where did you park the car?*

part•ner |pärt′ nər| *n., pl.* **partners** Either of a pair of persons dancing together: *The partners danced quickly across the floor.*

par•ty |pär′ tē| *n., pl.* **parties** A gathering of people for fun: *We went to a Halloween party.*

paste |pāst| *n., pl.* **pastes** A material, such as a mixture of flour and water, used to stick things together. *v.* **pasted, pasting** To stick with glue: *He pasted pictures in his scrapbook.*

pat |păt| *v.* **patted, patting** To touch gently with an open hand: *Don't pat the dog.*

patch |păch| *n., pl.* **patches** **1.** A piece of material used to mend a hole, rip, or worn place. **2.** A small area that is different from what is around it: *There is a patch of snow on the ground.* *v.* **patched, patching** To mend with a patch.

pay |pā| *v.* **paid, paying** To give or spend money for things bought or for work done: *I paid for my ticket.*

pear |pâr| *n., pl.* **pears** A yellow or brown fruit that has a round bottom and is narrow at the top. Pears grow on trees.
♦ *These sound alike* **pear, pair.**

pen·cil |pĕn′ səl| *n., pl.* **pencils** A thin stick of black or colored material used for writing or drawing.

pen·ny |pĕn′ ē| *n., pl.* **pennies** A coin used in the United States and Canada; cent. One hundred pennies equal one dollar.

peo·ple |pē′ pəl| *n., pl.* **people** Human beings; persons: *Many people came to the football game.*

per·fect |pûr′ fĭkt| *adj.* Without any mistakes: *My drawing is a perfect copy of yours.*

pic·nic |pĭk′ nĭk′| *n., pl.* **picnics** A party in which people carry their food with them and then eat it outdoors.

pic·ture |pĭk′ chər| *n., pl.* **pictures** A painting, drawing, or photograph of a person or thing: *Leo painted a picture of me.*

pie |pī| *n., pl.* **pies** A food made of a filling, such as of fruit or meat, baked in a crust.

pint |pīnt| *n., pl.* **pints** A measurement equal to two cups or half a quart.

pitch |pĭch| *n., pl.* **pitches** A throw of the baseball by a pitcher to a batter: *The third pitch was a curve, and the batter could not hit the ball.*

place |plās| *n., pl.* **places** **1.** A particular location, as a city: *In what place were you born?* **2.** A space for one person to sit or stand: *Save a place for me at the movies.* *v.* **placed, placing** To put in a particular place or order: *I placed cups and spoons on the table.*

place·ment |plās′ mənt| *n., pl.* **placements** The act of putting things in a special arrangement or order: *He will be in charge of the placement of the pictures on the wall.*

plan |plăn| *n., pl.* **plans** **1.** A way of doing something that has been thought out ahead of time: *What are your plans for the evening?* **2.** A drawing showing how the

ă	pat	ŏ	pot	û	fur
ā	pay	ō	go	*th*	the
â	care	ô	paw, for	th	thin
ä	father	oi	oil	hw	which
ĕ	pet	ōō	book	zh	usual
ē	be	ōō	boot	ə	ago, item
ĭ	pit	yōō	cute		pencil, atom
ī	ice	ou	out		circus
î	near	ŭ	cut	ər	butter

parts of something are put together: *We followed the plans to make the model car.*

play |plā| *v.* **played, playing** **1.** To amuse oneself: *We went out to play, and Dad went back to work.* **2.** To take part in a game of: *We will play baseball after school.*

plunge |plŭnj| *v.* **plunged, plunging** To throw oneself suddenly into water: *We plunged into the waves.*

point |point| *n., pl.* **points** A sharp end, as of a pencil. *v.* **pointed, pointing** To call attention to something with the finger: *The librarian pointed to the sign that said "Quiet."*

pond |pŏnd| *n., pl.* **ponds** A small body of water: *Frogs and fish live in the pond.*

po·ny |pō′ nē| *n., pl.* **ponies** A kind of horse that remains small when grown.

po·ster |pō′ stər| *n., pl.* **posters** A large sheet of paper with a picture or printing on it that is put up as an ad, a notice, or a decoration: *The poster showed that the circus was coming to town.*

pret·ty |prĭt′ ē| *adj.* **prettier, prettiest** Pleasing to the eye or ear.

prize |prīz| *n., pl.* **prizes** Something won in a game or a contest: *The first prize in the bike race is a new helmet.*

pro·gram |prō′ grăm| *n., pl.* **programs** A list of events and names: *The program showed the names of the actors in the play.*

prop |prŏp| *v.* **propped, propping** To keep from falling; support: *I propped myself up on the bed with pillows.*

pup·py |pŭp′ ē| *n., pl.* **puppies** A young dog.

pur·ple |pûr′ pəl| *n., pl.* **purples** A color between blue and red. *adj.* Of the color purple: *Grape juice is purple.*

Q

quar·rel |kwôr′ əl| *v.* **quarreled, quarreling** To argue: *The children quarreled over which book to read.*

quart |kwôrt| *n., pl.* **quarts** A measurement equal to two pints.

queen |kwēn| *n., pl.* **queens 1.** A woman who is the ruler of a country. **2.** A large female that lays eggs in a group of bees, ants, or termites.

quick |kwĭk| *adj.* **quicker, quickest** Very fast; rapid; not slow: *I turned on the light with a quick movement of my hand.*

quick·ly |kwĭk′ lē| *adv.* In a quick way; rapidly; not slowly: *Come here quickly!*

quit |kwĭt| *v.* **quit, quitting** To stop doing: *I quit work at five o'clock.*

R

rab·bit |răb′ ĭt| *n., pl.* **rabbits** A burrowing animal with long ears, soft fur, and a short, furry tail.

ran·ger |rān′ jər| *n., pl.* **rangers** A person who patrols or watches over a forest or park: *The ranger helped visitors at the national park.*

rare |râr| *adj.* **rarer, rarest** Not often found or seen: *Gina collects rare stamps.*

raw |rô| *adj.* **rawer, rawest** Uncooked: *I made a salad of raw vegetables.*

re- A prefix that means "again": *refill.*

re·cess |rē′ sĕs′| or |rĭ sĕs′| *n., pl.* **recesses** A short time for rest or play: *We played hopscotch at recess.*

re·make |rē māk′| *v.* **remade, remaking** To make again.

re·pair |rĭ pâr′| *v.* **repaired, repairing** To fix.

re·peat |rĭ pēt′| *v.* **repeated, repeating** To say or do again: *Please repeat your last question.*

re·place |rĭ plās′| *v.* **replaced, replacing 1.** To put back in place: *I replaced the dishes in the cupboard.* **2.** To take or fill the place of: *Cars replaced the horse and buggy.*

re·tell |rē tĕl′| *v.* **retold, retelling** To tell again; repeat.

re·use |rē yōoz′| *v.* **reused, reusing** To use again.

re·view |rĭ vyōo′| *v.* **reviewed, reviewing** To study again; check: *Let's review the chapter before we take the test.*

re·ward |rĭ wôrd′| *n., pl.* **rewards** Something that is given in return for a worthy act or service: *You deserve a medal as a reward for your bravery.*

re·write |rē rīt′| *v.* **rewrote, rewritten, rewriting** To write again: *She rewrote her messy paper.*

riv·er |rĭv′ ər| *n., pl.* **rivers** A large stream of water that is often fed by smaller streams flowing into it.

roar |rôr| *n., pl.* **roars** A loud, deep cry or sound, such as a lion makes: *We heard the roar of a huge tiger.*

round |round| *adj.* **rounder, roundest** Shaped like a ball or circle: *An orange is round.*

row |rō| *v.* **rowed, rowing** To move a boat with oars: *Do you want to row across the lake?*

rub |rŭb| *v.* **rubbed, rubbing** To move back and forth against a surface: *The cat rubbed its head against my arm.*

ruf·fle |rŭf′ əl| *n., pl.* **ruffles** A strip of pleated material, such as ribbon or lace, used as a decoration: *The curtains had ruffles at the bottom.*

ă	pat	ŏ	pot	û	fur
ā	pay	ō	go	*th*	**the**
â	care	ô	paw, for	th	**thin**
ä	father	oi	oil	hw	**which**
ĕ	pet	ōō	book	zh	usual
ē	be	ōō	boot	ə	ago, item
ĭ	pit	yōō	cute		pencil, atom
ī	ice	ou	out		circus
î	near	ŭ	cut	ər	butter

S

sad·ly |săd′ lē| *adv.* In a way that shows sorrow or unhappiness: *Carlo waved sadly to his grandparents as they left.*

said |sĕd| *v.* Past tense and past participle of **say**: *Did you hear what he said?*

sail |sāl| *n., pl.* **sails** A piece of strong cloth that is stretched out to catch the wind and move a boat or ship through the water. *v.* **sailed, sailing** To travel on a ship or boat with sails.
   ◆ *These sound alike* **sail, sale.**

sale |sāl| *n., pl.* **sales** A selling of things at less than usual prices.
   ◆ *These sound alike* **sale, sail.**

same |sām| *adj.* **1.** Exactly alike: *These books are the same size.* **2.** Being the very one or ones: *This is the same seat that I had yesterday.*

Sat·ur·day |săt′ ər dē| or |săt′ ər dā| *n., pl.* **Saturdays** The seventh day of the week.

save |sāv| *v.* **saved, saving 1.** To rescue from danger. **2.** To keep from wasting or spending.

saw |sô| *n., pl.* **saws** A tool that has a thin metal blade with sharp teeth for cutting hard material.

say |sā| *v.* **said, saying 1.** To speak: *Sandy always says hello to me.* **2.** To state: *The newspaper says that it will rain tonight.*

scald |skôld| *v.* **scalded, scalding** To burn with a very hot liquid: *She spilled boiling water and scalded her hand.*

scare |skâr| *n., pl.* **scares** A feeling of fear: *I got a scare when I went into deep water in swim class.*

scarf |skärf| *n., pl.* **scarfs** *or* **scarves** A piece of cloth that is worn around the neck or head.

scene |sēn| *n., pl.* **scenes 1.** A place as seen by a viewer; view. **2.** The place where an action or an event occurs: *The tow truck arrived at the scene of the wreck.* **3.** The place in which the action of a story or play occurs. **4.** A short section of a play or a movie.
   ◆ *These sound alike* **scene, seen.**

school |skōōl| *n., pl.* **schools 1.** A place for teaching and learning. **2.** The students and teachers at such a place.

score·board |skôr′ bôrd′| or |skōr′ bôrd′| *n., pl.* **scoreboards** A large board for showing the score of a game: *The winners' names were shown on the scoreboard.*

scratch |skrăch| *n., pl.* **scratches** A thin, shallow cut or mark made with or as if with a sharp tool: *The thorns on the rose bush made a scratch on my arm.*

scream |skrēm| *v.* **screamed, screaming** To make a long, loud cry or sound; yell.

screen |skrēn| *n., pl.* **screens 1.** A frame covered with wire mesh, used in a window or door to keep out insects: *Put a screen in the window to keep out the flies.* **2.** A flat surface on which slides or movies are shown.

seam |sēm| *n., pl.* **seams** The line formed by sewing two pieces of material together.
♦ *These sound alike* **seam, seem.**

search |sûrch| *v.* **searched, searching** To look carefully: *We searched along the beach for seashells.*

second¹ |sĕk′ ənd| *n., pl.* **seconds** A unit of time equal to 1/60 of a minute.

second² |sĕk′ ənd| *adj.* **1.** Coming after the first: *Elena won second prize.* **2.** Another: *May Sean have a second chance?*

see |sē| *v.* **saw, seen, seeing** To take in with the eyes: *I see my socks under the bed.*

seek |sēk| *v.* **sought, seeking** To try to find or get; look for: *We are seeking directions.*

seem |sēm| *v.* **seemed, seeming** To appear to be: *You seem worried.*
♦ *These sound alike* **seem, seam.**

seen |sēn| Past participle of **see:** *Have you seen my hat anywhere?*
♦ *These sound alike* **seen, scene.**

sell |sĕl| *v.* **sold, selling** To exchange something for money: *I sold my bike for $50.00.*

send |sĕnd| *v.* **sent, sending 1.** To cause to go: *They sent me home.* **2.** To mail: *Grandma sends me a letter every week.*

Sep·tem·ber |sĕp tĕm′ bər| *n.* The ninth month of the year. September has 30 days.

serve |sûrv| *v.* **served, serving** To present or offer food for others to eat: *Dad served dinner to the family.*

sew |sō| *v.* **sewed, sewn** or **sewed, sewing** To make, repair, or fasten a thing with stitches made by a needle and a thread.

shake |shāk| *v.* **shook, shaken, shaking** To move back and forth or up and down with short, quick movements: *Shake the orange juice to mix it up.*

shal·low |shăl′ ō| *adj.* **shallower, shallowest** Not deep.

sham·poo |shăm pōō′| *n., pl.* **shampoos** A liquid soap used to wash hair.

share |shâr| *v.* **shared, sharing** To have, use, or do together with another or others: *Let's share this last orange.*

she's |shēz| Contraction of "she is" or "she has": *She's my sister.*

shin·y |shī′ nē| *adj.* **shinier, shiniest** Bright: *We polished the car until it was shiny.*

shoe |shōō| *n., pl.* **shoes** An outer covering for the foot: *His left shoe hurts his big toe.*

shook |shŏŏk| *v.* Past tense of **shake:** *The strong winds shook our house.*

short |shôrt| *adj.* **shorter, shortest 1.** Not long: *Short hair is now in style.* **2.** Not tall. **3.** Covering a small distance or taking a small amount of time: *We took a short walk.*

should·n't |shŏŏd′ nt| Contraction of "should not": *We shouldn't leave the party too late.*

shut |shŭt| *v.* **shut, shutting 1.** To close: *Shut the door.* **2.** To stop entrance into: *Dad shut the beach house for the winter.*

side |sīd| *n., pl.* **sides 1.** A line or surface that forms an edge: *A triangle has three sides.* **2.** One of the surfaces of an object that connects the top and the bottom: *Let's paint that side of the house first.*

sight |sīt| *n., pl.* **sights 1.** The ability to see. **2.** Something seen or worth seeing: *The baby whale was a wonderful sight.*

sing·er |sĭng′ ər| *n., pl.* **singers** Someone who performs a song.

skin |skĭn| *n., pl.* **skins** The outer covering of a human or animal body.

skip |skĭp| *v.* **skipped, skipping** To move forward by stepping and hopping lightly: *We held hands and skipped in a circle.*

skit |skĭt| *n., pl.* **skits** A very short play: *We put on a skit for the first graders.*

skunk |skŭngk| *n., pl.* **skunks** An animal that has black and white fur and a bushy tail. A skunk can spray a bad-smelling liquid when it is frightened.

sky•scrap•er |skī′ skrā′ pər| *n., pl.* **sky-scrapers** A very tall building: *From the top floor of the skyscraper, we could see the whole city.*

sleet |slēt| *n.* Rain that is partly frozen into ice: *When the temperature dropped, the sleet turned into snow.*

sling |slĭng| *n., pl.* **slings** A band of cloth looped around the neck to support an injured arm or hand: *The doctor put Maria's broken wrist in a sling.*

slip•per |slĭp′ ər| *n., pl.* **slippers** A light shoe that is easily slipped on and off. Slippers are usually worn indoors: *She got out of bed and put on her warm slippers.*

slow |slō| *adj.* **slower, slowest** Moving or going at a low speed; not quick.

slow•ly |slō′ lē| *adv.* In a slow way; not quickly: *A turtle moves slowly.*

small |smôl| *adj.* **smaller, smallest** Little.

smart |smärt| *adj.* **smarter, smartest** Having a quick mind; bright.

smell |smĕl| *v.* **smelled** *or* **smelt, smelling** To notice the odor of something by using the nose: *I smell smoke. n., pl.* **smells** Odor; scent: *The smell of roses came from the perfume.*

smile |smīl| *n., pl.* **smiles** A happy look on the face. A person makes a smile by curving the corners of the mouth upward. *v.* **smiled, smiling** To have or make a smile.

smoke |smōk| *n.* The mixture of gases and carbon that rises from burning material: *Smoke rose from the burning wood.*

ă	pat	ŏ	pot	û	fur
ā	pay	ō	go	*th*	the
â	care	ô	paw, for	th	thin
ä	father	oi	oil	hw	which
ĕ	pet	o͞o	book	zh	usual
ē	be	o͞o	boot	ə	ago, item
ĭ	pit	yo͞o	cute		pencil, atom
ī	ice	ou	out		circus
î	near	ŭ	cut	ər	butter

snarl |snärl| *v.* **snarled, snarling** To growl with the teeth showing.

soak |sōk| *v.* **soaked, soaking** To make or become completely wet: *The rain soaked our clothes and hair.*

soap |sōp| *n., pl.* **soaps** A substance that is used for washing; *Use that bar of soap and a washcloth to wash your face.*

sock |sŏk| *n., pl.* **socks** A short covering for the foot that reaches above the ankle and ends below the knee.

soft |sôft| *adj.* **softer, softest** Not hard or firm: *The pillow is soft.*

soil |soil| *n., pl.* **soils** The loose top layer of the earth's surface in which plants can grow; dirt.

sold |sōld| *v.* Past tense and past participle of **sell**: *We sold the old car and bought a new one.*

some•one |sŭm′ wŭn′| *pron.* Some person; somebody: *I hoped that someone would answer the phone, but no one did.*

some•thing |sŭm′ thĭng| *pron.* A thing that is not named: *I bought something for my parents.*

some•times |sŭm′ tīmz′| *adv.* Now and then; at times: *I see them sometimes but not often.*

soon |so͞on| *adv.* **sooner, soonest** Within a short time: *We'll soon know the answer.*

sought |sôt| *v.* Past tense and past participle of **seek**: *We sought a way to make our sick cat feel better.*

sound |sound| *n., pl.* **sounds** Something that is heard: *The sound of the drum was very loud.*

sour |sour| *adj.* **sourer, sourest** Having a sharp taste: *Lemons, limes, and grapefruit are sour.*

space |spās| *n., pl.* **spaces 1.** The area without limits where the stars, planets, comets, and galaxies are. **2.** The open area between objects: *Leave a space for my chair.*

spark |spärk| *n., pl.* **sparks** A small bit of burning matter: *The burning logs crackled, and sparks flew everywhere.*

speak |spēk| *v.* **spoke, spoken, speaking** To say words; talk: *Mom will speak to our doctor about my fever.*

speak•er |spē′ kər| *n., pl.* **speakers** A person who speaks: *The speaker told his listeners about his trip to Chicago.*

splint |splĭnt| *n., pl.* **splints** A device that is used to hold a broken bone in place: *He had a splint on his broken finger.*

spoil |spoil| *v.* **spoiled** *or* **spoilt, spoiling 1.** To make less perfect or useful: *A storm spoiled our picnic.* **2.** To become unfit for use; ruin: *The milk spoiled.* **3.** To hurt people by giving them too much: *Don't spoil your younger brothers and sisters.*

spoon |spoon| *n., pl.* **spoons** A piece of silverware with a shallow bowl at the end of its handle. Spoons are used for measuring, serving, or eating food: *I need a spoon to eat my soup.*

spot |spŏt| *n., pl.* **spots 1.** A small mark or stain: *Red spots on your body may mean you have measles.* **2.** A place or location: *We found our favorite spot on the beach.*

spray |sprā| *v.* **sprayed, spraying** To make water or another liquid come out of a container in many small drops: *We sprayed the garden with water from the hose.*

spread |sprĕd| *v.* **spread, spreading** To open out wide or wider: *I spread the cloth on the table.*

spring |sprĭng| *n., pl.* **springs** The season of the year between winter and summer when plants begin to grow.

sprout |sprout| *v.* **sprouted, sprouting** To appear as new growth: *The corn sprouted after the rain.*

squeak |skwēk| *v.* **squeaked, squeaking** To make a high, thin noise such as a mouse makes.

squeak•y |skwē′ kē| *adj.* **squeakier, squeakiest** Making a high, thin noise: *The rusty hinges are squeaky.*

squeeze |skwēz| *v.* **squeezed, squeezing 1.** To press together with force: *The baby squeezed the rubber toy.* **2.** To force by pressing: *We squeezed through the door.*

stage |stāj| *n., pl.* **stages** The raised platform in a theater on which actors perform.

star |stär| *n., pl.* **stars 1.** A body that appears as a very bright point in the sky at night. **2.** A performer who plays a leading role in a play or movie.

start |stärt| *v.* **started, starting 1.** To begin to move, go, or act: *We started for the lake early in the morning.* **2.** To have a beginning: *Camp will start in June.*

step |stĕp| *n., pl.* **steps** An action taken to reach a goal: *We have taken the first step toward cleaning up the school grounds.*

stick |stĭk| *n., pl.* **sticks** A long, thin piece of wood, as a branch cut from a tree. *v.* **stuck, sticking** To fasten with something, such as glue: *I am sticking a stamp on the envelope.*

stick•er |stĭk′ ər| *n., pl.* **stickers** A small piece of paper with glue on the back.

stick•i•ness |stĭk′ ē nĕs| *n.* The quality or condition of being sticky: *I can't get the stickiness of the honey off my hands.*

stick•y |stĭk′ ē| *adj.* **stickier, stickiest** Tending to stick: *Glue is sticky.*

sting |stĭng| *v.* **stung, stinging** To hurt with a small, sharp point: *A bee stung me on the foot.*

stir |stûr| *v.* **stirred, stirring** To mix by moving in a circle again and again: *I stirred the vegetables into the soup.*

stop |stŏp| *v.* **stopped, stopping 1.** To end moving, acting, or operating: *Dad stopped at the red light.* **2.** To bring or to come to an end: *The rain finally stopped.*

storm |stôrm| *n., pl.* **storms** A strong wind with rain, hail, sleet, or snow.

sto•ry |stôr′ ē| *n., pl.* **stories** A tale made up to entertain people: *I have just read an adventure story.*

straight |strāt| *adj.* **straighter, straightest 1.** Not curving, curling, or bending; not crooked: *I have straight hair.* **2.** Without a break: *It snowed for five straight days.*

straw |strô| *n., pl.* **straws 1.** Stalks of grain, as wheat or oats, whose seeds have been removed: *Some straw is used as bedding for animals, and some is used to weave hats and baskets.* **2.** A thin tube made of paper or plastic through which a person can drink a liquid.

stream |strēm| *n., pl.* **streams** A small body of flowing water; a brook: *That stream flows into the river by our house.*

street |strēt| *n., pl.* **streets** A road in a city or town: *I live on this street.*

strength |strĕngkth| *n., pl.* **strengths** The quality of being strong; power: *Elephants have a huge amount of strength.*

stretch•er |strĕch′ ər| *n., pl.* **stretchers** A movable bed or cot on which a sick or injured person can be carried.

string |strĭng| *n., pl.* **strings 1.** A cord for fastening or tying: *Tie the pile of newspapers with string.* **2.** A series of things or

ă	pat	ŏ	pot	û	fur
ā	pay	ō	go	th	the
â	care	ô	paw, for	th	thin
ä	father	oi	oil	hw	which
ĕ	pet	ŏŏ	book	zh	usual
ē	be	ōō	boot	ə	ago, item
ĭ	pit	yōō	cute		pencil, atom
ī	ice	ou	out		circus
î	near	ŭ	cut	ər	butter

events: *A string of accidents have happened at that corner.*

strong |strông| *adj.* **stronger, strongest** Having much power, energy, or strength: *A strong horse pulled the heavy cart.*

strug•gle |strŭg′ əl| *v.* **struggled, struggling** To make a great effort: *Chuck and I struggled to climb the mountain. n., pl.* **struggles** A great effort: *Getting up a 6:00 A.M. is a struggle.*

stub•born |stŭb′ ərn| *adj.* **1.** Not willing to change in spite of requests from others: *The stubborn child refused to wear boots.* **2.** Hard to deal with: *I have a stubborn cold.*

stu•dent |stōōd′ nt| or |styōōd′ nt| *n., pl.* **students** A person who studies, as in a school: *The students studied for the test.*

stur•dy |stûr′ dē| *adj.* **sturdier, sturdiest** Strong: *The workbench has sturdy legs.*

style |stīl| *n., pl.* **styles** A special way of dressing, looking, or acting: *She dresses in an old-fashioned style.*

sub•way |sŭb′ wā′| *n., pl.* **subways** An underground train in a city: *We rode the subway all the way downtown.*

sud•den |sŭd′ n| *adj.* **1.** Happening without warning: *We were caught in a sudden snowstorm.* **2.** Rapid; quick: *With a sudden movement I caught the falling vase.*

suit•case |sōōt′ kās′| *n., pl.* **suitcases** A piece of luggage: *I put clothes for my trip in my suitcase.*

sum•mer |sŭm′ ər| *n., pl.* **summers** The hottest season of the year. Summer is between spring and autumn.

Sun·day |sŭn′ dē| or |sŭn′ dā| *n., pl.* **Sundays** The first day of the week.

sway |swā| *v.* **swayed, swaying** To swing back and forth or from side to side: *The willow trees were swaying in the wind.*

T

ta·ble |tā′ bəl| *n., pl.* **tables** A piece of furniture that has legs and a flat top: *Carl put plates and silverware on the table.*

talk |tôk| *v.* **talked, talking 1.** To say words; speak. **2.** To have a conversation.

tap |tăp| *v.* **tapped, tapping** To strike gently: *I tapped my friend on the shoulder.*

taught |tôt| *v.* Past tense and past participle of **teach:** *The teacher taught us a new song that she had learned.*

tax·i |tăk′ sē| *n., pl.* **taxis** A car that carries passengers wherever they want to go for a fare: *We asked the taxi driver to take us uptown.*

teach |tēch| *v.* **taught, teaching** To give lessons in: *Our teacher taught the class another dance.*

teach·er |tē′ chər| *n., pl.* **teachers** A person who teaches or gives instruction.

teeth |tēth| *n.* Plural of **tooth:** *Please brush your teeth.*

test |tĕst| *n., pl.* **tests** Questions or problems used to measure knowledge: *We had an arithmetic test yesterday.*

thank·ful |thăngk′ fəl| *adj.* Showing or feeling thanks; grateful: *We were thankful that no one was hurt in the fire.*

their |thâr| *pron.* Belonging to them: *They put their boots in the closet.*
♦ *These sound alike* **their, there, they're.**

there |thâr| *adv.* **1.** At or in that place: *Set the package there on the table.* **2.** To or toward that place: *I bicycled there and back. pron.* Used to start a sentence in which the verb comes before the subject: *There are several kinds of dogs.*
♦ *These sound alike* **there, their, they're.**

ther·mom·e·ter |thər mŏm′ ĭ tər| *n., pl.* **thermometers** An instrument that shows how hot or cold it is: *The thermometer showed that the temperature was zero.*

they |thā| *pron.* The persons, animals, or things last talked about; those ones: *Elephants are large, but they move quickly.*

they're |thâr| Contraction of "they are."
♦ *These sound alike* **they're, their, there.**

thick |thĭk| *adj.* **thicker, thickest** Having much space between opposite sides; not thin: *A thick board does not break very easily.*

thin |thĭn| *adj.* **thinner, thinnest 1.** Having little space between opposite sides; not thick: *The sun is shining through the thin curtains.* **2.** Not fat.

think |thĭngk| *v.* **thought, thinking 1.** To use one's mind to form ideas and make decisions: *I think that I should leave now.* **2.** To believe: *Pam thinks that it is too cold to go swimming.*

third |thûrd| *adj.* Coming after the second: *They picked the first two TV shows to watch, and I picked the third one.*

though |thō| *adv.* However; nevertheless: *The shirt is pretty; it doesn't fit, though.*

thought |thôt| *v.* Past tense and past participle of **think:** *I thought about what you said.*

three |thrē| *n., pl.* **threes** The number, written *3*, that is equal to the sum of 2 + 1. *adj.* Being one more than two.

threw |thro͞o| *v.* Past tense of **throw:** *Todd threw his model plane into the air.*
♦ *These sound alike* **threw, through.**

through |thro͞o| *prep.* In one side and out the other side of: *We walked through the park to the bus stop.*
♦ *These sound alike* **through, threw.**

throw |thrō| *v.* **threw, thrown, throwing** To send through the air by moving the arm quickly: *I will catch the towel if you throw it to me.*

Thurs·day |thûrz′ dē| or |thûrz′ dā| *n., pl.* **Thursdays** The fifth day of the week.

tie |tī| *v.* **tied, tying** To fasten with a cord or rope: *Wrap the package, and tie it with a string. n., pl.* **ties** A narrow band of cloth worn around the neck and tied in front; necktie.

tight |tīt| *adj.* **tighter, tightest 1.** Held firmly in place; not loose: *I tied a tight knot.* **2.** Leaving no extra room or time; crowded: *My schedule is tight today.*

tooth |tōoth| *n., pl.* **teeth** One of the hard, bony parts in the mouth that is used to chew and bite: *I broke a tooth when I bit into some taffy.*

tor·na·do |tôr nā′ dō| *n., pl.* **tornadoes** *or* **tornados** A twisting, dangerous storm. A tornado has a funnel-shaped cloud that comes down from a thundercloud.

tor·toise |tôr′ təs| *n., pl.* **tortoises** A turtle, especially one that lives on land.

tough |tŭf| *adj.* **tougher, toughest** Strong; not likely to break or tear.

town |toun| *n., pl.* **towns** A place where people live that is larger than a village but smaller than a city.

toy |toi| *n., pl.* **toys** Something that children play with.

trace |trās| *v.* **traced, tracing** To copy by following lines that have already been drawn or printed: *Jack traced the picture of the puppy from a magazine.*

track |trăk| *n., pl.* **tracks** A path or course made for racing or running: *The runners practiced on an indoor track in the gym.*

train·er |trā′ nər| *n., pl.* **trainers** A person who coaches sports players or show animals: *The trainer taught the seal to bounce a ball.*

trav·el |trăv′ əl| *v.* **traveled, traveling** To go from one place to another: *The whole family traveled around the world.*

tried |trīd| *v.* Past tense and past participle of **try:** *Carol tried to telephone Jeff, but no one was home.*

trim |trĭm| *v.* **trimmed, trimming** To make neat or even, especially by cutting: *Trim my bangs, so that I can see.*

ă	pat	ŏ	pot	û	fur
ā	pay	ō	go	*th*	**the**
â	care	ô	paw, for	th	**thin**
ä	father	oi	oil	hw	**which**
ĕ	pet	ōo	book	zh	usual
ē	be	ōō	boot	ə	ago, item
ĭ	pit	yōo	cute		pencil, atom
ī	ice	ou	out		circus
î	near	ŭ	cut	ər	butter

trou·ble |trŭb′ əl| *n., pl.* **troubles** A cause of unhappiness or difficulty: *We had trouble with our homework, so we asked for help.*

try |trī| *v.* **tried, trying** To make an effort; attempt: *She tried to win the prize.*

Tues·day |tōoz′ dē|, |tyōoz′ dē|, *or* |tyōoz′ dā′| *n., pl.* **Tuesdays** The third day of the week.

tu·lip |tōo′ lĭp| *or* |tyōo′ lĭp| *n., pl.* **tulips** A garden plant that grows from a bulb and has cup-shaped flowers: *Some tulips are light colors, while others are bright red.*

tune |tōon| *or* |tyōon| *n., pl.* **tunes** The musical part of a song: *I was so happy that I whistled several tunes.*

turn |tûrn| *v.* **turned, turning** To move or cause to move around a center; rotate: *I heard the key turn in the lock.*

two |tōo| *n., pl.* **twos** The number, written *2,* that is equal to the sum of 1 + 1. *adj.* Being one more than one: *I have two sisters.*

U

un- A prefix that means: **1.** Not: *unhappy.* **2.** Opposite of: *untie.*

un·clear |ŭn klîr′| *adj.* Not clear; not well organized: *The report is unclear.*

un·der |ŭn′ dər| *prep.* **1.** Below: *A boat passed under the bridge.* **2.** Beneath and covered by: *I hid the kitten under my coat.* **3.** Beneath the surface of: *The plumber laid a pipe under the ground.*

un·fair |ŭn fâr′| *adj.* **unfairer, unfairest** Not fair; not right: *We think the decision is unfair.*

un·hap·py |ŭn hăp′ ē| *adj.* **unhappier, unhappiest** Without joy or pleasure; not happy; sad.

un·hurt |ŭn hûrt′| *adj.* Not hurt; not injured: *The driver was unhurt in the accident.*

un·im·por·tant |ŭn′ ĭm pôr′ tnt| *adj.* Not important; having little meaning or value.

un·kind |ŭn kīnd′| *adj.* **unkinder, unkindest** Not kind; harsh or cruel.

un·like |ŭn līk′| *prep.* **1.** Not like; different from: *I had heard a sound unlike any other.* **2.** Not usual for: *It's unlike you not to say hello.*

un·tie |ŭn tī′| *v.* **untied, untying 1.** To loosen or undo: *I could not untie the knots in my shoelace.* **2.** The opposite of **tie.**

un·til |ŭn tĭl′| *prep.* **1.** Up to the time of: *They studied until dinner.* **2.** Before: *You can't have the bike until Monday.* *conj.* **1.** Up to the time that: *They studied until it was time for dinner.* **2.** Before: *You can't go out until you finish your homework.* **3.** To the point that: *They played soccer until they were tired.*

un·wrap |ŭn răp′| *v.* **unwrapped, unwrapping** To open by removing the wrapper from; to open a present: *May I unwrap my gifts, or must I wait until tomorrow?*

use·ful |yo͞os′ fəl| *adj.* Being of use or service; helpful; not useless: *Our map of Chicago was useful when we visited there.*

V

ver·y |vĕr′ ē| *adv.* **1.** To a high degree; extremely: *I am a very happy person today.* **2.** Exactly: *I said the very same thing.*

vi·o·let |vī′ ə lĭt| *n., pl.* **violets** A low-growing plant with tiny flowers that are bluish purple, yellow, or white.

vis·it |vĭz′ ĭt| *v.* **visited, visiting** To stay with as a guest: *I am visiting an old friend for a week.*

W

walk |wôk| *v.* **walked, walking** To move on foot at an easy, steady pace. *n., pl.* **walks 1.** An act of walking: *We took a walk on the beach.* **2.** A distance covered in walking: *The walk to school is less than a mile.*

wall |wôl| *n., pl.* **walls** A solid structure that forms a side of a building or room.

wal·rus |wôl′ rəs| *n., pl.* **walrus** or **walruses** A large sea animal that has tough, wrinkled skin and large tusks. Walruses live in the Arctic.

want |wŏnt| *v.* **wanted, wanting** To wish or desire: *They wanted to play outdoors.*

was |wŏz| or |wŭz| *v.* First and third person singular past tense of **be:** *He was late.*

wash·er |wŏsh′ ər| or |wô′ shər| *n., pl.* **washers** A machine for washing clothes.

was·n't |wŏz′ ənt| or |wŭz′ ənt| Contraction of "was not": *My friend wasn't home.*

watch |wŏch| *v.* **watched, watching 1.** To look at with care: *People stopped to watch the parade.* **2.** To be alert and looking: *Watch for the street sign. n., pl.* **watches** A small device for telling time that can be worn on the wrist or carried in a pocket.

weak |wēk| *adj.* **weaker, weakest** Not strong: *My left hand is weaker than my right hand.*
◆ These sound alike **weak, week.**

weak·ly |wēk′ lē| *adv.* In a weak way.
◆ These sound alike **weakly, weekly.**

weak·ness |wēk′ nĭs| *n., pl.* **weaknesses** The feeling of being weak: *The weakness in my ankle is due to a sprain.*

wear |wâr| *v.* **wore, worn, wearing** To have on the body: *I wear mittens on cold days.*

Wednes·day |wĕnz′ dē| or |wĕnz′ dā| *n., pl.* **Wednesdays** The fourth day of the week.

week |wēk| *n., pl.* **weeks 1.** A period of seven days: *We will be home in a week.* **2.** The period from Sunday through the next Saturday.
◆ These sound alike **week, weak.**

week·end |wēk′ ĕnd′| *n., pl.* **weekends** The time from Friday evening through Sunday evening.

week·ly |wēk′ lē| *adv.* Once a week or every week: *My aunt visits us weekly.*
◆ These sound alike **weekly, weakly.**

weigh |wā| *v.* **weighed, weighing 1.** To find out how heavy something is: *He weighed himself on a scale.* **2.** To have a certain heaviness: *The car weighs 2,800 pounds.*

well |wĕl| *adv.* **better, best** In a way that is good, proper, skillful, or successful: *Tammy skis well.*

were |wûr| *v.* **1.** Second person singular past tense of **be:** *You were in school yesterday.* **2.** First, second, and third person plural past tense of **be:** *We were there too.*

weren't |wûrnt| Contraction of "were not": *Sam and I weren't sick yesterday.*

ă	pat	ŏ	pot	û	fur
ā	pay	ō	go	*th*	the
â	care	ô	paw, for	th	thin
ä	father	oi	oil	hw	which
ĕ	pet	ōō	book	zh	usual
ē	be	ōō	boot	ə	ago, item
ĭ	pit	yōō	cute		pencil, atom
ī	ice	ou	out		circus
î	near	ŭ	cut	ər	butter

where |hwâr| *adv.* At, in, or to what or which place: *Where is the telephone? conj.* At, in, or to what or which place: *I am going to my room, where I can study.*

whis·tle |hwĭs′ əl| *n., pl.* **whistles** A device that makes a high, clear sound when air is blown through it: *The coach blew her whistle, and the game began.*

who's |hōōz| Contraction of "who is" or "who has": *Who's knocking at the door?*

wide |wīd| *adj.* **wider, widest 1.** Taking up a large amount of space from side to side; broad: *We live on a wide street.* **2.** Fully open: *The little child's eyes were wide with surprise.*

wild |wīld| *adj.* **wilder, wildest** Not grown, cared for, or controlled by people; not tame: *The polar bear is a wild animal.*

will |wĭl| *helping v.* **would** Something that is going to take place in the future: *They will arrive tonight.*

win·dow |wĭn′ dō| *n., pl.* **windows** An opening in a wall with a frame and panes of glass to let in light.

win•ter |wĭn′ tər| *n., pl.* **winters** The coldest season of the year, between fall and spring.

wis•dom |wĭz′ dəm| *n.* Good judgment in knowing what to do and being able to tell the difference between right and wrong; knowledge.

won't |wōnt| Contraction of "will not": *She won't forget to meet us.*

word |wûrd| *n., pl.* **words** A sound or group of sounds that has meaning: *Do you know how to say that word?*

work |wûrk| *n., pl.* **works 1.** The effort that is required to do something; labor: *Cleaning the house is hard work.* **2.** A job: *Our neighbor is looking for work as a teacher.* **3.** A way by which a person earns money. *v.* **worked, working 1.** To put out effort to do or make something: *I worked hard raking leaves while my little sister played on the swing.* **2.** To have a job: *My parents work in a hospital.*

wor•ry |wûr′ ē| *v.* **worried, worrying** To feel or cause to feel uneasy: *Your bad cough worries me.*

would |wŏŏd| *helping v.* Past tense of **will**: *They said that they would help.*

would•n't |wŏŏd′ nt| Contraction of "would not": *The sick cat wouldn't eat.*

wrap |răp| *v.* **wrapped, wrapping** To cover by winding or folding something: *Wrap the baby in a towel.*

wreath |rēth| *n., pl.* **wreaths** A circle of flowers or leaves: *She wore a wreath of daisies in her hair.*

wren |rĕn| *n., pl.* **wrens** A small brown songbird: *A wren was singing in the tree.*

wrench |rĕnch| *n., pl.* **wrenches** A tool for turning: *She used a wrench to loosen the bolts.*

wring |rĭng| *v.* **wrung, wringing** To twist or squeeze: *Wring out the wet mop when you finish washing the floor.*

write |rīt| *v.* **wrote, written, writing 1.** To make letters or words with a pen or pencil. **2.** To communicate by writing: *I wrote the good news to my friend.*

wrong |rông| *adj.* **1.** Not correct. **2.** Bad: *It is wrong to lie.* **3.** Not working correctly. **4.** Not fitting or suitable: *You picked the wrong time to call.*

X

x-ray *or* **X-ray** |ĕks′ rā| *n., pl.* **x-rays** *or* **X-rays 1.** A machine that takes pictures of parts of the body, such as organs and bones, that cannot be seen from the outside. **2.** A photograph taken by an x-ray machine: *The x-ray showed where the bone was broken.*

Y

yel•low |yĕl′ ō| *n., pl.* **yellows 1.** Having the color of the sun. **2.** Something having this color, as the yolk of an egg. *adj.,* **yellower, yellowest** Of the color yellow: *He wore a yellow shirt.*

Content Index

Credits

Series design and cover design by Ligature, Inc. Front cover and title page photograph: © Art Wolfe/Allstock

Illustrations

Meg Kelleher Aubrey: 29, 71, 89, 125, 149, 156, 165, 171, 185, 192, 195, 198, 207, 209, 213, 219.
Paul Breeden: 154, 155.
John Butler: 29, 35, 53, 59, 95, 113, 125, 137, 149, 159, 162, 167, 168, 174, 177, 180, 183, 201, 204, 210, 216.
Lorinda Cauley: 12, 14, 15, 18, 21, 35, 77, 137.
Doug Cushman: 82, 83.
Lois Ehlert: 13, 19, 25, 31, 37, 49, 55, 61, 67, 73, 85, 91, 97, 103, 109, 121, 127, 133, 139, 145, 157, 163, 169, 175, 181, 193, 199, 205, 211, 217.
Harriet Fishman: 282, 297, 300.
Ruth Flanigan: 281, 284, 291, 294, 299.
Nick Harris: 118, 119.
Diane Dawson Hearn: 41, 89, 95, 101, 125, 161, 173, 179, 197, 203, 215, 221.
Carol Inouye: 278, 285, 292.
Laurie Jordan: 17, 23, 24, 27, 30, 33, 35, 36, 39, 41, 48, 51, 53, 54, 57, 59, 60, 63, 66, 69, 72, 75, 77, 89, 95, 101, 107, 113, 131, 137, 143, 167, 173, 179, 209, 215, 221.
Fred Lynch: 29, 71, 107.
Cheryl Kirk Noll: 276, 283, 295, 303.
Robin Spowart: 17, 23, 65, 113, 131, 167, 197, 203.
George Ulrich: 258, 261, 263, 265.
Ashley Wolff: 17, 23, 41, 53, 59, 69, 71, 77, 84, 87, 90, 93, 96, 99, 102, 105, 108, 111, 120, 123, 126, 129, 131, 132, 135, 138, 141, 144, 147, 149, 161, 179, 185, 197, 203, 209, 215, 221.

Photographs

3–4 Nancy Sheehan
16 Gale Zucker/Stock Boston
22 Bryan Peterson/The Stock Market
28 Earth Scenes/Mickey Gibson
34 "Family Group—Reading", (Detail), Philadelphia Museum of Art: Given by Mr. and Mrs. J. Watson Webb.
40 Lewis Portnoy/The Stock Market
52 National Baseball Hall of Fame
58 Gary Irving/TSW-Click/Chicago, Ltd.
64 Circus World Museum, Baraboo, Wisconsin
70 George H. Harrison/Grant Heilman
76 Richard Pasley/Stock Boston
88 J. Zehrt/FPG
94 "The Rehearsal on Stage", (Detail), The Metropolitan Museum of Art, Bequest of Mrs. H.O. Havemeyer, 1929. The H.O. Havemeyer Collection. (29.100.39)
100 Stu Rosner/Stock Boston
106 Marvin E. Newman/Sports Illustrated, TIME, Inc.
112 J.H. Robinson/Photo Researchers
124 The Granger Collection
130 Charles Gupton/Stock Boston
142 Gary Braasch
148 Gary Lewis/The Stock Market
154 C.C. Lockwood/Bruce Coleman, Inc.
155 Animals, Animals/Joe and Carol McDonald
160 Mark Wagner/TSW-Click/Chicago Ltd.
166 The Granger Collection
172 © Recycled Paper Products, Inc.; Illustration by Lisa Blowers, Photo by Peter Chapman
178 *The Aesop for Children*, Illustrated by Milo Winter. © 1919, 1947; Checkerboard Press, A Division of Macmillan Publishing Co., All Rights Reserved. (left). *Aesop's Fables*, Retold in verse by Tom Paxton, Illustrated by Robert Rayevsky. Text copyright 1988 by Tom Paxton, Illustration copyright 1988 by Robert Rayevsky. By permission of Morrow Junior Books, A Division of William Morrow and Co. (right). Photo by Peter Chapman.
184 Jeffrey D. Smith/Woodfin Camp and Associates
190 (upper) James L. Ballard/Ligature, Inc.
190 (lower) James L. Ballard/Ligature, Inc.
196 Martin/Custom Medical Stock Photo
202 Animals, Animals/Richard Kolar
208 Bob Taylor Photography/The Stock Shop
214 Friend and Denny/The Stock Shop
220 Martha Swope
277 Ed Simpson/After Image
287 Animals, Animals/Leonard Lee Rue III
289 Ellis Herwig/Stock Boston
304 Charles Krebs/The Stock Market
305 Eric Futran/The Gartman Agency